Comparative
Programming
Languages

INTERNATIONAL COMPUTER SCIENCE SERIES

Consulting Editors **A D McGettrick** University of Strathclyde
J van Leeuwen University of Utrecht

SELECTED TITLES IN THE SERIES

Comparative Programming Languages

Leslie B. Wilson
Robert G. Clark

Department of Computing Science, University of Stirling

Addison-Wesley Publishing Company

Wokingham, England · Reading, Massachusetts · Menlo Park, California
New York · Don Mills, Ontario · Amsterdam · Bonn
Sydney · Singapore · Tokyo · Madrid · San Juan

The programs presented in this book have been included for their instructional value. They have been tested with care but are not guaranteed for any particular purpose. The publisher does not offer any warranties or representations, nor does it accept any liabilities with respect to the programs.

Many of the designations used by manufacturers and sellers to distinguish their products are claimed as trademarks. Addison-Wesley has made every attempt to supply trademark information about manufacturers and their products mentioned in this book. A list of the trademark designations and their owners appears on page vi.

Cover design by Marshall Henrichs.
Cover painting *The Tower of Babel* by Pieter Brueghel (1563), courtesy of
    The Künsthistorisches Museum, Vienna.
Illustrations by Chartwell Illustrators.
Typeset by CRB Typesetting Services, Ely.
Printed in Great Britain by The Bath Press, Avon.

First printed 1988.

British Library Cataloguing in Publication Data
Clark, Robert G.
    Comparative programming languages.
    1. Programming languages (Electronic
    computers)
    I. Title   II. Wilson, L.B.
    005.13   QA76.7

    ISBN 0-201-18483-4

Library of Congress Cataloguing in Publication Data
Clark, Robert G. (Robert George), 1944–
    Comparative programming languages.

    Bibliography: p.
    Includes index.
    1. Programming language (Electronic computers)
    I. Wilson, Leslie B.   II. Title.
    QA76.7.C55   1988   005.13   87-27063
    ISBN 0-201-18483-4

To Mandy, Judy, Julia and Alan

TRADEMARK NOTICE

Preface

Aims and objectives

In this book we consider the principal programming language concepts and show how they are dealt with in both the traditional imperative languages, such as FORTRAN and Pascal, and in the newer functional, logic and object-oriented languages. Since new languages are continually emerging, there is a need to re-evaluate the programming language scene at regular intervals. Examples of recent significant developments are:

(1)   languages that have been around for several years but whose importance and potential have been realized only recently (for example, PROLOG);
(2)   the re-awakening of interest in functional languages; and
(3)   the development of new imperative languages like Ada and Modula-2, which are the culmination of several decades of language design.

The programming language scene has always been bedevilled by protagonists pushing their favourite language. This often leads to a reluctance to examine rival languages and to a 'love me, love my language' approach. The lack of a scientific approach to languages tends to emphasize the differences between them, even when these are quite minor. Our approach is to find common ground between languages and to identify the underlying principles. Although the approach of logic languages, functional languages and object-oriented languages is different from that of the traditional imperative languages, there are many areas of similarity, and seeing these helps us to understand the differences better.

This approach is important at the present time when there are major and important controversies as to which way we should be heading. Should we stick with the old faithfuls like FORTRAN and COBOL trying to adapt them to new hardware and software ideas? Should we throw these old languages away and standardize on a modern imperative language like Ada or Modula-2? Are imperative languages themselves outdated? Is the future likely to be dominated by the newer functional languages like Hope and ML, by logic languages like PROLOG or by object-oriented languages like

Smalltalk? Are fourth-generation languages about to end the rule of COBOL as the most widely used programming language? Many of these questions are quite impossible to answer at present, but it is important to address these issues.

Another reason for the production of this book is a dissatisfaction with existing texts for teaching purposes. This is not to say that existing books on programming languages are bad, but many contain far too much material for a normal semester course. We therefore set out to write a relatively short book on comparative languages. The book has, in the end, turned out slightly larger than we hoped. It provides an updated version of the ACM Curriculum 78 Course CS8 'Organization of Programming Languages'. Some of the topics in that syllabus are now of less importance than they were 10 years ago while others, such as functional, logic and object-oriented languages, which were not even mentioned in the syllabus in 1978, have now assumed an important position and their omission from a comparative language course would be a major deficiency.

The type of course taught in our department is, we think, fairly typical. It combines both theoretical and practical work and so there is a limit to the amount of material that can be covered. We feel that it is important to get the balance right. A purely theoretical approach usually leaves most computer science students unable to fit the theory with their practical experience, while an approach that merely piles one language on top of the other leaves the student ignorant of the common threads in language design.

Intended audience

Although this book is intended primarily as a student text for a comparative language course, we hope it will also be read by practising computer programmers. It is easy to be overwhelmed by the large number of available programming languages and we hope this book provides some guidance through the programming language jungle.

We have assumed a reading knowledge of Pascal together with proficiency in a structured imperative language such as Pascal, PL/I, C or Ada. We have not assumed any prior knowledge of languages such as LISP and PROLOG.

Structure and contents

Many books on comparative programming languages have separate chapters on each of the main languages covered. We have not adopted this approach, but have organized the book so that there are separate chapters on the main language concepts with examples and discussion of how they are dealt with in particular languages. The emphasis is on imperative languages and although a wide range of languages is covered, Pascal and Ada are used in a central role.

- **Chapter 1   Introduction**: This shows how programming languages fit into the software development process and the effect this has had on language design. [pages 1–15]

- **Chapter 2   Historical Survey**: This provides a historical survey so that the development of present day languages can be traced. [pages 17–60]

- **Chapter 3   Types, Objects and Declarations**: This deals with variables, types and declarations. It is shown that many of the differences between languages can be explained in terms of the binding time of their attributes. [pages 61–89]

- **Chapter 4   Expressions and Statements**: This discusses expressions and statements with the emphasis on structured control statements. [pages 91–118]

- **Chapter 5   Subprograms**: This looks at program structure and the importance of subprograms. Particular attention is paid to parameter-passing mechanisms. [pages 119–158]

- **Chapter 6   Data Structures**: This deals with arrays, records and dynamic data structures. [pages 159–190]

- **Chapter 7   Modules**: This considers the problem of programming in the large and the need to decompose large programs into self-contained units with small strictly defined interfaces. This leads to a discussion of information hiding, abstract data types and object-oriented languages. [pages 191–225]

- **Chapter 8   Concurrency**: This describes how concurrency is handled in Ada, Modula-2 and occam and how these languages deal with inter-process communication and synchronization. [pages 227–248]

- **Chapter 9   Functional Languages**: This introduces functional languages and describes both the traditional LISP approach and the approach taken in the newer purely functional languages such as FP and Hope. [pages 249–280]

- **Chapter 10   Logic Programming**: This deals with logic programming and is mainly concerned with the language PROLOG. [pages 281–300]

- **Chapter 11   Input and Output**: This describes input and output, which always seems to be the Cinderella of language design. [pages 301–320]

- **Chapter 12   The Future**: This reviews the present situation and attempts to predict the direction in which language design is likely to go. [pages 321–333]

- **Appendix 1   Language Summaries**: This summarizes the features of the principal languages dealt with in the text. [pages 335-349]
- **Appendix 2   Language Texts**: This gives an annotated bibliography for a wide range of programming languages. [pages 351-356]

Chapters 1, 2, 3, 4, 5, 6 and 7 introduce the basic concepts and are best read in the given order, while Chapters 8, 9, 10 and 11 build on earlier material and, as they are largely self-contained, can be taken in any order. Each chapter contains a synopsis, outlining the major topics to be covered, a concise end-of-chapter summary, exercises and an annotated bibliography. Solutions to selected exercises are given at the back of the book.

Finally, we should make it clear what this book is not. It is not a language reference manual or a text on language implementation. We make no attempt to teach any particular language, but the annotated bibliography at the end of the book gives suggestions for further reading in all the languages covered. It is also not a book on the principles of program construction, although throughout the book we view each language construct from the point of view of whether or not it helps or hinders the construction of readable and reliable programs.

Acknowledgements

We would particularly like to thank our colleagues in the Computing Science Department at the University of Stirling who have acted as an ideal sounding board. Their helpful criticisms of various chapter drafts of this book have prevented us from straying too far into error.

Leslie B. Wilson
Robert G. Clark
May 1988

Contents

CHAPTER 1

Introduction

This chapter looks at the different stages involved in the development of software and concludes that the main purpose of a programming language is to help in the construction of reliable software. It also discusses how designers have tried to include expressive power, simplicity and orthogonality in their languages while noting that pragmatic matters such as implementation and error detection have a significant influence.

Finally, the basic building blocks used in the construction of a language are considered; that is, the character set, the rules for identifiers and special symbols, and how comments, blanks and layout are handled. The reader is assumed to be familiar with one of the methods used to define language syntax, such as Backus-Naur form or syntax diagrams, but no such assumptions are made about the reader's knowledge of the methods used to formally describe the semantics of language constructs. As the latter require a much higher level of mathematical sophistication than is assumed, formal semantic notations are not used in this book. Brief outlines of the three main methods are, however, given and the interested reader is referred to the more theoretical treatment given by Tennent (1981).

1.1   The Diversity of Languages

Although over a thousand different programming languages have been designed by various research groups, international committees and computer companies, most of these languages have never been used outside the group that designed them while others, once popular, have been replaced by newer languages. Nevertheless, a large number of languages remain in current use and newer languages continue to emerge. This situation can appear very confusing to students who have mastered one language, usually Pascal, and perhaps have a reading knowledge of a couple of others. They might well ask: 'Does a lifetime of learning new languages await them?'

Fortunately, the situation is not as bleak as it appears because, although two languages may seem to be superficially very different, they often have many more similarities than differences. Individual languages are not usually built on separate principles; in fact, their differences are often due to quite minor variations in the same principle.

The aim of this book is to consider the principal programming language concepts and to show how they have been dealt with in various languages. By studying these features and principles we can better understand why languages have been designed in the way they have. Furthermore, when faced with a new language, we can identify where the language differs from those we already know and where it provides the same facilities disguised in a different syntax.

1.2   The Problem-Solving Process

A computer is a tool that solves problems by means of programs (or **software**) written in a programming language. The development of software is a multi-stage process and Figure 1.1 shows the different stages involved. First, it is necessary to determine what needs to be done. This is called the **requirements analysis** and often necessitates extensive discussion with potential users – that is, the customers. The next step is to produce a document, the **specification**, that defines as accurately as possible the problem to be solved; in other words, it determines what the system is to do. Requirements analysis and specification are the most difficult stages of software development.

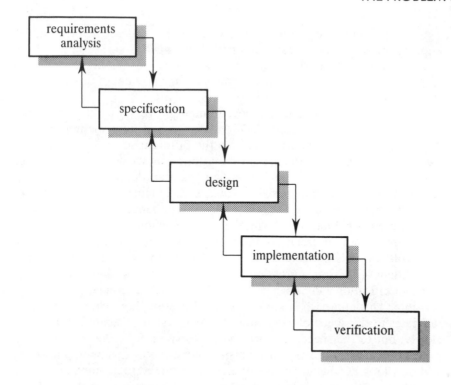

FIGURE 1.1
Software development.

Having defined what the system is to achieve, the next step is to **design** a solution, which can then be implemented on a computer. It is only at this last stage (**implementation**) that a programming language is directly involved.

The aim of the fifth stage (**verification**) is to show that the implemented solution satisfies the original specification. Although there has been a lot of theoretical work on verification, or **program proving**, it is usually still necessary at this stage to run the program with carefully chosen test data. But the problem with program testing is that it can only show the *presence* of errors, it can never prove their absence.

The final stage of software development, usually termed **maintenance**, covers two quite distinct activities:

(1) The correction of errors that were missed at an earlier stage but have been detected after the program has been in active service.

(2) Modification of the program to take account of additions or changes in the user's requirements.

It is important to realize that the software development process is iterative, not sequential. Therefore, knowledge gained at any one of the stages outlined can (and should) be used to give feedback to earlier stages.

Although a programming language is only explicitly involved in the implementation stage, it has traditionally influenced the other stages of the process. Designers are, for example, usually aware of the implementation language to be used and bias their designs to take account of the language's strong points.

In describing the software development process, the different stages of requirements analysis, specification, design and implementation were discussed, but the boundaries between the different stages are not always clear cut. For example, the need for a notation in which a specification or design can be written down has led to the development of both **specification** and **program design languages**. Such languages are at a higher level and give fewer details than implementation languages. Furthermore, as they are mathematical in form, they are amenable to proof techniques. As a specification or design contains all the information necessary to solve the problem, it is possible, at least in theory, to execute them directly, rather than generating a program in an implementation language. Indeed, some specification and design languages have been developed so that this is possible. This approach is known as **rapid prototyping**, where rapid does not refer to the speed of execution, for such systems usually execute very slowly, but to the speed at which the prototype can be developed. However, languages of this type are outside the scope of this book and so we will only look at what are conventionally considered to be implementation languages, although some of the functional languages, such as Hope, described in Chapter 9 have been used for rapid prototyping.

Using a systematic program development process has greatly influenced both language design and how languages are used. For example, Pascal was designed to support the ideas of **structured programming** while Ada and Modula-2, which were developed from Pascal, have additional features to enable them to be used effectively and safely in the construction of large systems. In modern languages, more validity checking takes place at compile time, which is a considerable help in program testing. Also, the problems of program maintenance have led to the introduction of features that allow large systems to be broken down into self-contained modules. It is clear, therefore, that programming languages do not exist in a vacuum; rather, the design of modern languages is a direct response to the needs and problems of the software development process.

1.3   Language Design

The primary purpose of a programming language is to support the construction of reliable software. However, a language should also be user friendly so that it is straightforward to design, write, test, run, document and modify programs written in that language. To understand how these objectives may be achieved, the issues of language design can be divided into several broad categories:

- expressive power,
- simplicity and orthogonality,
- implementation,
- error detection and correction,
- correctness and standards.

Expressive power

A programming language with high expressive power enables solutions to be expressed in terms of the problem being solved rather than in terms of the computer on which the solution is to be implemented. Hence, the programmer can concentrate on problem solving. Such a language should provide a convenient notation to describe both algorithms and data structures in addition to supporting the ideas of structured programming and modularization.

Another aspect of expressive power is the range of operations and operators provided. If a language does not include a suitable range of operators, then the programmer generally has to provide these by function declarations, thereby distracting the programmer's attention to the lower level aspects of solving the problem. Often, languages may have high expressive power in some areas, but not in others; for example, FORTRAN has a range of numerical operations that give it expressive power for numerical work, but it is much less effective in data processing applications.

Also included under the heading of expressive power is readability; that is, the ease with which someone familiar with the language can read and understand programs written by other people. Readability is considerably enhanced by a well-designed comment facility, and good layout and naming conventions. In practice, it should be possible to write programs that act, to a large extent, as their own documentation, thereby making maintenance and extension of the program much easier.

Simplicity and orthogonality

Simplicity implies that a language allows programs to be expressed concisely in a manner that is easily written, understood and read. This objective is often underrated by computer scientists, but is a high priority for non-professional programmers. The success of BASIC and fourth-generation languages is an eloquent commentary on the importance users place on simplicity.

A simple language either avoids complexity or handles it well. Inherent in most simple languages is the avoidance of features that most human programmers find difficult. Simple languages should not allow alternative ways of implementing constructs nor should they produce surprising results from standard applications of their rules.

An orthogonal language is one in which any combination of the basic language constructs is allowed and so there are few, if any, restrictions or special cases. An example of an orthogonal language is ALGOL 68 which was, in fact, designed with the aim of keeping the number of basic concepts as small as possible. The idea was that the resulting language would be simple as it would only consist of combinations of features from this small set of basic concepts.

There can, however, be a clash between the ideas of orthogonality and simplicity. For example, Pascal, which is not orthogonal, is simpler to learn and use than ALGOL 68. Where a new special construct is introduced in Pascal, the same effect is achieved in ALGOL 68 by the combination of simpler existing constructs. Although the ALGOL 68 approach is elegant and powerful, the more pragmatic approach (Wirth, 1975) taken in the design of Pascal has led to a more understandable language.

What is generally agreed is that the use of constructs should be consistent; that is, they should have a similar effect wherever they appear. This is an important design principle for any language although it is obviously of great importance in an orthogonal language which gets its expressive power from the large number of combinations of basic concepts. Whether simplicity or orthogonality is the goal, once the basic constructs are known, their combination should be predictable. This is sometimes called the **law of minimum surprise**.

Implementation

The ease with which a programming language can be implemented and the efficiency of the resulting code can be major factors in a language's success. Large languages, for example, have an inherent disadvantage in this respect because the compiler will, almost inevitably, be large and indeed may be beyond the scope of small computers.

Some language designers, notably Wirth the designer of Pascal and Modula-2, have made many of their design decisions on the basis of the ease with which a feature can be compiled and executed efficiently. One of the many advantages of having a close working relationship between language design and language implementation teams is that the designers can obtain early feedback on constructs that are causing trouble. Often, features that are difficult to translate are also difficult for human programmers to understand. ALGOL 60 and ALGOL 68 are prime examples of languages that have had a relative lack of success due in part to the fact that they were designed by committees who largely ignored implementation considerations, as they felt that such considerations would restrict the ability to produce a powerful language. In contrast, the implementation of FORTRAN, Pascal and Modula-2 went hand in hand with their design and the Ada design team was dominated by language implementors.

However, it is necessary to achieve a proper balance between the introduction of powerful new features and their ease of implementation. ISO Standard Pascal, for example, has features that were omitted from the original version of the language on the grounds that they were too expensive to implement.

Error detection and correction

It is important that programs are correct and satisfy their original specification. However, demonstrating that this is indeed the case is no easy matter. As most programmers still rely on program testing as a means of showing that a program is error free, a good language should assist in this task. It is therefore sensible for language designers to include features that help in error detection and to omit features that are difficult to check.

Ideally, errors should be found at compile time when they are easier to pinpoint and correct. The later an error is detected in the software development process, the more difficult it is to find and correct without destroying the program structure.

As an example of the importance of language design on error detection, consider the FORTRAN method of type declarations where the initial letter of a variable name implicitly determines the type of the variable. Although this method is convenient and greatly reduces the number of declarations required, it is in fact inherently unsound since any misspelling of variable names is not detected at compile time and leads to run-time errors. Conversely, explicit type declarations have the following advantages. Firstly, they provide additional information that enables more checking to be carried out at compile time and, secondly, they act as part of the program documentation.

Correctness and standards

The most exacting requirement of correctness is proving that a program satisfies its original specification. As yet, such proofs of correctness have not had a major influence on language design. However, the basic ideas of structured programming do support the notion of proving the correctness of a program, as it is clearly easier to reason about a program with high-level control structures than about one with unrestricted **goto** statements.

To prove that a program is correct, or to reason about the meaning of a program, it is necessary to have a rigorous definition of the meaning of each language construct. (Methods for defining the syntax and semantics of a language are discussed in Section 1.4.) However, although it is not difficult to provide a precise definition of the syntax of a language, it is very difficult, if not impossible, to produce a full semantic definition, and as far as most programmers are concerned it is unreadable anyway. It is therefore vital in the early stages of a language's development to have an informal description that is understandable by programmers. As in many aspects of computer science, there needs to be a compromise between exactness and informality.

A programming language should also have an official standard definition to which all implementors adhere. Unfortunately, this seldom happens as implementors often omit features that are difficult to implement and add features that they feel will improve the language. As a result, program portability suffers. The exception to this is Ada. An Ada compiler must be validated using a specially constructed suite of test programs before it can be called an Ada compiler. It is interesting that one of the aims of these tests is to rule out supersets as well as subsets of the language. This is an excellent idea and it is hoped that it will become the norm.

1.4   Lexical Elements

The conventions allowed in writing programs in a particular language are often known as the **lexical elements** and cover such items as the character set, the rules for identifiers and operators, the use of keywords or reserved words, how comments are written, and the manner in which blanks and layout are handled.

Character set

The character set can be thought of as containing the basic building blocks of a programming language – letters, digits and special characters such as arithmetic operators and punctuation symbols. Two approaches can be taken when deciding on the character set to be used in a language. One is to choose all the characters deemed necessary. This is the approach taken with APL and ALGOL 60, but it has the drawback that either special input/output equipment has to be used or changes have to be made in the published language when it is used on a computer.

The alternative approach is to use only the characters commonly available with current input and output devices. Hence, the character set of an early language like FORTRAN is restricted by the 64 characters available with punched cards whereas Pascal is constrained by the character set available with the CDC 6000 series computer on which it was originally implemented. Consequently, only the 26 capital letters A–Z, the digits 0–9 and 13 special characters, namely = + - * / ( ) : , . ' $ plus the blank space, are available with FORTRAN. In contrast, ALGOL 60 allows both upper and lower case letters in addition to many more special characters. In most modern languages such as Pascal, capital letters and their lower case counterparts are considered to be the same, and so they are suitable for use both on devices with large and small character sets.

Since the early 1970s, most input and output devices have supported internationally accepted character sets such as ASCII (American Standard Code for Information Interchange) and this has been reflected in the character sets of languages. The ASCII character set has 128 characters of which 95 are printable; the remaining characters are special control characters. The printable characters are the upper and lower case letters, digits, punctuation characters, arithmetic operators and three different sets of brackets ( ), [ ] and { }.

Composite symbols are often used to extend the range of symbols available. Commonly used examples are the relational operators <= and >= and the assignment operator :=. FORTRAN uses .LE. and .GE. instead of <= and >=.

Identifiers and reserved words

The character set is the collection from which the symbols making up the vocabulary of a programming language are formed. Clearly, a language needs conventions for grouping characters into words so that names (usually known as **identifiers** in computing) can be given to entities such as variables, constants, etc. (Naming conventions are discussed in Chapter 3.)

Some of the words in a programming language are given a special meaning. Examples of this are DO and GOTO in FORTRAN, and **begin**, **end** and **for** in Pascal. Two methods are used for including such words in a language. The method adopted by FORTRAN is to allow such words to have their special well-defined meaning in certain contexts. The words are then called **keywords**. This method was also adopted by the designers of PL/I since it limited the number of special words that the programmer had to remember – the scientific programmer using PL/I is unlikely to know all the business-oriented keywords, while the business programmer is unlikely to know all the scientific keywords. However, the drawback of this method is that the reader of a program written in a language with keywords has the task of deciding whether a keyword is being used for its *special* meaning or is an occurrence of an *ordinary* identifier. Furthermore, when an error occurs due to the inadvertent use of an unknown keyword, it is not always clear when a word has its special meaning, without consulting all the declarations.

The alternative method, used initially by COBOL and adopted by most modern languages, is to restrict the use of such words to their special meaning. The words are then called **reserved words**. The advantage of the reserved word method is best seen in languages like Pascal where the number of such words is quite small. In COBOL, however, the number of reserved words is much larger – over 300 – and so the programmer has the task of remembering a large number of words that must not be used for such things as variables.

In ALGOL 60 programs, reserved words are written in a different typeface, either underlined or boldface, depending on the situation. The drawback of this is that many input devices cannot cope with underlined words, so less attractive alternatives, such as writing reserved words in quotes, are used. In hand-written versions of programs in Pascal and Ada, for example, reserved words are often underlined so that they stand out while in books they are often printed in boldface. In the version presented to a compiler, however, they are typed in the same way as ordinary identifiers.

Comments

Almost all languages allow comments, thereby making the program more readily understood by the human reader. Such comments are, however, ignored by the compiler. In early languages such as FORTRAN, which has a fixed format of one statement per line, comments are terminated by the end of a line. In FORTRAN's case, the comment lines are also preceded by a C in column 1. A similar method is used in other early languages such as COBOL and SNOBOL4.

ALGOL 60 uses a different method for comments: they begin with the reserved word **comment** and terminate with a semicolon. However, the problem with this method is that programmers often fail to terminate comments correctly, using a fullstop instead of a semicolon. Consequently, the compiler, interpreting the program exactly, ignores the next declaration or statement. Errors caused in this way are then difficult to find as the error message, if one is generated, is usually quite unrelated to the actual error.

Most later languages enclose comments in brackets. Pascal, for example, uses either (* and *) or { and } while PL/I and C use /* and */. But this approach still leaves the problem of terminating a comment unresolved. Some compilers alleviate this problem by giving a warning if a statement separator – that is, a semicolon – occurs within a comment. Ada, in contrast, commences a comment with two hyphens and ends it by the end of a line, so reverting to the methods of the earliest high-level languages.

Blanks and line termination

Programming languages vary considerably in the importance they attach to blanks (spaces). At one extreme, languages such as ALGOL 60 (and FORTRAN within columns 7 to 72 of a line) ignore blanks wherever they occur while, at the other extreme, SNOBOL4 uses blanks as separators and as the primitive operation of concatenating two strings. Most languages, however, use blanks as separators in a manner similar to that of natural language. Several blanks may also be used wherever one is allowed. Blanks in identifiers are normally forbidden, but to aid readability many languages include the underscore character so that identifiers like *current_account* and *centre_of_gravity* can be used.

The significance of the end of a line also varies according to the language. FORTRAN and COBOL, because they were card oriented in their early years, adopted the convention that the end of a line terminated a statement. If the statement could not be contained within one line, a continuation character was then used in the following line. The current COBOL convention is that a fullstop terminates a statement, but FORTRAN has continued to use the end-of-line terminator for statements. Most recent high-level languages use the semicolon either to separate or to terminate statements. This method is often known as free format since it means that a new line can be started anywhere that a space may occur in a statement.

1.5   Syntax and Semantics

The **syntax** of a programming language describes the correct form in which programs may be written while the **semantics** denotes the meaning that may be attached to the various syntactic constructs. This book assumes that readers are aware of how the syntax of a programming language can be defined, either by a notation such as **Backus-Naur Form** (**BNF**) or by means of **syntax diagrams**; readers who are interested in studying the syntax of a language in detail can consult most texts on Pascal as these usually include an appendix giving the grammar of Pascal in terms of syntax diagrams. When the syntax of a language is expressed in such a simple and unambiguous notation, it is clear to the language user and implementor alike which constructs are legal and which are not.

In contrast to the early progress made in the formal definition of syntax, the task of formulating a suitable definition for the semantics of programming languages has presented many problems. Endless attempts have been made by researchers to arrive at a readable, concise and unambiguous notation for the definition of semantics, and, although considerable progress has been made, an easily understandable solution to the semantics of programming languages is still not available. BNF was first used in the definition of ALGOL 60, but as the working committee was unable to come up with a solution to the semantic problem to match the BNF syntactical description, the committee resorted to the English language for the semantic explanations. Unfortunately, the use of English prose is ambiguous, so that two readers can often arrive at different interpretations of a typical sentence.

The three methods that are currently used to describe the semantics of a language are the **operational** approach, the **denotational** approach and the **axiomatic** approach. These notations are not easy to follow and require a much higher level of mathematical sophistication than is assumed in this book. However, for completeness, a brief overview of each notation will be given.

The operational approach defines a simple abstract machine that has a set of data structures and operations whose semantics is assumed to be known. The semantics of a programming language is then defined by the rules governing how programs written in that language can be executed on the abstract machine. Although the abstract machine is unlikely to be similar to any existing computer, the operational semantics of a language can be of direct benefit to the language implementor. This notation does, however, often contain too much implementation detail to be of much use to the language user.

The **Vienna Definition Language** is an example of the operational approach. Its intention was to present a formal definition of PL/I, but unfortunately the result was massive and impenetrable by normal mortals. The reason for this was not that operational semantics are bad *per se*, but that combined with the complexities of PL/I the result was hard to follow and interpret.

The denotational approach is more abstract than the operational method. Language constructs are modelled by appropriate mathematical objects, usually numbers or functions, whose meaning is already known. It is hierarchical in nature with high-level features being defined in terms of lower level features whose meaning has already been defined. As it gives information about the effect of program execution, rather than about how the execution is to be carried out, it is, unlike the operational approach, of more use to language designers than language implementors.

The axiomatic method, which is based on symbolic logic, uses **rules of inference** to deduce the effect of executing a construct. The meaning of a statement, or group of statements, S is described in terms of:

(1)   the set P of conditions (called the **pre-condition**) that are assumed or asserted to be true before S is executed, and

(2)   the set Q of conditions (the **post-condition**) that can be deduced to be true after execution of S.

This is usually written as:

$\{P\}\ S\ \{Q\}$

The post-condition that holds after the execution of one group of statements can of course act as the pre-condition for the next.

Unlike the other two approaches, the meaning of S is not described directly; instead, it is described indirectly by its effect in transforming P into Q. This means that the axiomatic method is of most use in verifying and reasoning about the effect of programs.

As these three methods are useful under differing circumstances, they can be seen to be complementary to one another, rather than competitors.

SUMMARY

- Although there are many different programming languages in existence, these languages do, in fact, have more similarities than they have differences.

- The stages in software development are requirements analysis, specification, design, implementation, verification and maintenance. A programming language is not directly involved until the implementation stage.

- The evolution of a systematic software development process has greatly influenced language design.

- The primary purpose of a programming language is to support the construction of reliable software.

- A programming language should be simple, have high expressive power and language constructs that are consistent – that is, they should have a similar effect wherever they appear.

- It is important to have a proper balance between the introduction of powerful language features and their ease of implementation.

- Languages should support the detection of as many errors as possible at compile time.

- A language should have a single official definition to which all implementors adhere.

- The lexical elements of a language cover such items as the character set and the rules for identifiers and special symbols.

- FORTRAN and PL/I have keywords while most other languages such as Pascal have reserved words.

- The syntax of a programming language is usually defined using BNF.

- In most language reference manuals, the semantics of language constructs are not described formally; rather, they are given in a natural language such as English.

- There are three approaches to formal semantics: operational, denotational and axiomatic. These methods are complementary to one another.

Bibliography

The approach taken in this book to focus on language concepts and show how these concepts are realized in different programming languages is similar to that adopted by Horowitz (1983), Ghezzi (1982) and Meyer (1986). The book by Barron (1977) also takes this approach, but is heavily weighted towards ALGOL 68, while Tennent (1981) takes a more theoretical view.

The alternative approach of having separate chapters on the main programming languages has been adopted by Tucker (1986) and MacLennan (1987). Pratt (1984), on the other hand, has combined both approaches: the language features are discussed in the first part of the book while the second part is devoted to individual languages. The result is comprehensive, although it leads to a very large text. Both Pratt and MacLennan also contain a large amount of material on language implementation.

A very different approach has been taken in the book by Ledgard (1981). Instead of using examples from a range of existing languages, they describe language concepts through a specially designed series of 'mini-languages'.

Barron, D. W. (1977), *An Introduction to the Study of Programming Languages*, Cambridge University Press.

Ghezzi, C. and Jazayeri, M. (1982), *Programming Language Concepts*, John Wiley.

Horowitz, E. (1983), *Fundamentals of Programming Languages*, Springer-Verlag.

Ledgard, H. and Marcotty, M. (1981), *The Programming Language Landscape*, Science Research Associates.

MacLennan, B. J. (1987), *Principles of Programming Languages* (Second Edition), Holt, Rinehart and Winston.

Meyer, H. G. (1986), *Programming Languages*, Burgess Communications.

Pratt, T. W. (1984), *Programming Languages: Design and Implementation* (Second Edition), Prentice-Hall.

Tennent, R. D. (1981), *Principles of Programming Languages*, Prentice-Hall.

Tucker, A. B. (1986), *Programming Languages* (Second Edition), McGraw-Hill.

Wirth, N. (1975), 'On the Design of Programming Languages', *IFIP*, **74**, pp. 386–393, North-Holland.

CHAPTER 2

Historical Survey

There are two main reasons for studying the history of programming languages. Firstly, the languages available today are only explicable by examining how they grew up. One has to look at their development to understand why, for example, two of the major languages, FORTRAN and COBOL, are still in use over 30 years after their first appearance. There is in fact a huge inertia in the programming environment, which means that once a language has been successful, it is very difficult to supersede it by a newer language. The large investment in established systems ensures the continued use of old languages.

The second reason for looking at the history of programming languages is to pinpoint some of the errors made in the past and so try to avoid repeating them. A prime example where this was not the case was the rise of the microprocessor whose development paralleled that of the early computers in many respects. Unfortunately, many of the same mistakes were repeated because the software designers were unaware of the historical lessons.

This chapter starts its survey from the languages used with the early computers and traces their development as far as Ada, PROLOG, Modula-2 and Smalltalk. While every attempt has been made to be historically accurate, the main purpose of this survey is to give the flavour of programming language development and to try to recapture the feelings of programmers at the time when new languages arrived on the scene.

2.1   Early Machines

The birth of programming languages is a matter for some conjecture. Some people might consider that Ada, Countess of Lovelace, was the first programmer because she worked with Charles Babbage on the Analytical Engine. However, such academic speculations are best left to the historians. Likewise, the early work on the machines and languages of the late 1940s is of little interest in the development of programming languages.

The early languages, called **order codes** or **instruction codes**, were in fact very primitive, even in comparison with assemblers. They used numbers for operation codes as well as for storage locations and special registers which were called accumulators. Often, there were no mnemonics or floating point, and library routines, which were used for routine calculations and for input and output, were not called, but were inserted in the code. Also, loops, in which the instructions were changed, were far from the modern **for** loop in ease of operation although their purpose was the same.

An example of machine code instructions typical of the early machines (in this case, for the Ferranti Pegasus computer) is as follows:

```
1.3     521
3.0     1125
```

The first instruction (21) multiplies the number in location 1.3 by the number in accumulator 5. The result is a double-length number which is held in accumulators 6 and 7. The second instruction (12) transfers the contents of accumulator 1 to location 3.0, which is then modified by the number in accumulator 5.

Although order codes with mnemonics were used on machines such as the EDSAC I, programming at this level was soon seen to be a considerable drawback in the advance of computers. Machine codes were both hard to learn and difficult to use, which meant that early programs were full of errors and the 'patch' – that is, actually changing the executable code – was the standard method of correction. However, the middle and late 1950s saw a surge in the attempt to improve programming languages on both sides of the Atlantic.

First attempts to improve machine code

SHORTCODE for the UNIVAC, Speedcode for the IBM 701 and Matrix Interpretive schemes were all the result of early attempts to improve machine code. An example of an early autocode program is as follows.

Autocode instruction	Comment
`v10=TAPEB*`	Read in n, then n numbers
`n1=v10`	Set n1 = n
`n0=n1`	
`v0=0.0`	Initialize v0
`1)v0=v0+v(10+n0)`	Form sum of the numbers
`n0=n0-1`	
`⇾1,n0≠0`	
`v1=v0/n1`	Mean
`n2=0`	Initialize counter n2
`2)v2=v(10+n1)`	
`⇾3,v1>=v2`	
`n2=n2+1`	If number > mean add one to counter
`3)n1=n1-1`	
`⇾2,n1≠0`	
`PRINTv1,1025`	
`PRINTn2,2025`	Print answers
`(⇾0)`	

Although this program was specifically written for the Ferranti Pegasus computer, it is fairly typical of autocodes. It has two types of variables, floating-point variables v1, v2, v3 ... and integer variables n0, n1, n2 ... which are used mainly as indices, or what are now called subscripts. The program itself reads in a list of numbers and finds the mean and the number of values that are greater than the mean.

Although autocodes were not high-level languages, they did have the beauty of being very simple and, therefore, easy to learn. They also avoided two of the problems inherent in early machines: fixed-point working and the transfer of information between the high-speed store and the backing store (usually a magnetic drum). However, as each instruction of an autocode program is interpreted, they were inefficient at run time. When programs became large, they not only ran slowly but were not very readable. Despite these drawbacks, autocodes were widely used.

2.2   FORTRAN

The birth of FORTRAN

The big breakthrough in the early years was the development of 'The IBM Mathematical FORmula TRANslating system', known then and subsequently as FORTRAN. This was by no means an isolated development, but depended very much on the previous attempts to raise the level of programming languages. The manual for FORTRAN 1 was released in 1956, but it was not until 1958 before successful compilers were running programs correctly. Following this, FORTRAN took off in a manner that probably surprised even its most ardent advocates.

One of the principal designers of FORTRAN, Backus, has made it clear that the motivating factor behind the language was not the beauty of programming in a mathematical notation but the economics of programming at that time (Wexelblat, 1981). Programming and debugging costs exceeded running costs and the situation was worsening with the advent of faster computers, which included hard-wired floating point. The only solution was to design a language for scientific computations that allowed the programmer to use mathematical notation. However, the designers of FORTRAN felt that this had to be done in a way that produced efficient object code, otherwise practising programmers would reject the language if they could produce a hand-coded version that ran much faster than the compiled FORTRAN program. Such worries have left their mark on FORTRAN and, as can be seen, considerations of run-time efficiency played a major role in its design, as did the IBM 704 machine and its punched card input.

Since FORTRAN was designed primarily for scientific calculations, string handling facilities were almost non-existent, and the only data structure was the array. Although the array was hedged about with limitations, it did represent a considerable step forward. Other FORTRAN features that were equally acceptable to its new devotees were:

- Comments.

- Assignment statements that allowed mathematical expressions of some complexity on the 'right-hand' side.

- The simplicity of writing loops with the DO statement.

- Subroutines and functions: the idea of the subroutine and function was not new, but FORTRAN did improve on them by employing a symbolic notation close to mathematics.

- Formats for input and output: input and output conversions were notoriously difficult on early computers, but FORTRAN formatting took a lot of the pain away.

- Machine independence: a FORTRAN program could be run on different machines.

Considering the state of ignorance about compiling in the late 1950s, the early FORTRAN compilers were remarkably good; but even so they were unable to achieve the aim of their designers, which was to produce code that was as efficient as hand-coded versions. Despite this, FORTRAN became enormously popular in a very short time, the main reasons for its success being the following:

- It made efficient use of programmers' time.
- It was easy to learn and opened the door to the computer for non-specialist programmers.
- It was supported by IBM, which soon became the most powerful firm in computing; in effect, FORTRAN and IBM arose together.
- When it was introduced, most applications and users were scientific, and FORTRAN had the right facilities for such users.
- It simplified several areas of computing in which programming was very tedious; notably, input and output.

The development of FORTRAN

The success of FORTRAN was not without its problems, the principal one being that programmers were reluctant to use any other language. Thus, FORTRAN was used in circumstances for which it lacked the relevant language features – for example, for data processing applications and as an interactive language.

Another problem encountered was that there was no standard for FORTRAN and so slightly different versions were used in the compilers. Hence, a program that ran successfully on one FORTRAN compiler would more than likely fail when used with a different compiler. The clear need for a standard was underlined by the development of ALGOL 60 with its more precise definition. Eventually, the American National Standards Institute (ANSI) developed a standard for FORTRAN in 1966 while a new standard, called FORTRAN 77, emerged in 1978. However, the ability of the language to reflect new ideas in programming has been slow – only recently have the ideas of structured programming been incorporated into the standard FORTRAN. It was a batch language and could not reflect interactive programming ideas. Furthermore, Backus has recently pointed out (1978) that FORTRAN is very firmly based on the von Neumann computer architecture, as indeed are most of the current high-level languages. While this promotes run-time efficiency, it considerably limits the programmer's thinking and inhibits the problem-solving process. The development of FORTRAN and its associated languages is shown in Figure 2.1.

A FORTRAN PROGRAM

In Section 2.1, a simple autocode program was given for finding the mean of a list of numbers and the number of values that are greater than the mean. Here is the same problem solved in FORTRAN.

```
C     FORTRAN PROGRAM TO FIND MEAN OF N NUMBERS AND NUMBER OF
C     VALUES GREATER THAN THE MEAN
      DIMENSION A(99)
      REAL MEAN
      READ(1, 5)N
   5  FORMAT(I2)
      READ(1, 10)(A(I), I = 1, N)
  10  FORMAT(6F10.5)
      SUM = 0.0
      DO 15 I = 1, N
  15  SUM = SUM + A(I)
      MEAN = SUM/FLOAT(N)
      NUMBER = 0
      DO 20 I = 1, N
      IF (A(I) .LE. MEAN) GOTO 20
      NUMBER = NUMBER + 1
  20  CONTINUE
      WRITE(2, 25) MEAN, NUMBER
  25  FORMAT(8H MEAN = , F10.5, 5X, 20H NUMBER OVER MEAN = , I5)
      STOP
      END
```

Notes

(1)   The first two lines are comments.

(2)   In the third line, the array has to be declared and its size given; in this case, 99 elements with subscripts from 1 to 99. (The ALGOL 60 program in Section 2.3 shows the use of an array with variable bounds.)

(3)   Most FORTRAN variables are declared implicitly by use. However, MEAN is declared explicitly as REAL because if it was declared implicitly, it would be an INTEGER variable, as its first letter is between I and N.

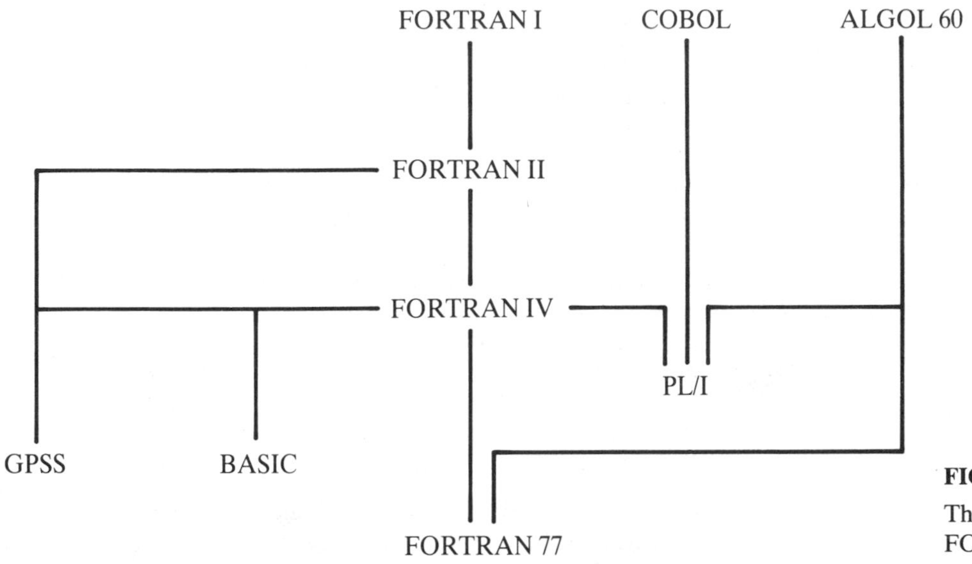

FORTRAN I   COBOL   ALGOL 60

FORTRAN II

FORTRAN IV

PL/I

GPSS   BASIC

FORTRAN 77

FIGURE 2.1
The development of
FORTRAN.

2.3 ALGOL

The period of the late 1950s was a very important one in the history of programming languages. Not only did it see the development of FORTRAN and COBOL but also a third major language – namely, ALGOL. No other language has had such a profound influence on programming language design and definition as that of ALGOL.

ALGOL emerged from a joint committee of European and American programming language experts that was set up with the aim of producing a common language (Wexelblat, 1981). Originally, this language was called IAL (International Algebraic Language) but later it became known as ALGOL (ALGOrithmic Language). The objectives of the language were stated as follows:

- It should be as close as possible to standard mathematical notation and be readable without too much additional explanation.

- It should be possible to use it for the description of computing processes in publications.

- It should be mechanically translatable into machine programs.

The committee's first product, usually known as ALGOL 58, was never implemented but the criticisms raised did help in the development of a subsequent version, ALGOL 60. The 'Report on the Algorithmic Language ALGOL 60' (Naur, 1960) was a major event in the history of programming languages and the 'Revised Report' (Naur, 1963), published three years later, was a classic. It may seem surprising to make such a song and dance about a language that was never in widespread use in the United States. However, its influence has been greater than that of FORTRAN and no other language has added so much to programming language theory.

The major concepts introduced by ALGOL were:

- Language definition: BNF was used to define the syntax for the first time, a concept that led naturally to syntax-directed compilers. The semantics, however, proved more difficult and the definitions in English did lead to some ambiguity.

- ALGOL was structured: it was the original block-structured language and variables in ALGOL were only valid within the block in which they were declared.

- Arrays could have variable bounds at compile time, although the bounds had to be fixed when the block, in which the array was declared, was entered at run time so that suitable storage could be allocated.

- ALGOL contained several structured control statements. The **if** statement and **for** statement were considerable advances on similar constructs in FORTRAN although the ALGOL control statements were simplified in later ALGOL-like languages.

- ALGOL 60 was the first language to introduce recursion using recursive procedures. However, there was some argument as to whether the original committee realized the full import of their proposals in this area. Originally, recursion was decried as 'academic' and of little practical utility. But this view was partly caused by the difficulties the earlier ALGOL compilers had in implementing the concept. However, there is no doubt now that the ability to use recursion is a very important programming skill and with improved compilers it is not inefficient.

As already indicated, ALGOL was intended as a reference and publication language as well as a language for writing programs to run on computers. This led to its use by, amongst others, the Association for Computing Machinery (ACM) to communicate algorithms between users. But despite its powerful and improved facilities, ALGOL 60 was unable to supersede FORTRAN as the main scientific language. Several reasons have been advanced for this, but it was probably a combination of factors that kept FORTRAN well ahead, namely:

- Since ALGOL 60 compilers came out approximately three years after FORTRAN, the latter was strongly entrenched and programmers were reluctant to change. Although this phenomenon is very prevalent amongst programming languages, this was the first (but not last) instance of a new language being unable to supersede an established competitor.

- Since ALGOL had more features, it was harder to learn.

- Although IBM initially supported ALGOL, they eventually decided that its customers were happy with FORTRAN and so did not wish to change. The great success of IBM in the 1960s helped to boost FORTRAN.

- FORTRAN compilers were simpler and ran programs faster than similar ALGOL programs.

- ALGOL had no official input/output (I/O). It was decided to leave this to the individual manufacturers so that they could tailor it to their computers. Although this seemed a reasonable decision, if a semi-official standard I/O had been agreed, then many manufacturers would have used it and a *de facto* standard ALGOL would have been formulated.

The development of ALGOL-like languages

ALGOL has had a strong influence on many subsequent languages as is shown diagrammatically in Figure 2.2. The immediate successor to ALGOL 60 was ALGOL W (Wirth, 1966). In essence, this represented a major tidying up of ALGOL 60 with a few new features. The most important changes and additions were:

- Records and references: they provided data structures other than arrays and allowed linked lists, trees and graphs.

- The **case** statement.

- Changes that separated the **for** and **while** statements and made the **for** statement more restricted and less prone to error.

- Procedure and function parameters could be called by value, result and value-result. The call-by-name method of parameter passing introduced by ALGOL 60 used the obvious mathematical approach of replacing a formal parameter by the corresponding actual

AN ALGOL 60 PROGRAM

The following ALGOL 60 program solves the problem of finding the mean of a list of numbers and how many numbers are greater than the mean.

```
begin comment this program is the ALGOL 60 version of finding the mean
              and the number of those greater than the mean;
    integer n;
    read(n);
    begin real array a[1 : n];
        integer i, number; real sum, mean;
        for i := 1 step 1 until n do read (a[i]);
        sum := 0.0;
        for i := 1 step 1 until n do
        sum := sum + a[i];
        mean := sum/n;
        number := 0;
        for i := 1 step 1 until n do
        if a[i] > mean then number := number + 1;
        write("MEAN =", mean, "NUMBER OVER MEAN =", number)
    end
end
```

Notes

(1)   Unlike FORTRAN, the array declarations in ALGOL 60 could have variable bounds, as the array a has in this program. Variable bounded arrays can only be declared in an inner block and the value of the variable bound must be known before the block is entered at run time.

(2)   There are no implicit declarations in ALGOL 60 – all variables must be declared.

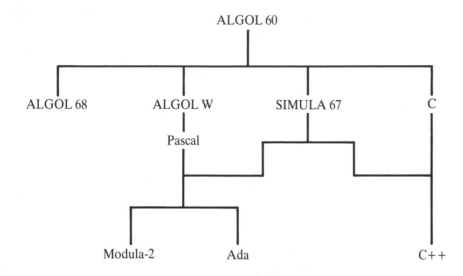

FIGURE 2.2

The main members of the ALGOL family.

parameter wherever it occurred. However, this method had been found to be inefficient and in some instances it led to unexpected results. Although it was still available in ALGOL W, it was discouraged.

- *Long real* and *complex* data types were introduced to enable double-length and complex arithmetic.
- The *bits* data type gave low-level processing ability.
- Assert statements were allowed and the assertions tested during a program run.
- Some string facilities were included, but they were still very primitive.

ALGOL W was indeed a worthy successor to ALGOL 60 and although not widely available, it was well liked by its users.

The next ALGOL-like language was ALGOL 68, which was produced amid much controversy by the International Federation of Information Processing (IFIP) ALGOL working party in 1968. Its initial specification was so abstruse that there was some delay in its implementation and simple guides were produced before even partial acceptance of the language was achieved. Although ALGOL 68 had many virtues, these were rather lost in the controversy about its specification. Consequently, the large claims made for ALGOL 68 were never achieved. The idea of it being a universal language and ideally suited for data processing applications may have had some validity, but this made little impact on practising programmers.

The better points of ALGOL 68 were:

- An economy of concepts: the idea was to produce a core language with a small number of powerful concepts. (Note that PL/I, which is discussed in Section 2.5, went the other way by trying to be a comprehensive language.)
- Uniformity: it tried to avoid special cases.
- Orthogonality: having determined how a feature worked in one situation, it could be expected to behave in a similar way in any other situation; that is, there were no interaction effects between concepts.

2.4   Business Data Processing Languages

In the early stages of their development, computers were thought of as instruments for carrying out scientific calculations. However, it was soon realized that computers manipulated symbols and that these symbols did not necessarily have to be in the form of numbers. This realization led to some consideration of how the computer could be used to help solve the data processing problems inherent in large businesses. One of the major problems that existed in trying to develop a language for this purpose was the lack of a recognized notation – applications of this type were quite different from scientific calculations for which the language of mathematics had for years been the notational basis. One possible language that provided a basis on which to build a notation was the English language; however, on examination, it was found to have too many ambiguities and was unsuited in its natural form to the precision of a computer.

The first business programming language, started in about 1955, was FLOW-MATIC and this led on to the development of COBOL. FLOW-MATIC used English words for operations and data and the data designs were written independently of the manipulation routines. It was planned and implemented only on the UNIVAC 1.

COBOL

COBOL (COmmon Business Oriented Language) was yet another important language developed in the late 1950s. Its development was co-ordinated by a committee consisting mainly of representatives of computer manufacturers in the United States (US Department of Defense: 1960,

1961). Although the major influence on the design of COBOL was FLOW-MATIC, other earlier languages, notably Commercial Translator and AIMACO, also had some effect. COBOL was in fact a development from previous languages and ideas rather than a designed language. Its use has been widespread and for many years it was the single most-used programming language in the world. Undoubtedly, the policy of the US Department of Defense (DOD) had a considerable influence on the success of COBOL. Apart from being one of the prime protagonists of the early meetings and committees when COBOL was introduced, the Department made it its policy to award contracts only where a COBOL compiler was available, and all computers purchased with Government funds had to have such a compiler. In fact, the DOD made COBOL a *de facto* standard long before it had an ANSI (1968) definition.

Since COBOL is essentially a data processing language, it differs significantly from FORTRAN and ALGOL, which emerged at about the same time. It places considerable emphasis on data and its input and output while keeping language features necessary for calculations very simple. As the language statements have an English-like syntax, COBOL is verbose. This was a deliberate design feature, its intention being that managers as well as programmers would find the final programs readable. The verbosity does cause some experienced programmers anguish and attempts were made, via systems like Rapidwrite (Humby, 1964), to allow a shorthand version of COBOL to be written by the professional programmer, from which the compiler could produce full COBOL.

While COBOL was never intended as an innovative language – indeed, it has had very little influence on subsequent languages – it did introduce the basic idea of distinguishing between the description of the data, the physical environment in which the computing was to be done and the actual processes performed on the data. Thus, the logical description of the data of the problem could be described independently of the physical characteristics of the media on which it was stored and manipulated; that is, the description is machine independent without being too inefficient. This separation is an important feature of COBOL and represented a major advance in its time.

A COBOL program is divided into four parts:

(1)   The identification division, which provides commentary and program documentation.

(2)   The environment division, which contains machine-dependent program specifications. Thus, it specifies the connections between the COBOL program and the external data files.

(3)   The data division, which gives a logical description of the data.

(4)   The procedure division, which contains the algorithms necessary to solve the problem.

A COBOL PROGRAM

Programming in COBOL, as in most business data processing, uses the concept of a file as the central data entity. Since the problem given previously is not really suitable for COBOL, as it is essentially scientific, the following COBOL program is a simple data processing application – it reads in one file, extends each record and writes out a new file.

```
      IDENTIFICATION DIVISION.
      PROGRAM-ID. INOUT.

      *Comments are placed on a line that has an asterisk
      *in the first column. It is a good idea to put
      *your NAME and the date of writing on your program.
      *You should also include a brief description of the
      *function of the program.
      *This program reads in one file, extends each record
      *and writes out a new file.
      *

      ENVIRONMENT DIVISION.

      INPUT-OUTPUT SECTION.
      FILE-CONTROL.

          SELECT INP-FIL ASSIGN TO INFILE.
          SELECT OUT-FIL ASSIGN TO OUTFILE.

      DATA DIVISION.
      FILE SECTION.

      FD  INP-FIL
          LABEL RECORDS STANDARD
          DATA RECORD IS REC-IN.
      01  REC-IN.
          05  ALPHA-IN    PIC A(4).
          05  SP-CH-IN    PIC X(4).
          05  NUM-IN      PIC 9(4).

      FD  OUT-FIL
          LABEL RECORDS STANDARD
          DATA RECORD IS REC-OUT.
```

```
01  REC-OUT.
    05  ALPHA-OUT   PIC A(4).
    05  SP-CH-OUT   PIC X(4).
    05  NUM-OUT     PIC 9(4).
    05  EXTRAS      PIC X(16).

WORKING-STORAGE SECTION.

01  EOF             PIC X VALUE IS 'N'.

PROCEDURE DIVISION.

AA.

    OPEN INPUT INP-FIL
    OPEN OUTPUT OUT-FIL

    PERFORM CC
    PERFORM BB THRU CC UNTIL EOF = 'Y'

    CLOSE INP-FIL, OUT-FIL
    DISPLAY "End of Run"

    STOP RUN.

BB.

    MOVE REC-IN TO REC-OUT
    MOVE 'EXTRA CHARACTERS' TO EXTRAS
    WRITE REC-OUT.

CC.

    READ INP-FIL
        AT END MOVE 'Y' TO EOF.

************* END OF LISTING **************
```

Note

(1)   This shows how COBOL divides programs into the four standard parts:
IDENTIFICATION DIVISION, ENVIRONMENT DIVISION, DATA DIVISION and PROCEDURE DIVISION.

Not all of the design features of COBOL have proved successful. For example, few programmers consider that the English-like form of the COBOL statement makes the overall program easily comprehensible. Even at the statement level, possible misunderstandings can arise. As an example, consider the COBOL statement:

```
DIVIDE CAKE INTO 3.
```

When executed in COBOL, the number 3 is divided by the value of the variable CAKE, which is not the result expected from the English translation. The difficulties of readability are even more noticeable when a complete COBOL program is examined and the lack of structure in the language evident.

The development of COBOL

The development of COBOL for use in business data processing paralleled that of FORTRAN in the scientific community in many respects. However, the proliferation of different dialects of COBOL never happened to the extent that it did with FORTRAN due to its tightly controlled development. The syntax of COBOL was formalized very early in its development (1965). (The meta-language used was not the BNF of ALGOL 60 but one more suited to COBOL's statements and structures.) The control of COBOL has been exercised through the Executive Committee of CODASYL (COnference on DAta SYstems Languages), which was instrumental in its initial development. This control has led to an orderly maintenance and enhancement of the language, something that is not so necessary for a dynamic, new language but essential for a language that is intended for wide use in business data processing.

Although the tight control on COBOL has had some good effects – for example, making it effectively a universal language for data processing – it has had the drawback that the language has hardly changed in the first 25 years of its active life. Those changes (for example, the 1974 and 1985 standards) that have come about have been mainly to keep up with major equipment advances, but these have been relatively modest.

RPG

RPG (Report Program Generator) was introduced by IBM in the early 1960s in response to customer requests for a simple language for the generation of reports. This request arose mainly from the users of small IBM computers who found the COBOL compiler too large and the assembler too difficult to use.

The original RPG was not a great success due to technical difficulties, which made the process of using it slow and unwieldy. However, when IBM introduced the new 360 series of machines in 1965, an improved version of the language, RPG II, was brought out with considerably enhanced features. Further improvements to RPG occurred in the 1970s but these were mainly to do with supporting terminal processing.

RPG has a fixed coding structure with formats for:

- input specification (files and data),
- switch specification (Booleans),
- calculation and process,
- output specification.

Underlying the compiler is a 'fixed' logic cycle of input–process–output which is, nevertheless, flexible and has quite sophisticated options. It supports procedures and subroutine calls and is easily linked with other RPG or assembler programs. It also supports any reasonable range of inputs and outputs, including sequential, indexed sequential and random files, and handles arrays and binary (as opposed to decimal) calculations. An unusual and very successful feature is a built-in matching logic that handles file-matching problems of considerable complexity – a very common requirement in data processing. The fixed format and 'fixed' logic of RPG make its programs almost self-documenting, and thus maintenance and modifications are easier.

The newer versions of RPG are effective alternatives to COBOL, or PL/I, for a wide range of commercial work and are better adapted to access via terminals.

Fourth-generation languages

Programming languages are sometimes classified by their generation. Machine codes formed the first generation, autocodes and symbolic assemblers the second generation while high-level languages such as FORTRAN, COBOL and Pascal are often referred to as being of the third generation. A feature that distinguishes third-generation languages from their predecessors is their independence from particular computer hardware. The aim of the fourth generation is to make languages much more problem oriented.

Fourth-generation languages (4GLs) are languages that were developed as a result of the dissatisfaction of business users with large conventional languages like COBOL. These users were often not professional programmers who wished to obtain quick results from data stored in a computer. The availability of terminals and, more recently, IBM PCs and their clones has had a major influence on the use of 4GLs. A business manager sitting at a desk with a PC wants quick results and is neither able nor prepared to embark on a large programming exercise to get them.

The problem in discussing 4GLs is their bewildering number and variety. Most are commercially produced for a particular computer or range of computers and the distinction between a language and a package is not always clear. The following tries to distinguish the main strands in this somewhat confused area.

Application generators

These languages generate solutions for routine applications. Typical operations include data entry, ideally with full checking, and updating of files or databases.

Query languages

These languages are used with databases and allow the user to ask questions relating to several fields of the basic data records. More sophisticated languages in this category also allow the user to update the database.

Decision-support languages

The intention of the designers of languages of this type was to help the user make informed and therefore better decisions. Such languages provide the user with facilities to build databases and to then perform statistical calculations, such as an analysis of trends on the data. Decision-support languages are usually business oriented and are typically used in the planning stage for analyzing projected financial investment. They may include graphics facilities to enhance the display of material and vary from the simple, but effective, spreadsheets of VISICALC and LOTUS 1-2-3 to languages with sophisticated statistical and operations research features for decision making. Most of them also include windowing and data scrolling as important facilities.

In practice, 4GLs are not clearly divided into these three categories. While many 4GLs include report generators and graphics facilities as part of the language, others have such facilities provided as separate packages. Certainly, the ability of such languages to provide easy access to interactive graphics is an important factor for the business user on his or her PC.

4GLs are currently the most fluid area in programming language design with new languages springing up and others withering away through lack of users. What is not being produced are well designed and thought out languages carefully tailored to the needs of the customer and which take into account current and future computer hardware.

2.5   General or Multipurpose Languages

In the late 1950s and early 1960s, language designers started working on the integration of the data processing ideas that had resulted in COBOL with the principles underlying scientific languages such as ALGOL and FORTRAN. The first multipurpose language to emerge was JOVIAL (Jules Own Version of the International Algorithmic Language), which was developed at System Development Corporation (SDC). The major influence on its design was IAL (or ALGOL 58 as it is now more commonly known). The language is, therefore, much closer to the ideas of ALGOL than FORTRAN. As the language was developed to program a very large real-time system called SAGE, which had previously been written in machine code, the major objective in developing JOVIAL was to produce a language for programming large complex systems. In effect, JOVIAL combined the ability of doing numerical scientific computations with non-trivial data handling, manipulation and storage as well as adequate input/output facilities.

PL/I

In the early 1960s, two categories of programmer could be fairly clearly distinguished. On the one hand, there was the scientific programmer, usually using FORTRAN, whose needs were floating-point arithmetic, arrays, procedures and fast computation, usually via batch job processing. On the other hand, there was the commercial user who merely required decimal arithmetic in addition to fast and asynchronous input/output, string handling facilities and efficient searching and sorting routines. However, there was also a growing band of special-purpose users who had diverse requirements, such as efficient real-time working, pattern matching facilities, variable length bit string arithmetic and list processing.

IBM was very much in the forefront of progress at this time and saw the opportunity in providing a computer system suitable for a wide range of users. The system that emerged was the IBM 360. To accommodate this new hardware, a new programming language was to be developed. Originally, this language was called NPL, but the acronym was later dropped in favour of PL/I (Programming Language I) because of confusion with the National Physical Laboratory at Teddington, UK.

This new programming language was originally designed by a committee of IBM and their users who solicited views from a wide range of people as well as studying the major current languages FORTRAN, ALGOL, COBOL and JOVIAL. The guiding principles of the designers were as follows.

- the programmers' time is an important asset and should not be wasted,
- there is a unity in programming which the current division between scientific and commercial languages did not reflect.

The designers hoped, therefore, to produce a language that was comprehensive, easy to learn, teach and use, and capable of extension and subsetting. There were to be as few machine dependencies as possible while allowing the programmer to have full access to machine and operating system facilities without resorting to assembly language coding.

To accomplish all these design criteria, a large language was obviously going to be required. However, the designers felt that the programmers need not know all the features of the language to be able to use it efficiently. The result was the crucial and controversial idea at the heart of PL/I – namely, default. Every attribute of a variable, every option and every specification had a default interpretation and this was set to be the one most likely required by a programmer who does not know that alternatives exist. However, the implications of the default criterion were much wider than users had at first envisaged.

As the original version of PL/I (the NPL version) was too broad and incompletely specified, IBM took on the task of clarifying and refining the original specification. The version of PL/I that finally emerged combined many of the ideas of FORTRAN, ALGOL and COBOL. From FORTRAN, came the parameter-passing mechanisms, independently compiled subprograms, formatted input/output and COMMON blocks; from ALGOL, block structure and structured statements; from COBOL, record input/output, PICTURE type declarations and heterogeneous data structures. There were, however, ideas culled from elsewhere; namely, list processing concepts, control structures and methods for storage management. One new feature was exception handling by means of ON-conditions.

Before PL/I, language designers had either opted for run-time efficiency at the expense of flexibility (as was done, for example, in FORTRAN and COBOL) or had allowed flexibility at the expense of run-time efficiency (for example, SNOBOL and LISP). PL/I, in contrast, attempted to have both run-time efficiency and flexibility, but the penalty it paid was language complexity. It did by its existence highlight the problems involved in trying to design a general-purpose language that strives to satisfy all programmers. Nevertheless, it represents one extreme in design philosophy; that is, providing features for all applications within a fixed framework – what might be called a 'complete' language.

The alternative strategy to PL/I, probably best (although not ideally) represented by ALGOL 68, was to have a small core of basic language features that could be easily extended. The argument of core vs complete languages was much debated in the late 1960s and early 1970s but no worthwhile conclusions were reached.

A PL/I PROGRAM

Here is a PL/I solution to the problem of finding the mean of a list of numbers and the number of values that are greater than the mean:

```
EXAMPLE : PROCEDURE OPTIONS (MAIN);
 /* This is the PL/I version of the mean and the number
    of values greater than the mean */
 GET LIST (N);
 IF N > 0 THEN BEGIN;
   DECLARE MEAN, A(N) DECIMAL FLOAT,
     SUM DEC FLOAT INITIAL(0), NUMBER FIXED INITIAL (0);
   GET LIST (A);
   DO I = 1 TO N;
     SUM = SUM + A(I);
   END;
   MEAN = SUM/N;
   DO I = 1 TO N;
     IF A(I) > MEAN THEN
       NUMBER = NUMBER + 1;
   END;
   PUT LIST ('MEAN = ', MEAN, 'NUMBER GREATER THAN MEAN = ', NUMBER);
END EXAMPLE;
```

Notes

(1)   PL/I allows both explicit and implicit declarations which can include initialization as in the case of SUM and NUMBER above.

(2)   It allows operations with entire arrays like GET LIST (A).

(3)   The final END can be used to terminate any inner blocks as well as the outermost block.

The future of general-purpose languages

PL/I suffered from considerable teething problems and, indeed, without the massive backing of IBM, it would probably have died an early death. IBM's support kept it alive but even they could not force users to accept it. At one stage, IBM tried to replace FORTRAN and COBOL by PL/I making it the universal language. However, customer resistance was too strong and many people threatened to take their business elsewhere if IBM would not provide FORTRAN and COBOL compilers. Hence, IBM being a sound commercial organization, capitulated. So PL/I had to exist and justify itself in competition with FORTRAN and COBOL.

The size of PL/I produced large compilers and hence slow compile times, particularly with small machines where the overlaying of code for the compiler was necessary. The increase in core storage and the production of optimizing compilers did help to alleviate these problems but, even so, PL/I never replaced either FORTRAN or COBOL, never mind both.

The search for a universal language did not stop with PL/I, although its lack of success considerably dented the hopes of designers. The latest candidate in this respect is Ada which has the massive support of the DOD. It has been dubbed by its detractors as "The PL/I of the eighties".

2.6   Interactive Languages

Early computers only ran one program at a time, but as computers developed and became more complex, operating systems were designed to use the available facilities – high-speed store, backing store, input/output devices – more efficiently. For example, the slowness of the input/output operations in comparison with the speed of the central processor led to **time sharing** with many remote stations sharing the time of the central computer. Eventually, the remote terminal became the normal tool of the programmer. Changes such as these started in the early 1960s and gradually gathered momentum until by the mid 1970s it was commonplace.

Although programming languages began to adapt to these changing circumstances, the provisions varied widely. Most language compilers were available to programmers at their terminals in more or less the same way as that for batch processing. Programmers put their programs into a file and then ran the appropriate language compiler using the file as the source program. Errors, if there were any, were output to the terminal and, if necessary, placed in a scratch file for reference. The programmer could then modify the original file and re-run the compiler. There were, however, some attempts to provide the programmer with better interactive facilities for on-line programming.

JOSS (Johnniac Open Shop System), developed in the early 1960s at the RAND Corporation, was probably the first interactive language. It demonstrated the value of on-line access to a computer and provided simple calculating facilities, a feature that was particularly useful to non-specialist engineers. QUIKTRAN, which emerged a little later, was the result of an attempt to adapt an existing language, FORTRAN, for use on a remote terminal: features of FORTRAN that were unsuitable for an interactive environment were omitted while a number of features that facilitated on-line debugging were added. QUIKTRAN was kept compatible with FORTRAN so that programs developed and debugged on a terminal could also use the regular FORTRAN compiler in batch mode.

For quite different reasons, two interactive languages, BASIC and APL, have made a considerable impact on programming.

BASIC

BASIC (Beginner's All-purpose Symbolic Instruction Code) was developed at Dartmouth College by Kemeny and Kurtz in the mid 1960s. Their intention was to produce a language that was very simple for students to learn and one that was easy to translate. The idea was that students could be merely casual users or go on from BASIC to more sophisticated and powerful languages, and that a casual programmer who has done nothing for six months can still remember how to program in BASIC (JOSS also claims this benefit). As someone described it, it is like learning to ride a bicycle or swim, once learned never forgotten. For many programmers, BASIC was like a return to the early autocodes: it could be learnt very quickly and programs written after one or two days' practice. However, it was not without its problems, particularly when larger more comprehensive work was required.

Like FORTRAN, a decade earlier, the success of BASIC surprised its inventors. However, this success was, no doubt, due mainly to the need for a simple high-level language for the new microcomputers of the mid 1970s, and BASIC was available, well known and certainly simple. It caught on in a big way.

In addition to the normal statements of a traditional programming language, BASIC has a few simple user commands which represent the interactive part of the language. The NEW command is used to create a BASIC program, which may be listed by the LIST command, edited by the DELETE command, executed by the RUN command and saved by the SAVE command. Any previously saved program can be retrieved for further use by the OLD command. BASIC is therefore not just a language, but incorporates sufficient operating system commands to make it complete in itself.

A BASIC PROGRAM

The solution to the problem of finding the mean and the number of values greater than the mean is given here in BASIC for comparison:

```
10 REM THIS IS A BASIC PROGRAM FOR FINDING THE MEAN
20 DIM A(99)
30 INPUT N
40 FOR I = 1 TO N
50 INPUT A(I)
60 LET S = S + A(I)
70 NEXT I
80 LET M = S/N
90 LET K = 0
100 FOR I = 1 TO N
110 IF A(I) < M THEN 130
120 LET K = K + 1
130 NEXT I
140 PRINT "MEAN IS ", MEAN
150 PRINT "NUMBER GREATER THAN MEAN IS ", K
160 STOP
170 END
```

Note

(1)   Variables cannot be declared, are single letters and automatically initialize to zero.

APL

APL (A Programming Language) was originally defined by Iverson as a mathematical language for the concise description of numerical algorithms. In its original form, it contained a large number of operators – the standard operators +, − and × in addition to more exotic ones for operating on arrays. However, when the language was eventually implemented on a computer, several operators were omitted, but it still remained in its programming language form a remarkably 'rich' language.

APL has a large alphabet (52 letters, 10 digits and 52 other characters) and the following unusual characteristics:

- The primitive objects are arrays (lists, tables, matrices).

- It is an operator-driven language. Although branching operations are possible, they are little used in practice as the power of the language mainly comes from its array operators.

- There is no operator precedence: all statements are parsed from right to left.

APL generally requires a programming technique very different from that used with the traditional scientific languages. Indeed, many programmers find the ability to program in a traditional language is more of a hindrance than a help when using APL. To be successful, a programmer needs to envisage what effect different operators, either on their own or in conjunction with other operators, have on arrays. Programs often contain, therefore, a succession of such operators. The designer Iverson recommended beginners to 'play' with the language to get a feel for the effect of the operators, both on their own and in conjunction.

Although there has been a lot of controversy about APL, it nevertheless seems to attract devotees who consider it the only language for the programmer. It has also been suggested that it brings computing and mathematics closer together.

2.7 Special-Purpose Languages

A large number of programming languages have been developed for a specific purpose; for example, SNOBOL which illustrated string manipulation techniques. This section looks at some of the languages that are important either in their own right or because of their influence on the development of other programming languages.

String manipulation languages

The first effective string manipulation language was COMIT, which provided a means of searching a string pattern and performing transformations when that pattern was found. COMIT was developed at the Massachusetts Institute of Technology (MIT) in the period 1957–1961. A more widely used and influential string manipulation language was SNOBOL, which was developed at Bell Laboratories several years after COMIT. The early versions of SNOBOL had several teething troubles and when discussing the language, it is usually SNOBOL4, which came out in 1967, that is considered as the definitive version. These early string manipulation languages were used in areas such as symbolic mathematics, text preparation and natural language applications.

In SNOBOL4, the basic element is the character string. Although there are operations for joining and separating these character strings, the most fundamental operation in SNOBOL4 is the pattern match. This operation examines a string to see if it possesses a particular substring or other property. If a match is found, then various possibilities, such as replacement, can take place.

SNOBOL4 has two types of data structure: ARRAY and TABLE. ARRAY is a collection of data items that need not be of uniform type. The items are indexed by numeric subscripts in the normal way. TABLE, on the other hand, is an associative array with each element indexed by a unique associative value that is not necessarily an integer; for example, it could be a string such as COLOUR['RED'].

Although SNOBOL4 has had little influence on the major general-purpose languages, whose string handling facilities fall far short of those provided by SNOBOL, the ideas embedded in SNOBOL did have an impact on the designers of text editors. It should be remembered that the more sophisticated operations in SNOBOL, such as pattern matching with replacement, can extend the length of the original string, but that to do this satisfactorily requires dynamic storage allocation. However, as this is not something language implementors are keen to provide, string operations in other languages are usually restricted to string comparison, string movement and other operations that do not lengthen the string. The effect of this is that strings have a fixed maximum length throughout the execution of a program.

SNOBOL, with its emphasis on strings and string manipulation, jumps and labels and with no declarations, is a maverick among modern languages. It shows an alternative way of doing things which, in many cases, is not as bad as 'the structuralists' would have people believe. The main complaint against SNOBOL is its unfortunate habit of making spaces significant in some operations. Once such an error is made it can be very troublesome to find.

List-processing languages

In the early scientific languages (FORTRAN and ALGOL), the only data structure was the array. All of its elements were of the same type and, in the case of FORTRAN, it was of fixed size. Although COBOL had a data structure that allowed elements of different types, in none of these early languages was there scope for altering the basic structure of the array. This is in essence what list processing accomplishes, usually by having an element divided into an information part and a pointer part. The pointer part can, in the case of a linked list, reference the next element in the list, but in tree structures there are usually at least two pointers. In general, the linkage can be as complex as required by the problem although in languages such as LISP the pointers are implicit.

The early list-processing languages were developed to show the value of such processing in the programming environment. The first such language was IPL-V, which was developed at the Carnegie Institute of Technology in the period 1957–1961. IPL-V was really an assembly level set of commands for doing list processing on a hypothetical machine – the commands were interpreted. The significance of IPL-V was to define the concept of a list and to show how it could be implemented, albeit very crudely. It was used mainly by those programming artificial intelligence problems and it pioneered many of the fundamental concepts of list processing – in particular, the idea of a **free space list** from which storage space for new elements of the list could be obtained and to which storage space could be returned when no longer required.

The other early list-processing language, LISP, has had a more lasting effect on programming language design. It was developed by John McCarthy at MIT in the late 1950s and he and his co-workers produced a workable language in the early 1960s.

The principal features of LISP are as follows:

- It performs computations with or on symbolic expressions rather than numbers. This arose because the designers were mainly mathematicians who were particularly interested in applying computing to artificial intelligence problems (game playing, theorem proving, natural language processing).

- It represents symbolic expressions and other information in the form of list structures in computer memory – this idea originated from IPL.

- It uses a small set of constructor and selector operations to create and extract information from lists. These operations are expressed as functions and use the mathematical idea of the composition of functions as a means of constructing more complex functions.

- Control is recursive rather than iterative.

- Data and programs are equivalent forms. Thus, programs can be modified as data and data structures executed as programs.

In addition to these features, LISP was probably the first language to implement storage management by garbage collection. Furthermore, there is an affinity between LISP and Lambda calculus which it seems was not planned by the designers.

LISP as implemented on a computer is somewhat different from the 'pure' LISP of the original definitions. It does, however, come close to being a **functional language** (as pure LISP is). A functional language has as its fundamental operation the evaluation of expressions. This is in contrast to the majority of languages (FORTRAN, COBOL, Pascal, BASIC, ALGOL), known as **imperative languages**, which use a sequence of commands to carry out the desired operations. Interest in functional languages has increased significantly during the 1980s. A major reason for this is that, as functional programs achieve their effect by creating new objects rather than by modifying existing ones, they are easier to reason about than their imperative counterparts.

LISP has survived as a language despite the death of most list-processing languages for several reasons. It is an elegant mathematical system with a simple basic functional structure capable of expressing the ideas of Lambda calculus. These features, together with the fact that LISP systems allow programs to be developed interactively, make LISP well suited to artificial intelligence applications. Finally, the survival of LISP has been helped by an agreement on a standard version of the language known as COMMON LISP.

The early 1960s saw a rash of list-processing languages: for example, L6, IPL, SLIP and WISP. However, their day was soon over when the general-purpose languages (ALGOL W, ALGOL 68, PL/I, Pascal and Ada) started to incorporate list-processing facilities within the language.

Simulation languages

The simulation of discrete systems was one of the first problems that computers were used to solve. These systems were modelled by a series of state changes that often occur in parallel. Complex interactions could arise between the elements of the system as they compete for restricted system resources. The simulation technique itself follows the system elements through their changes of state gathering quantitative information. This information is then used to predict the properties of the system under hypothetical situations. For example, simulation of a traffic system can predict how the proposed model will perform as traffic densities increase and hopefully show where bottlenecks could occur.

The earliest simulation language to be widely used was GPSS (General-Purpose Simulation System). Although it was first described in 1961, it was somewhat later before the system was available to programmers. In GPSS, the system being simulated is described by a block diagram in which the blocks represent the activities and the lines joining the blocks indicate the logical sequence in which the activities can be executed. When there is a choice of activities, this is represented by several lines leaving a block and the conditions under which this choice is made is stated in the block.

GPSS provided the user with a set of different block types to simulate a system. The activities of the system (often called **transactions**) are created in GENERATE blocks. Although each transaction can only be in one block at any instant of time, it may be transferred instantaneously to another block at a specific time. Many transactions can move through a block diagram simultaneously and many transactions can be in the same block at any instance. Transactions have priorities and can have associated data attributes. Clock time is used and a block type, ADVANCE, is concerned with representing the expenditure of time.

A GPSS program operates by moving a transaction as far as it can go and then seeing if there are other transactions due to move at the same time instant. When all such movements have been completed, the program advances the clock to the time of the next imminent event and repeats the process. When the simulation is terminated, the program automatically prints an output report. In addition, certain block types are available for gathering statistics.

GPSS has often been criticized for the slow execution time of its programs. While not denying the slow run time, which is due mainly to the use of interpretive programming to implement the block diagram, the designers point out that the ease of using GPSS means that the overall time for developing the model and obtaining the final results is shorter than that in many other languages.

Not long after the arrival of GPSS, the RAND Corporation developed a simulation language called SIMSCRIPT. In SIMSCRIPT, the system being simulated is described in terms of entities, attributes (the properties associated with entities) and sets (groups of entities). For example, an entity could be a student, the attributes might be name, sex, courses and address, and the sets could be the collections of students in various departments. Unlike the block diagram approach of GPSS, in SIMSCRIPT the programmer models the action of the system by writing FORTRAN-like statements. Another difference is that the SIMSCRIPT approach is based on subprograms rather than coroutines.

In Europe in the early 1960s a small group led by Ole-Johan Dahl and Kristan Nygaard at the Norwegian Computer Centre were also constructing a simulation language which eventually became known as SIMULA 67, although this was not the first working version of the language. It was designed for system description and simulation, a system in this case being a collection of independent objects with a common objective. Systems were simulated by examining the life cycle of the elements of the system.

SIMULA was based on ALGOL 60 with one very important addition – the **class** concept. Using this concept, it is possible to declare a class, generate objects of that class, name these objects and form a hierarchical structure of class declarations. Although this concept was only introduced to describe the life cycles of the elements in the discrete simulation, it was later recognized as a general programming tool ideal for describing and designing programs in an abstract way. The basic idea was that the data (or data structure) and the operations performed on it belonged together, and this forms the basis for the implementation of abstract data types.

The class concept has been adapted and used in many modern languages, such as Concurrent Pascal, Modula-2, CLU and Ada. It has also proved useful in concurrent programming. Classes in SIMULA are based on procedure declarations and the block structure of ALGOL 60, but free the latter concept from its inherently nested structure by allowing several block instances to co-exist.

When viewed objectively, SIMULA is more like a general-purpose language of the ALGOL W type rather than a special-purpose simulation language. Indeed, the simulation is usually done by using two supplied classes SIMSET and SIMULATION. Nevertheless, SIMULA 67 has survived and had a considerable influence on programming languages as diverse as Smalltalk, C++ and Ada.

Systems programming languages

In the 1960s there was considerable resistance to the use of any high-level languages on the part of programmers who were writing systems programs (such as compilers and operating systems). They argued that the needs of efficiency dictated the use of assembly level languages. One of the first applications of higher level languages in the systems field was syntax-directed compilers. Gradually, systems programmers moved away (often reluctantly) from low-level programming to high-level languages such as PL/I. However, they still tended to retreat back into low-level code for the 'vital' parts of the system because, basically, the general-purpose languages did not contain the low-level facilities required in systems work. What was really needed was a specialist systems programming language, but unfortunately there seemed to be no agreement on what such a language should contain. Hence, the result was a proliferation of such languages – it almost seemed that you could not be considered an advanced systems programming group if you did not have your own language.

Systems programming languages is rather a broad term, covering a wide range of applications such as operating systems and real-time systems. Such languages should have facilities for activating several processes simultaneously, synchronizing these processes as appropriate and responding to interrupts. The ideas of concurrent processing (or parallel programming) were developed more intensively in the 1970s and are discussed in Section 2.8.

BCPL and Coral 66, introduced during the late 1960s and early 1970s, were the most popular systems programming languages in the UK, the latter being more widely used because of the support given to it by the UK Ministry of Defence. In the United States, the situation was less clear as several languages (for example, JOVIAL, BLISS and XPL) were being used. The most widely used systems programming language is now C, which is examined in more detail in Section 2.8.

An interesting new development in this area is the language occam, which was developed for use with a particular computer – the transputer. The idea is to build powerful computers from a network of transputers operating in parallel. Communication and synchronization are therefore central to the design of both the transputer and of the language occam.

Occam is a simple language that has the process as the central concept. What would be subprograms in a conventional language are processes in occam. Processes communicate with one another by sending messages over channels – this corresponds closely to the hardware links between transputers. The general approach to communication and synchronization is in fact very similar to that used in Ada and is discussed in Chapter 8.

Packages

Packages are not strictly programming languages at all, but it is sometimes very difficult to tell where a package ends and a language begins. There has been a large increase in the use of packages over the past 10 years, mainly at the expense of specialist languages. Hence, users, instead of learning a specialized language for their field, are provided with a package that often requires very little extra knowledge to use.

Possibly the most widely used package is SPSS (Statistical Package for Social Scientists). SPSS has replaced simulation languages in many applications even though it provides less sophisticated facilities. However, it is much easier to use and can be employed by people with very little knowledge of computers and how they operate. This fact leads many users to treat such a package as a black box, with little idea of how it works, which itself has dangerous implications and does require such users to take care in checking the validity of what they are doing and the results obtained.

Packages are heavily used in scientific calculations and, as numerical methods become standardized, new and improved algorithms are incorporated. SSP (Scientific Subroutine Package) was the forerunner, but has been superseded by the NAG (Numerical Algorithms Group) library in Britain and Europe and by ISML in the United States. In both these cases, a specialist group keeps the packages up to date by adding new accredited algorithms and improving existing ones.

2.8   Programming Languages in the 1970s and Early 1980s

The 1960s saw the establishment of many programming languages – notably, FORTRAN, ALGOL, COBOL, PL/I and BASIC. These languages consolidated their grip on the market and made it exceedingly difficult for any new language to make a major impact. Of the languages that emerged during the 1970s, three are certain to survive into the 1990s and beyond. These are Pascal, which is exerting a strong influence as an initial teaching language; C, which is currently the main language for systems programmers and is boosted by the continuing and growing importance of the UNIX operating system; and Ada, which appeared at the very end of the decade and is more correctly considered a language of the 1980s. Another language that arrived in the late 1970s but made little impact until the 1980s is PROLOG. Modula-2 also emerged in the 1970s from the Wirth stable which was responsible for the design of ALGOL W, PL360 and Pascal. Object-oriented programming which is based on two primitives, objects and messages, is also attracting a lot of attention. Its main representative language is Smalltalk.

Pascal

Pascal was developed by Professor Niklaus Wirth in the late 1960s and early 1970s. His aims were to produce a language that could be efficiently implemented on most computers and be suitable for teaching programming as a logical and systematic discipline, thus encouraging well-structured and well-organized programs. Pascal was influenced more by ALGOL-like languages than FORTRAN. However, there was a determined effort by Wirth to make his language efficient. He felt that this was the only way to challenge the strong grip FORTRAN had on programming, particularly in the United States. Thus, Pascal contains certain features for efficiency reasons.

The static array is probably the most controversial feature of Pascal. In most ALGOL-like languages, the size of an array does not have to be specified until a block is entered at run time. Although this allows for more flexible programming and a more efficient use of storage, it does usually slow down program execution. Pascal adopted the static array, as used in FORTRAN, where the size is determined at compile time. In addition, the passing of array parameters in procedures also used fixed sized arrays. This was an even more controversial decision because of the restrictions it imposed, particularly on those doing numerical calculations. However, this restriction was removed when the ISO Standard for Pascal was published in 1982 (ISO, 1982).

One of the positive aspects of Pascal is the inclusion of features that encourage well-written and well-structured programs. For example, although **goto** statements are included, they are a restricted and minor feature of the language. Pascal also includes ALGOL-like structured loops with the addition of a **repeat** ... **until** construct. Data types are a prominent feature of Pascal and they can be built up from the primitive, unstructured types *integer*, *real*, *Boolean* and *char*. The unstructured user-defined types are defined either by enumeration of the possible values, as in:

```
type suit = (clubs, diamonds, hearts, spades, notrumps);
```

or by subrange, as in:

```
type letter = 'A' .. 'Z';
     digit = 0 .. 9;
```

The structured user-defined types include arrays, records, sets and files. In addition, pointer types may be used, usually in conjunction with records, to form linked lists or tree structures. Strings can be declared and manipulated in Pascal, but the rigid size of the string and the lack of suitable string operations make string handling clumsy.

Pascal only started to be widely used in the late 1970s when many universities adopted it as their initial teaching language for computer science students and by the mid 1980s it had become the dominant teaching language. The reasons for this movement were the need for a language that provided a comprehensive set of data structures and which encouraged good programming style. Although the switch to Pascal has been slower in industry, there is now considerable interest in the language, particularly at the small computer end of the market. Previously, microcomputer programmers used low-level languages, with BASIC as the common high-level language because of the smallness of its interpreter. However, Pascal compilers are usually small enough to fit comfortably into micros and many users prefer the programming facilities of Pascal to those provided by the unstructured BASIC.

The C language

Historically, C evolved from BCPL through the language B and was the programming language used to implement the UNIX operating system together with most of its commands. C and the UNIX system were in fact developed together at Bell Laboratories. Some aspects of the design of C – for example, the ++ operator – reflect its origins and features that were available on the PDP-11 computer for which the first compiler was written.

The strength of C lies in the fact that it combines the advantages of a high-level language with the facilities and efficiency of an assembly language. The flexibility required by a systems programming language is provided by the lack of type checking and the ability to perform arithmetic on store addresses and operations on bit patterns. This flexibility, combined with the availability of a wide range of operators that may be freely combined, means that it is possible to write very compact and efficient code. However, the major drawback is that the code is often far from readable and the lack of type checking means that it is much easier to write erroneous programs in C than in a language like Pascal.

Apart from the fact that it does not allow the nesting of subprograms, C has all the facilities expected of a modern imperative language; that is, structured control statements, recursion, records and dynamic data structures. It is also a relatively small language and the existence of a portable C compiler means that it can be implemented relatively easily on a new machine. An object-oriented extension of C, called C++, has recently been developed and, in line with modern thinking, it has much stricter type checking.

Although it originated as a systems programming language, the use of C has spread into other areas and so it must now be regarded as a general-purpose language. It is, however, a language for experienced programmers rather than novices.

A C PROGRAM

A C program to solve the problem of finding the mean of a list of numbers and how many are greater than the mean is as follows:

```
main( )
/* this is the C version of the program to find the
   mean and the number of those greater than the mean */

{ float a[100], mean, sum;
  /* the array a has 100 elements – a[0] .. a[99] */
  int n, i, number;
  scanf("%d", &n);
  for(i = 0; i < n; i++) scanf("%f", &a[i]);
  sum = 0.0;
  for(i = 0; i < n; i++)
     sum += a[i];
  mean = sum/n;
  number = 0;
  for(i = 0; i < n; i++)
  {  if (a[i] > mean) number++;
  }
  printf("MEAN = %f\n", mean);
  printf("NUMBER OVER MEAN = %d\n", number);
}
```

Note

(1)   The three statements:

$$i++; \qquad i += 1; \qquad i = i + 1;$$

all have the same effect.

Ada

The US Department of Defense, the largest user of computers in the world, decided to sponsor the development of a new programming language in the mid 1970s. The main reason for this was that it was dissatisfied with the conglomeration of different languages used in its computer systems and it wanted a standard programming language for embedded computer systems. The latter are computer systems used to control part of a larger system, such as an industrial plant, an aircraft or a hospital life support system. These applications are normally very large, highly complex, contain a high degree of concurrency and change with time. The other important requirement of such systems is high reliability combined with the ability to recover from errors.

The original requirements for this new language were given in a document called 'Strawman' and were further refined in documents called 'Woodenman', 'Tinman', 'Ironman' and 'Steelman'. At the 'Tinman' stage, it was decided there was no suitable existing language and so an international design competition was organized. This was won by a group from CII-Honeywell Bull of France headed by Jean Ichbiah. The resulting language was called Ada after Ada, Countess of Lovelace, who worked on Babbage's Analytical Engine and was considered by many to be the first programmer.

Although Ada is Pascal based, it is a much larger and more complex language. It not only extends Pascal constructs but contains features that have no analogue in Pascal. One of the key features of Ada is the package, which is designed for the description of large software components. A package has affinities both with the class concept of SIMULA 67 and the module of Modula-2. It contains type definitions and data objects in addition to operations for manipulating these objects. So, like the class concept, it is a further abstraction of the well-known procedure idea. Packages aid information hiding because both the representation of data and the implementation of the operations may be hidden from the user. Ada also has the notion of a library of packages, thereby enabling the programmer to create a system from combinations of existing packages, rather than writing a new program from scratch.

Apart from a broad range of built-in data types, there is a powerful set of data typing mechanisms. Ada is a strongly typed language, which means that all type checking can be done at compile time. Sequencing and control statements are similar to those used in Pascal – namely, **if** ... **then** ... **else**, **case**, **while** and **for** – but the **goto** statement is only given in a restricted form. An interesting feature of Ada is the loop structure which includes an **exit when** construct. This allows general loops with a test at the beginning, like the traditional **while** statement, at the end, like the **repeat** ... **until** statement, or in the middle of the loop. Procedures and functions are again similar to those in Pascal, but the parameter-passing mechanisms using **in**, **out** and **in out** correspond to ALGOL W's value, result and value-result.

The task facility in Ada is included to permit parallel processing and there is a *clock* data type to exercise control and allow the programmer to handle real-time applications. Ada also contains an extensive set of features for interrupt and exception handling. These are on the same lines as the PL/I ON-conditions, but are more powerful and somewhat better designed. In the opinion of the authors, the ramifications of these complex facilities are not fully understood by the language designers and the lack of a formal semantics supports this view.

Ada is undoubtedly a very comprehensive language and the support of the US Department of Defense will ensure it has a prominent place in the programming environment. The strongest criticism of the language is Tony Hoare's ACM Turing Lecture entitled 'The Emperor's Old Clothes' (1981). His principal objection to Ada is that it is too big and far too complex, to which the Ada designers reply that large, real-world problems cannot be solved with small simple languages. No doubt this argument will continue to rage for many years but it is just possible that a simpler language has already emerged in the form of Modula-2.

Modula-2

The language Modula-2 was designed by Wirth and thus, not surprisingly, is a descendant of Pascal and Modula. Modula-2 is, in effect, Pascal with the module concept and some multiprogramming facilities added. Modula was Wirth's first attempt to extend Pascal in this way and, although not wholly successful, pointed the direction for Modula-2.

The extensions to Pascal in Modula-2 are:

- The module concept and, in particular, the separation of specification and implementation.

- A more systematic syntax so that each programming structure starts and ends with a keyword.

- The inclusion of low-level facilities for mapping structured data on to storage without structure. This enabled Modula-2 to be used as a systems programming language.

- The concept of processes and their synchronization, modified by the notion of coroutines.

- Procedure types, which extend the normal idea of a procedure to allow the declaration of types whose values are procedures.

The concept of a module in Modula-2 is on the same level as the package in Ada and both are improved versions of the class concept, as used in SIMULA 67. Modules are in fact the key feature of Modula-2: by using specific modules, machine-dependent items can be isolated and controlled; a collection of standard modules can be written for low-level activities such as input/output conversion, file handling and process scheduling; and a library of modules for handling standard operations like input and output can be built up and made available when a program is loaded.

As with Ada, the module is intended to aid information hiding in the sense that the user knows how to use it and what it does, but not the details of implementation. Thus, the inner body of the module is protected from outside access and hence cannot be corrupted. In addition, the algorithms used in the module can be modified without having to change any of the modules that use it. This is accomplished by having a definition part which includes all the information the user needs to know about the module together with an explicit export list giving the objects that may be imported into other modules. There is then the hidden part of the module, called the implementation part, which is for the module designer only. This includes the algorithms used in the module and they can be altered without changing the definition part.

As yet, Modula-2 is only in its early days as a programming language and the question of whether it will eventually become a major language is uncertain. The programming philosophy for a user is not dissimilar to that of Ada, the difference being that the module, not the package, is the key element. Modula-2 does have the advantage of being less complex and hence much easier to implement than Ada but whether this will outweigh the backing of Ada by the Department of Defense remains to be seen.

PROLOG

PROLOG was originated by the Groupe d'Intelligence Artificielle at the University of Marseilles in the early 1970s. Its development, including the writing of compilers, was carried out at Marseilles and the Department of Artificial Intelligence, University of Edinburgh in the mid and late 1970s. However, the first book on PROLOG was not published until 1981 (Clocksin, 1981). Although PROLOG represented the first step towards programming in logic, it is not the complete logic programming language.

PROLOG's approach to programming is quite different from that of conventional languages, perhaps because it started as a language for solving artificial intelligence problems. Using the language of logic, a PROLOG programmer provides a specification for a problem by giving the known facts together with the relationships between the objects and what relationships are true. Unlike the programmer of languages like FORTRAN and COBOL, there is very little explicit control of how the problem is to be solved – the solution to the problem is produced by inference from the given facts and rules.

A PROLOG program consists of a series of clauses, which are of three basic types.

(1) Those declaring facts about objects and their relationships. Such facts are always deemed to be unconditionally true.

(2) Those defining rules about objects and their relationships.

(3) Those asking questions about objects and their relationships. Such questions ask the program whether some statements are true or false.

A more detailed description of PROLOG is given in Chapter 10 together with a simple example showing facts, rules and questions.

Interest in PROLOG has grown rapidly in the last few years, particularly since Japan announced that PROLOG would probably have an important part to play in their fifth-generation computer initiative.

There has been considerable discussion of the merits of logic programming as opposed to functional programming, particularly as regards the use of PROLOG and LISP programs to solve the same problems. It is doubtful whether such detailed comparisons will result in any definite conclusions. (Those who are interested in such comparisons should read the paper by O'Keefe (1983).) In contrast to LISP, which is effective when list processing is required, PROLOG is best used in searching applications with databases and expert systems. PROLOG is not ideally suited for data processing work and the lack of compound expressions in the language can make some applications very clumsy. Furthermore, a strictly logical approach to programming can often lead to severe inefficiencies at run time. Although PROLOG programmers have found ways to avoid some of these difficulties, these methods appear *ad hoc* and represent a move away from the purity of mathematical logic.

Smalltalk

This book is concerned with programming languages. Languages do not, however, exist in a vacuum; before a program can be run, it is necessary to interact with a computer's operating system and use such tools as an editor and the appropriate compiler. The approach taken in Smalltalk is to fully integrate the language with its support tools, thus providing a complete programming environment. Indeed, with Smalltalk, it is impossible to say where the language stops and the environment begins.

The first version of Smalltalk was developed by Xerox at their research centre in Palo Alto in the early 1970s for use with powerful graphics workstations. The current version is known as Smalltalk-80. Its support tools (pop-up menus, windows, icons and mouse input) have led the way in providing a user-friendly interface for both the expert and non-expert user. The Apple Macintosh is currently the best known of the systems that have been influenced by these ideas.

A powerful and friendly graphics interface is not the only radical feature introduced by Smalltalk. The fundamental concept in Smalltalk is the object; that is, some local data together with a set of procedures that operate on that data. All calculations are performed by sending messages to objects and problems are solved by identifying real-world objects and modelling them by Smalltalk objects. This has led to what is known as object-oriented programming, which is discussed in Chapter 7. As Smalltalk has been influenced by SIMULA, objects are referred to by their class, not their type as in Pascal.

Message passing and the support of a sophisticated environment are both expensive in terms of computer resources. In the early days of computing, computer time was very expensive compared with people's time. Languages and systems were therefore developed so that they made the best use of machine resources. The Smalltalk philosophy, on the other hand, is that computers are cheap and so systems should be developed to make the best use of people's time. The recent developments in computer design and reduction in computer costs have made this approach attainable.

SUMMARY

- High-level languages (often called third-generation languages) developed from the needs to make programming easier for the non-specialist programmer and to make languages independent of specific computer hardware.

- FORTRAN was the first widely used high-level language. It was immensely successful when it emerged in the late 1950s and is still widely used today in its FORTRAN 77 version for scientific and engineering applications.

- ALGOL 60, which appeared a few years after FORTRAN, was not as successful as FORTRAN in terms of numbers of users, but it had a much greater influence on subsequent languages, such as Pascal and Ada. It introduced many new concepts into programming languages including recursion, block structure, syntax definition and structured statements.

- COBOL was the first effective high-level language for commercial data processing. It is still a major language today although its pre-eminence in the business computing world is under challenge from the many and varied 4GLs.

- PL/I attempted to provide a general multipurpose language by combining many of the features of FORTRAN, ALGOL 60 and COBOL. However, it proved to be too large and unwieldy.

- The use of terminals attached to a central computer led to the introduction of interactive languages in the 1960s, one of which, BASIC, has become very popular because of its simplicity and the fact that its interpreter will fit into the memory of small machines.

- A vast number of special-purpose languages were designed in the 1960s, but often these were only used by the group who implemented them. The main survivors are SNOBOL4, which is a string manipulation language, and GPSS, which is a simulation language.

- LISP is oriented towards the manipulation of symbols, rather than numbers, and for two decades has been the dominant language in artificial intelligence.

- LISP is a list-processing language and is close to being a functional language. Functional languages are easier to reason about than their imperative counterparts.

- Pascal is now the major teaching language and has had a beneficial influence on programming style.

- C has proved to be the most successful systems programming language.

- Ada and Modula-2 are the most important of the modern generation of general-purpose imperative languages. Both are based on Pascal and incorporate the ideas of modularity and information hiding.

- PROLOG has introduced programmers to the delights of logic programming. Its impact has been enhanced by the support it has received from Japan's fifth-generation initiative in intelligent knowledge-based systems.

- Object-oriented programming has received increasing attention in recent years, the main object-oriented language being Smalltalk.

EXERCISES

2.1 What were the original design goals of FORTRAN and how far were they realized? What new concepts did FORTRAN introduce into programming languages and what influence did it have on later languages? Summarize the new features introduced into FORTRAN 77 and give reasons for their introduction.

2.2 ALGOL 60 was less successful than FORTRAN, but it has had a much greater impact on the design of later languages. Explain this apparent paradox.

2.3 (a)   Many programming languages have rather poor string handling facilities. Why is this? Compare the string handling facilities of SNOBOL4 with those of Pascal.

(b)   Consider a text editor known to you and compare its string handling facilities with those typically found in programming languages.

2.4 How important in the rise or fall of a new programming language is the availability of efficient compilers for a wide range of computers? What factors affect the provision of suitable compilers?

2.5 Identify Ada facilities that:

(a)   are similar to those in Pascal,

(b)   extend a Pascal construct,

(c)   differ significantly from anything in Pascal.

Choose an example from each group and suggest reasons why the Ada construct was designed as it was.

2.6 James Martin (1985) claims that computer science departments have ignored 4GLs. How far do you think his comments are justified? Are universities ignoring languages that are of fundamental importance?

2.7 Discuss how programming in PROLOG differs from programming in conventional languages such as Pascal.

Bibliography

The development of programming languages is well covered by the following books and articles. Two good starting points are the article by Wegner (1976) and the paper by Knuth entitled 'Early Development of Programming Languages'

(Metroplis, 1980), which is excellent on languages up to and including FORTRAN I. Much more detail is provided in the massive book by Sammet (1969) which gives all the major, and many minor, languages from the 1950s and 1960s. The only criticism is that it is very oriented towards languages from the United States. Two further papers by Sammet (1972, 1981) bring the history of languages up to date.

In a conference in 1981 (Wexelblat, 1981), the designers of the major languages of the 1950s and 1960s were asked to give their view of the language's design and development. The languages covered with the speaker's name in brackets are:

FORTRAN (John Backus), ALGOL (Alan Perlis and Peter Naur), LISP (John McCarthy), COBOL (Jean Sammet), APT (Douglas Ross), JOVIAL (Jules Schwartz), GPSS (Geoffrey Gordon), SIMULA (Kristen Nygaard), JOSS (Charles Baker), BASIC (Thomas Kurtz), PL/I (George Radin), SNOBOL (Ralph Griswold), APL (Kenneth Iverson).

ANSI (1968), *USA Standard COBOL*.

Backus, J. (1978), 'Can Programming be Liberated from the Von Neumann Style?', *Comm. ACM*, **21**, pp. 613–641.

Clocksin, W. F. and Mellish, C. S. (1981), *Programming in PROLOG*, Springer-Verlag.

Dijkstra, E. W. (1968), 'Goto Statement Considered Harmful', *Comm. ACM*, **11**, pp. 147–148.

Hoare, C. A. R. (1981), 'The Emperor's Old Clothes', *Comm. ACM*, **24**, pp. 75–83.

Humby, E. (1964), 'ICT COBOL Rapidwrite' in *Introduction to System Programming* (P. Wegner, Ed.), Academic Press, pp. 166–177.

ISO (1982), *Specification for Computer Programming Language Pascal*, ISO 7185-1982.

Martin, J. (1985), 'Excerpts from: An Information Systems Manifesto', *Comm. ACM*, **28**, pp. 252–262.

Metroplis, N., Howlett, J. and Rota, G.-C. (1980), *A History of Computing in the Twentieth Century*, Academic Press.

Naur, P. *et al.* (Eds.) (1960), 'Report on the Algorithmic Language ALGOL 60', *Comm. ACM*, **3**, pp. 299–314.

Naur, P. *et al.* (Eds.) (1963), 'Revised Report on the Algorithmic Language ALGOL 60', *Comm. ACM*, **6**, pp. 1–17.

O'Keefe, R. A. (1983), 'PROLOG Compared with LISP?', *ACM SIGPLAN Notices*, **18** (5), pp. 46–56.

Sammet, J. E. (1969), *Programming Languages: History and Fundamentals*, Prentice-Hall.

Sammet, J. E. (1972), 'Programming Languages: History and Future', *Comm. ACM*, **15**, pp. 601–610.

Sammet, J. E. (1981), 'An Overview of High-Level Languages' in *Advances in Computers*, **20**, Academic Press, pp. 199–259.

US Department of Defense (1960), *COBOL, Initial Specification for a Common Business Oriented Language*.

US Department of Defense (1961), *COBOL, Revised Specification for a Common Business Oriented Language*.

Wegner, P. (1976), 'Programming Languages – the First 25 Years', *IEEE Transactions on Computers*, **C-25**, pp. 1207–1255.

Wexelblat, R. L. (1981), *History of Programming Languages*, Academic Press.

Wirth, N. and Hoare, C. A. R. (1966), 'A Contribution to the Development of ALGOL', *Comm. ACM*, **9**, pp. 413–431.

CHAPTER 3

Types, Objects and Declarations

This chapter looks at the declaration of simple variable and constant objects and at the binding time of their various attributes. Objects can be divided into two groups: simple or scalar objects and structured objects. (Structured objects such as arrays and records are built from simpler objects and are the subject of Chapter 6.)

The efficiency and flexibility of a language is largely governed by whether the attributes of objects are bound early (for example, at compile time) or whether the binding is delayed until run time. This chapter distinguishes between static and dynamic scope and between the scope (name-declaration binding) and the lifetime (declaration-reference binding) of a variable.

An important attribute of an object is its type. This chapter looks at the numeric data types integer, real, fixed point and complex as well as the logical type Boolean, the character type, enumeration types and pointers. In addition, it shows how languages have developed so that a programmer can express a solution in terms of the problem to be solved rather than in terms of the computer being used.

3.1 Names

A program may be regarded as the specification of a series of operations that are to be performed on data objects. Languages vary as to the types of object that are allowed, the operations that can be applied and the method of controlling the sequencing of the operations. (Operations are dealt with in detail in Chapter 4.)

The type of an object determines its allowed values together with the set of operations that can be used to manipulate these values. Data objects have a **value** and a **type** and may be stored in what are known as **variables**. Variables have a **name**, various **attributes** and refer to an area of computer store. Although the details of the storage are not usually the concern of the high-level programmer, he or she is very much concerned with the naming of the variables and defining their type. It is necessary to keep clear the distinction between:

- the name of a variable (its identifier),
- the area of store (its **reference** or address),
- the data object stored.

The connection between names, references and values is shown diagrammatically in Figure 3.1 using a graphical notation developed by Barron (1977).

The names of variables are often called **identifiers**. Typically, an identifier is a combination of letters and digits with the first character being a letter. As was stated in Chapter 1, spaces are not normally allowed within identifiers except in languages such as ALGOL 60, which ignore spaces wherever they occur. Names such as:

left link, *buffer size*, *customer account*

seem quite natural and so languages such as Ada and C have found a compromise by using the underscore character:

left_link, *buffer_size*, *customer_account*

Languages differ in their approach to the allowed length of an identifier. FORTRAN, for example, restricts the length to six characters while languages such as Pascal allow identifiers of any length; however, some implementations only treat the first eight characters as significant. The recent trend in languages such as C, Ada and Modula-2 is to have no limit.

FIGURE 3.1

Connection between names, references and values.

No consensus seems to have been reached on whether or not upper and lower case letters should be distinct. In ALGOL 60, C and Modula-2 the case matters, while in Pascal and Ada it does not.

3.2   Declarations and Binding

One of the most important factors controlling the power, flexibility and efficiency of a language is the time at which different language features are associated with, or bound to, one another. This is known as their **binding time**. Binding can take place at compile time, load time, subprogram entry or during statement execution. In general, the ability to bind two features early (for example, at compile time) leads to efficient programs while binding that is delayed until run time leads to more flexibility.

Name-declaration binding

This section looks first at the binding between a variable and its attributes such as its name, its reference (that is, where it is held in store), its current value and its type. In most modern programming languages, variables are introduced into a program by a **declaration**. They are then used in program statements. The connection between the use of a name in a statement and its declaration is referred to here as **name-declaration binding**. To look at this, consider the following Pascal example:

```
program example(input, output);
var x, y : real;

   procedure inner;
   var y, z : integer;
   begin
      ...
      y := 34;
      y := y + 1;
      x := 27.4;
      ...
   end {inner};
```

```
begin
   ...
   x := 3.768;
   ...
   y := x;
   ...
end {example}.
```

Four variables have been declared: x and y of type *real* in the main program *example* and y and z of type *integer* in the procedure *inner*.

The main program *example* and the procedure *inner* are both examples of what are known as **blocks.** Blocks may be nested within other blocks and in this example block *inner* is nested within block *example*. Essentially, a block is a piece of program text, containing both declarations and statements, which is used to control the visibility of identifiers. The rules governing the visibility of identifiers are called the **scope rules**.

Names declared in a block are not visible from outside that block; hence, the integer variables y and z are not visible outside procedure *inner*. They are called **local variables**. On the other hand, blocks inherit names declared in enclosing blocks and so the real variable x can be used within procedure *inner* as well as in the main program. In both cases, its use is bound to the declaration of x in the main program. Variables used in one block, but declared in an enclosing block, are called **non-local** or **global variables**.

Consider now the declarations of y as a real variable in block *example* and as an integer variable in block *inner*. Variables are bound to their most local declaration; hence, the use of the name y in the statement:

$$y := x$$

which occurs in the main program is bound to the declaration of the real variable y while the use of y in the statement:

$$y := 34$$

which occurs in procedure *inner* is bound to the declaration of the integer variable y. It is not possible within *inner* to refer to the real variable y. This is referred to as a 'hole in the scope'. Ada follows the same rules as Pascal, but it would allow the real variable y to be accessed from within a procedure like *inner* by giving it the expanded name of *example.y*; that is, the variable y declared in block *example*.

In languages such as FORTRAN, PL/I, Pascal, Ada and Modula-2, the visibility of identifiers and the binding of names to declarations is determined at compile time. This is called **static scope** and it has the consequence that the binding of names to types (**name-type binding**) is also fixed at compile time. The advantage of static scope is that it allows type checking to be performed by the compiler; that is, it enables the compiler to check that variables are always used in their proper context. When the types of all objects can be determined at compile time, the language is said to be **strongly typed** . Ada and ALGOL 68 are strongly typed but, as will be seen later, there are loop holes in the type checking of most other widely used languages.

Static scope allows programmers to determine the connection or binding between the use of an identifier and its declaration by looking at the program text. In **dynamic scope**, the binding between the use of an identifier and its declaration depends on the order of execution, and so is delayed until run time. The difference between static and dynamic scope is best seen through an example. Consider the following outline Pascal program:

```
program dynamic(input, output);
var x : integer;

   procedure A;
   begin
     ... write(x); ...
   end{A};

   procedure B;
   var x : real;
   begin
     ... A; ...
   end{B};

begin
   ... B; ... A; ...
end {dynamic}.
```

As Pascal has static scope rules, the use of the variable x in procedure A is bound to the declaration of the integer variable x in the main program. However, if the name-declaration binding is dynamic, the use of x in procedure A would be bound to the most recent declaration of x. Hence, when procedure A is called from procedure B, the use of x in A would be bound to the declaration of the real variable x in procedure B, while when A is called from the main program, the use of x would be bound to the declaration of the integer variable x in the main program.

With dynamic binding, the type of a non-local variable such as x in procedure A therefore depends on where A has been called from. Although this means that type checking is not possible at compile time, dynamic scope does give more flexibility while static scope leads to programs that are more efficient and easier to understand. Many implementations of LISP use dynamic scope.

In languages such as APL, SNOBOL4 and LISP, the type of a variable depends on its current value: a value such as 7 has an integer type and a value such as 94.7 a real type. Name-type binding is therefore delayed until run time. This allows little or no type checking at compile time, but it does allow considerable flexibility at run time, even if this flexibility is at the expense of running speed. Such languages are said to be **weakly typed**.

Although LISP is a weakly typed language, recent functional languages such as Hope have type definitions with name-type binding occurring at compile time in the same way as with traditional imperative languages. Chapter 9 shows how what are called polymorphic functions allow the advantages of early name-type binding to be combined with the flexibility enjoyed by weakly typed languages.

Declaration-reference binding

A description of the execution of a program in an imperative language is most easily given in terms of the traditional von Neumann computer where a store is composed of individually addressable storage locations. Program variables are allocated to these storage locations and the value of a variable then corresponds to the location's contents.

The **lifetime** (sometimes called the **extent**) of a variable is when, during the execution of a program, that variable has storage space allocated to it. In Pascal and other ALGOL-like languages, a variable is only allocated storage on entry to the block in which it is declared. Hence, the real variables x and y in program *example* are allocated storage when program execution starts, but the integer variables y and z are only allocated storage when procedure *inner* is called, this space being deallocated when *inner* is left. The lifetime of the real variables x and y therefore lasts throughout the execution of the program whereas the integers y and z have a new incarnation each time *inner* is called. Consequently, the declarations of y and z may be bound to different storage locations (that is, different references) on different calls of procedure *inner*.

Before proceeding further, it is important to be clear about the distinction between the scope and the lifetime of a variable. The scope property is concerned with name-declaration binding and, in languages like Pascal, is a compile-time feature, and so can be discussed purely in terms of the program text. The lifetime of a variable, on the other hand, is concerned with **declaration-reference binding** which occurs at run time. The distinction between these two properties is shown diagrammatically in Figure 3.2.

Binding the declaration of a local variable to a different storage location (or reference) each time a block is entered has the consequence that, on block entry, a local variable does not inherit the value it had when

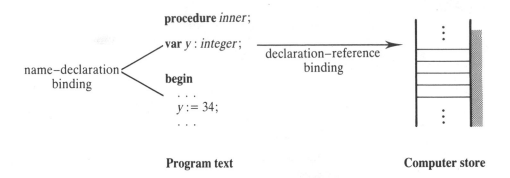

Program text   **Computer store**

FIGURE 3.2
Scope and extent.

the block was last executed. The value of a local variable is, therefore, undefined on block entry. Occasions do arise when it is useful for a procedure to 'remember' information from one call to the next. The only way this can be achieved in Pascal is by using global variables, and so to increase the lifetime of a variable its scope must be extended, thereby making it accessible to regions of the program from which we would rather it was hidden.

To handle this problem, ALGOL 60, C and PL/I allow the declaration of **static local variables** in addition to ordinary local variables. In ALGOL 60, these are known as **own variables**. Static local variables obey the same scope rules as ordinary local variables, but declaration-reference binding occurs at the beginning of program execution (that is, at load time) rather than on block entry. This means that a static local variable exists throughout program execution and its declaration remains bound to the same storage location. However, as problems arise with deciding how a static variable is to be initialized the first time a block is entered, such variables have been dropped from recent language designs. Chapter 7 describes how Ada and Modula-2 use modules to solve this problem in an elegant way.

Reference-value binding

The binding of a variable to a value occurs as a result of either an input or an assignment statement. Typically, during the execution of a program, a variable will be bound to a succession of different values. Consider, for example, the statement:

$$y := y + 1;$$

whose effect is to increment the value of y by 1. At first sight, this seems trivial until it is realized that y on the left-hand side refers to a place where a value may be stored (that is, it is a reference) while the y on the right-hand side refers to the current value of y. The binding of a variable to its value, therefore, involves three bindings:

(1)   The binding of the variable's name to its declaration (name-declaration binding).

(2)   The binding of its declaration to a store location (declaration-reference binding).

(3)   The binding of the storage location to a value (**reference-value binding**).

The process of finding the value, given the reference, is known as **dereferencing**. In the assignment statement just given, the y on the right-hand side is dereferenced to find its value so that 1 can be added to it. The resulting value is then assigned to the location whose reference is obtained from the left-hand side. A reference is sometimes called an **L-value** and the value of a variable an **R-value** where L and R stand for left and right, respectively.

It is worth noting at this point that it is the assignment operation, with its notion of updating a storage location, that requires store locations and references to be introduced into the computational model. When a language has no assignment statement, names can be directly bound to values, as will be seen in Chapter 9 which discusses purely functional languages.

Constants

Some data objects in a program do not change once they have been given an initial value, and these objects should be declared as **constants**. In Pascal, for example, constants are declared in the following way:

```
const pi = 3.14159265;
      lowestprime = 2;
      lastletter = 'z';
```

where the type is determined from the value.

The name-value binding for a constant is shown in Figure 3.3. It has a name and a value, but as a constant identifier cannot appear on the left-hand side of an assignment statement, there is no need for a reference. In Pascal, the name-value binding of a constant occurs at compile time while with a variable it occurs during statement execution.

Ada has generalized Pascal's constant declarations and brought them more in line with variable declarations. In Ada, both variables and constants can be given values within a declaration. Hence, the effect of the

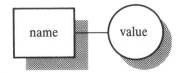

FIGURE 3.3
Name-value binding for
a constant.

Ada declaration:

>   *size* : *integer* := 20;

is to declare an integer variable whose initial value is 20 whereas the effect
of the declaration:

>   *size* : **constant** *integer* := 20;

is to declare an integer constant whose value is always 20. The values in
such variable and constant declarations may be given by expressions that
cannot be evaluated until run time. Consequently, in Ada, the name-value
binding of a constant may have to be delayed until block entry.

3.3   Type Definitions

The most important attribute of an object is its type. As has been seen, the
characteristics of a type are its allowed values together with the set of
operations that can be used to manipulate these values. At the lowest level,
data is usually just a collection of 1s and 0s, but a collection of such bits can
be viewed as an integer or real number, an array of numbers, a character or
even (although it is of no concern here) an instruction.

Scalar types that appear in most programming languages are:

- Numeric data types: integer, floating point and sometimes fixed
  point and complex.
- A logical type (often called Boolean).
- A character type.

Scalar types can be split into two categories: **discrete** (or **ordinal**)
types, where each value (except the maximum and the minimum values)
has a predecessor and a successor, and others such as *float* for which this is
not the case. *integer*, *Boolean* and *character* are discrete types. Hence, the
integer 42 has 41 as its predecessor and 43 as its successor, but it does not
make sense to talk about the successor of a floating-point number such as
42.734.

Table 3.1 Built-in data types of some common languages.

FORTRAN 77	Pascal	C	Ada
INTEGER	integer	int	integer
REAL	real	float	float
LOGICAL	Boolean		Boolean
CHARACTER	char	char	character
DOUBLE PRECISION		double	long_float

A distinction can be made between the **built-in** or **primitive** types, which are immediately available to the programmer, and other types, which can be constructed from the primitive types, although this distinction is becoming less important. In a language like Ada, new types can be added to the set of built-in types in such a way that the user cannot easily distinguish between the two groups. Table 3.1 gives the principal built-in types of some common languages.

Specifying type information

In FORTRAN and ALGOL 60, variables can be declared to be either one of the primitive types or a structured type. Some languages also have implicit or default declarations. For example, in FORTRAN, it is assumed that all undeclared variables with names starting with a letter in the range I to N are of type *integer* while those starting with any other letter are of type *real*. Although this method saves the programmer the somewhat tedious task of making declarations at the start of a program, it does suffer from the serious defect that misspelt variable names are taken to be references to new variables. In ALGOL 60, on the other hand, all variables must be declared before they can be used. Typical declarations are:

> **integer** a, b;
> **integer array** $c[1 : 10]$, $d[1 : 5]$;

In PL/I, additional information can be given about the attributes of a variable, as in:

```
DECLARE A FIXED(6), B FIXED DECIMAL(4),
        C(10) FIXED DECIMAL(7), D(5) FIXED DECIMAL(6);
```

which declares the same objects as in the ALGOL 60 example, but also indicates the number of decimal digits to be used for each of the integers. This additional information is given as part of the variable declaration and as a result the declaration becomes rather cluttered.

In Pascal, a variable can be declared to be of a type that is a subrange of another type, such as an integer; for example:

> **var** *a* : 1 .. 10;

However, instead of giving the range constraints as part of the variable declaration, it is possible, and preferable, to define a new named type, as in:

> **type** *index* = 1 .. 10;
> **var** *a* : *index*;

Details of the new type are thus brought together in one place rather than being distributed throughout the program in separate variable declarations. This is necessary when variables with the same constraint are to be declared in different parts of a program or are to be passed as parameters to subprograms. Also, by choosing meaningful type identifiers, the reader can be provided with additional information.

The description of name-declaration binding given earlier in Section 3.2 involved the use and declaration of variables. Here, name-declaration binding involves types with the use of the name *index* in:

> **var** *a* : *index*;

being bound to its declaration in:

> **type** *index* = 1 .. 10;

In Ada, a distinction is made between new types (called **derived types**) and new **subtypes**. The Ada declaration:

> **subtype** *index* **is** *integer* **range** 1 .. 10;
> *count* : *index*;

has a similar effect to the earlier declaration in Pascal. Hence, provided its value does not go out of range, an object of subtype *index* can be used anywhere that an object of type *integer* can be used. The type declaration:

> **type** *new_index* **is new** *integer* **range** 1 .. 10;
> *new_count* : *new_index*;

on the other hand, creates a new integer type called *new_index*. A consequence of this type declaration is that for each operator available on objects of type *integer* there is now a corresponding, but distinct, operator on objects of type *new_index*. Hence, the expression *count* + 1 has the integer addition operator while *new_count* + 1 has the *new_index* addition operator. Integer literals are available with type *integer* and all types derived from type *integer*.

Consider now the expression:

count + new_count

This expression is illegal as the two operands are of different types. Explicit conversion between type *integer* and type *new_index* can be made through the use of what is known as a **type mark**. In the expression:

new_index(count) + new_count

the type mark *new_index* is used to convert the value of *count* from type *integer* to type *new_index*. The type of the expression is, therefore, *new _index* while the expression:

count + integer(new_count)

is of type *integer*.

Strong typing and the introduction of types such as *new_index* do offer the programmer several advantages. For example, programs often have objects that are logically distinct although they may be represented in the same way on a computer (for example, as integers). Thus, by declaring these objects to be of different types, it is possible to guard against them being combined in ways that are logically inconsistent, and this allows many logical errors to be detected at compile time.

3.4   Numeric Data Types

Numeric data types are usually modelled on the machine representation of integer and floating-point (real) numbers. Although this gives the advantage of speed, it does mean that the range and precision of the numbers represented will vary from one machine to the next; thus, a program may give different answers on different machines.

The arithmetic operators (+, −, *, /) for addition, subtraction, multiplication and division are normally available with most programming languages and correspond directly to machine code instructions. However, as computers have different machine code instructions for integer and floating-point arithmetic, the effect of these operators depends on the context in which they are used. Hence, the expression 2 + 3 involves integer addition while 6.5 + 3.7 involves floating-point addition. When the effect of an operator depends on the type of its operands, the operator is said to be **overloaded**.

Languages such as ALGOL 60, Pascal and Modula-2 have a separate operator (**div**) for integer division with / being reserved for real division. In ALGOL 60 and Pascal, the result of evaluating 7 **div** 2 is 3 while the result of 7/2 is 3.5. In Modula-2, on the other hand, the operation 7/2 is illegal as the / operator is only defined for real operands.

Not all languages have two division operators. Both an early language like FORTRAN and later ones like Ada and C make do with a single overloaded division operator. In these languages, 7/2 gives the integer result 3 while real division is obtained by writing 7.0/2.0.

As will be seen in Chapter 4, neither Ada nor Modula-2 allow expressions that contain both integer and real operands. A division operator that takes integer operands and gives a real result does not comply with this, which is why this form of the division operator was dropped from the design of these languages.

The exponentiation operator in FORTRAN is ** while in ALGOL 60 it is ↑ . As part of the move for simplicity, this operator is not available in Pascal on the grounds that it was used too casually by programmers who did not realize how expensive it was in processing time. When R is a positive number of type REAL the FORTRAN expression X ** R is actually evaluated as:

```
EXP(R * ALOG(X))
```

where ALOG is the natural logarithm and EXP is the exponential operator. As both these functions are available in Pascal, the only real disadvantage of not having the exponentiation operator is a lack of ease of use, which discourages casual use. Ada has restored the operator **, but has added the restriction that the exponent must be an integer.

Other operators available with numeric types are the relational and equality operators. The result of a relational expression is of type *Boolean*. Most languages use <, <=, >, >= for the relational operators, but there is no agreement about 'not equals'; Pascal uses <>, C uses ! = and Ada / =. C is unusual in that it uses == as the equality operator with = being used for assignment.

A major difference between integer and real numbers is that integers are always represented exactly while the floating-point representation of a real number is only approximate. This is for the same reason that it is not possible to write down a finite decimal expansion for the number one-third. A consequence of this is that the equality operators do not always give the expected result when dealing with floating-point quantities and their use in this context is bad practice.

Integers

integer is the simplest of the built-in types. The range of possible integers is dependent on the machine hardware and the representation used. With a 32-bit word, integers in the range -2^{31} to $2^{31} - 1$ may be represented when the **two's complement representation** is used. Integer values, or **literals**, are written as a series of digits and, except in the case of languages where spaces are not significant, without any spaces.

Integers are often used by programmers in two contrasting ways: firstly, in the normal mathematical sense, although with a finite range, and, secondly, as counters in a loop or as an array index. The range of integers permissible is usually excessive for the second application while it can at times be insufficient for the first. This dilemma has led to several developments.

Languages such as C have the integer types *short* and *long* to provide integers of different lengths, but the actual length of each of these types depends on the implementation. So, on a 16-bit machine like the PDP-11, variables of type *int* typically have the same range as variables of type *short* on 32-bit machines. However, it is possible for a C compiler to implement *short*, *int* and *long* in the same way since it is stated that "you should only count on short being no longer than long", which seems rather to defeat the object of the exercise.

As has already been seen, the required number of digits can be given in PL/I in a declaration such as:

```
DECLARE I FIXED(6);
```

This declaration will, in fact, be usually implemented as at least the number of digits specified so that a suitable machine representation can be chosen, but it does have the advantage that it is less machine dependent than the C approach.

Subrange declarations in Pascal can reduce storage requirements, but their main advantage to the programmer is in the detection of logical errors. For example, given the declaration:

```
var count : 1 .. 10;
```

then the following:

```
for count := 0 to 10 do
```

will result in the error being picked up at compile time.

Like C, Ada has three predefined integer types: *short_integer*, *integer* and *long_integer*. The drawback that the allowed range of each of these types is implementation dependent is overcome by not expecting the

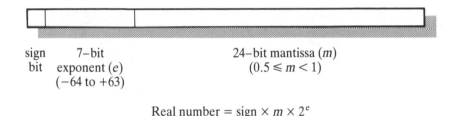

sign   7–bit   24–bit mantissa (m)
bit   exponent (e)   ($0.5 \leqslant m < 1$)
      (-64 to $+63$)

$$\text{Real number} = \text{sign} \times m \times 2^e$$

FIGURE 3.4

Representation of a loating-point number.

programmer to use these types directly, but instead to define a derived type. For example, in a declaration such as:

    type *my_integer* **is range** 1 .. 20000;

the compiler will select the most appropriate built-in integer type. Hence, although this type may be derived from type *long_integer* on an implementation on a 16-bit machine and from type *integer* on a 32-bit machine, this need not concern the programmer.

Floating-point numbers

Floating-point numbers are the most common type used in mathematical calculations. The name *real* has been used to denote this type in most of the older languages while C and Ada use the term *float*.

    The range and precision of floating-point numbers is determined by the implementation. Often, a real number is represented by 32 bits, as shown in Figure 3.4: one bit for the sign, seven bits for the exponent and the remaining 24 bits for the mantissa. The representation chosen is, essentially, a compromise as more bits for the exponent will increase the range and decrease the precision, since there will be fewer bits for the mantissa.

    Real literals may be written with or without an exponent. Examples in Pascal are:

    3.75   4.0   2.5E7   0.1786E-5

The literal 2.5E7 is read as 'two point five times ten to the power seven'. The number 4.0 is a real literal while 4 is an integer literal. In ALGOL-like languages, there must be at least one digit after the decimal point, hence 4.0, while in FORTRAN 4. is allowed. There are few other differences between languages except that 3E5 is treated as a real literal in Pascal and as an integer literal in Ada.

When declaring a real variable in PL/I as FLOAT DECIMAL, the number of decimal digits of precision can be stated, as in:

DECLARE X FLOAT DECIMAL(8);

Similarly, in Ada, although the built-in floating point type is *float*, other floating-point types may be declared. For example, the declaration:

type *real* **is digits** 8;

will define a floating-point type that has at least eight significant decimal digits. At first sight, this appears to give great flexibility, but as it is usually necessary in computer hardware to give an integral number of words to a floating-point number, this flexibility is largely illusory. Furthermore, in both PL/I and Ada implementations, a maximum precision is often imposed.

Using the representation given earlier for a 32-bit word, a floating-point number will have about seven decimal places of accuracy. Although this is sufficient for many calculations, there are times when more accuracy is required; for example, in certain algorithms used in numerical analysis where errors can accumulate. Languages intended for scientific use, therefore, usually provide a type that gives more precision. In ALGOL W and ALGOL 68 it is called *long real*, in FORTRAN it is called DOUBLE PRECISION and in C it is called *double*. The normal approach taken is to provide two words of storage for the floating-point number, instead of one. The sign and exponent parts are usually unchanged and the mantissa extended to include the second word. Thus, extending the earlier example to two 32-bit words would give a mantissa with 56 bits and 17 decimal places of accuracy. Unfortunately, this additional accuracy is not without its penalties. Since two words are used, there is an increase in processing time as well as the occupation of extra space.

Fixed-point numbers

Floating-point types are required in scientific calculations where very large and very small fractional numbers need to be represented. Many business calculations also require fractional numbers, but they do not need a large range, and so fixed-point numbers are more appropriate. For example, in PL/I the declaration of a variable X that was accurate to six decimal places, including two after the decimal point, could be written as:

DECLARE X FIXED DECIMAL(6, 2);

The number 5.01 is then represented to three decimal places of accuracy while 1005.01 is given to six. This is in contrast to floating-point numbers where the accuracy is relative and so is always to the same number of decimal digits.

Fixed-point numbers are also available in Ada and so it might be thought that an Ada type of the same range and accuracy could be defined as:

> **type** *dollars* **is delta** 0.01 **range** 0.0 .. 9999.99;

However, this is not the case. Fixed-point types in Ada are similar to floating-point types in that their representation is approximate. The value after **delta** specifies that all variables of type *dollars* are to be represented within an accuracy of 0.01 – that is, 1/100. As a binary representation is used, the number 0.01 will either be represented as 1/64 or as 1/128 and the one thing that can be guaranteed is that one hundred times 0.01 will not equal 1. This situation is confusing, especially for those with experience of fixed-point types in earlier languages.

Complex numbers

The type COMPLEX in FORTRAN consists of a pair of REAL numbers together with suitable predefined operations. However, it does not occur as a built-in type in most languages and facilities in languages like Ada make it easy to define such a type from its components. Chapter 7 looks at how this can be done.

3.5 Logical Types

If a program always obeyed the same series of statements in exactly the same order, it would not be a very flexible or powerful tool. Conditional control statements are, therefore, very important. As such statements depend on logical expressions that may be true or false, most languages have a logical type. In FORTRAN and ALGOL W, this is given the name LOGICAL, but in most languages the name given is *Boolean*, in honour of George Boole the Irish mathematician who invented an algebraic approach to logical notation. Theoretically, it is possible to represent Boolean values by a single bit, but this is seldom done as single bits are not usually separately addressable.

In FORTRAN, the logical values are written as .FALSE. and .TRUE.. In more recent languages, the predefined identifiers *false* and *true* are used although in ALGOL 60 and ALGOL 68 these identifiers are reserved words. C and PL/I do not have logical literals as such. In C, a false logical expression returns the integer value 0 while a true logical expression returns the value 1, although any non-zero value is treated as being true. This is a common source of error by programmers who convert to C from other languages such as Pascal. As they are used to writing = as the equality operator, rather than ==, it is easy to incorrectly write:

>   **if** $(a = 3)$ ...

instead of:

>   **if** $(a == 3)$ ...

Both statements are syntactically correct. The expression $a == 3$ is only true when a is equal to 3 while the effect of $a = 3$ is to assign the value 3 to a. Assignments in C have a value. In this case, it is 3, which is interpreted by the **if** statement as the result true!

In PL/I, the value *false* is written as '0'B and the value *true* as '1'B. Examples of the use of the logical operators (**and**, **or**, **not**) are given in Chapter 4.

3.6   Character Types

The early languages FORTRAN and ALGOL 60 had few facilities for processing strings of characters. The main use of characters was within a string to describe the results being output. The specialist string processing language SNOBOL4, on the other hand, included all the high-level facilities required to manipulate strings. However, the slow running of SNOBOL4 programs highlighted the difficulty involved in attaining both efficiency and ease of programming.

Most high-level languages now include the type *character* as a built-in type in addition to character operations. Character values are usually enclosed by single quotes as in:

>   'a'   'A'   ';'   ' '   '3'

which represent, respectively, the characters a, A, semicolon, space and 3. Apart from input, output and assignment, the main operations on characters involve the relational and equality operators.

Most languages do not define the character set to be used and so this depends on the implementation. In Pascal, all that can be assumed is that the digits and the lower and upper case letters are in their normal order; that is:

```
'0'  <  '1'  <  '2'  <  ...  <  '9'
'a'  <  'b'  <  'c'  <  ...  <  'z'
'A'  <  'B'  <  'C'  <  ...  <  'Z'
```

Ada goes one step further and states that type *character* gives the 128 characters of the ASCII character set.

The inclusion of strings of characters in languages such as C, Pascal, Modula-2 and Ada is accomplished by a data structure such as an array of characters. As data structures are the subject of Chapter 6, the discussion of strings will be deferred until then.

3.7   Enumeration Types

So far, the types discussed have either been primitive types or they have been derived from primitive types, usually by constraining the range of allowed values. Enumeration types are user-defined types and their use leads to much more readable programs. For example, consider the construction of a program that deals with the days in a week. One way of doing this would be to define the integer subrange type:

> **type** *days* = 1 .. 7;

and remember that 1 represented *Sunday*, 2 represented *Monday*, etc. However, a much better solution would be to define what is known as an **enumeration type**. This can be accomplished by the declaration:

> **type** *days* = *(Sunday, Monday, Tuesday, Wednesday,*
> *Thursday, Friday, Saturday)*;

where the possible literal values of type *days* are listed in order. This facility, which was first provided by Pascal, is a good example of the general trend in language design to provide the programmer with facilities to express a solution in terms of the problem to be solved rather than in terms of the computer being used.

Relational and equality operators are available with enumeration types with the relative values of the enumeration literals depending on their order in the declaration; hence:

> *Sunday < Monday < ... < Saturday*

In Pascal, successor and predecessor operations (*succ* and *pred*) are also available. Hence, the value of *succ(Monday)* is *Tuesday* while *pred*(*Monday*) is *Sunday*. *Sunday* has no predecessor and *Saturday* no successor.

In Section 3.1, the characteristics of a type were defined to be its allowed values together with the set of operations that can be used to manipulate these values. However, one drawback of using:

> **type** *days* = 1 .. 7;

to represent the days of the week is that all the operations on integers are still available, and it does not make sense, for example, to multiply two *days* together. The problem of having too rich a set of operations is removed by using an enumeration type although the reverse problem now exists; that is, all the necessary operations on *days* are not available. Thus, additional operations such as *daybefore* and *nextday* will be needed so that *daybefore*(*Sunday*) is *Saturday* and *nextday*(*Saturday*) is *Sunday*. Similarly, if an *integer* subrange is used to represent days, it is necessary to ensure that the successor of 7 is 1!

In Pascal, the definition of a new type and its new operations cannot be grouped together in the program text and so it is not obvious to the reader that they are logically related. This problem is resolved in Ada and Modula-2 by the use of modules and will be discussed in Chapter 7.

Also, in Pascal, enumeration values cannot be input or output. This restriction on their use has been lifted in Ada where it is possible to read them in and write them out. It is also possible in Ada to convert an enumeration literal to its representation as a character string and vice versa; thus:

> *days*'*image*(*Friday*)   is the string   "FRIDAY"
> *days*'*value*("FRIDAY")   is the literal   *Friday*

There is no counterpart of this in Pascal.

In Pascal, Ada and Modula-2, type *Boolean* is a predefined enumeration type that is declared behind the scenes as:

> **type** *Boolean* = (*false*, *true*);

In Pascal and Modula-2, the literals in different enumeration types must be distinct. In Ada, however, the following is legal:

> **type** *light* **is** (*red*, *amber*, *green*);
> **type** *flag* **is** (*red*, *white*, *blue*);

As the enumeration literal *red* is overloaded, it must always be clear from the context which version of *red* is being used; if it is not, it is necessary to *qualify* the use of *red* and either write *light*'(*red*) or *flag*'(*red*).

The *character* type in Ada is also an enumeration type and this allows other character sets to be defined. Type *character* normally uses the ASCII character set; however, if the Extended Binary Coded Decimal Interchange Code or EBCDIC character set was required instead, it could be defined by listing all the EBCDIC characters in order as the literals of an enumeration type definition. In this way, type *hexadecimal* could be defined as:

> **type** *hexadecimal* **is** ('0', '1', '2', '3', '4', '5', '6',
>   '7', '8', '9', 'A', 'B', 'C', 'D', 'E', 'F');

In Pascal and Modula-2, enumeration literals must be identifiers and so the above is not allowed.

3.8   Pointers

Pointer variables have as their value an address – that is, a reference to another data object. Such data types were not available in early languages such as FORTRAN, ALGOL 60 and COBOL although most later languages have included this facility.

Pointers, or references, may be used as simple variables or as components of a record. Typically, as in Pascal, pointers can be assigned values, used in equality comparisons and dereferenced. They can also have a special value **nil** (**null** in Ada and C) which indicates that the pointer variable is currently pointing nowhere. This is used to indicate the end of a linked list and can be thought of as being similar to the zero of ordinary integer arithmetic.

Pointer variables in PL/I can point to objects of any type and so there is no type checking at compile time. Later languages are, however, more restrictive than PL/I and the type of object being pointed at must be given as part of the pointer declaration.

The language C makes extensive use of pointers. The declaration:

> **int** *ci*, **cipoint*;

declares an integer variable *ci* and a variable *cipoint* whose type is 'pointer to integer'. So, after execution of the assignment statements:

> *ci* = 34;
> *cipoint* = &*ci*;

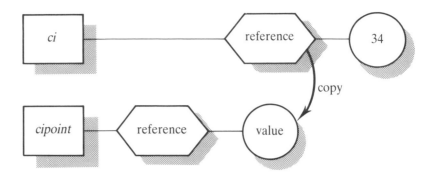

FIGURE 3.5

Effect of *cipoint* = &*ci*.

where the operator & can be read as 'the address of', the value of *cipoint* is the address of the variable *ci*. This is shown diagrammatically in Figure 3.5. Thus, the value of *ci* in an expression can now be referred to in the normal way, as in *ci* + 27, or it can be referred to indirectly by dereferencing *cipoint,* as in **cipoint* + 27. Both these expressions have the value 61. Note that any change to the value of *ci* will be reflected in the value obtained by dereferencing *cipoint*. When there is more than one way of referring to an object – that is, when the object has more than one name – the object is said to have an **alias**. It is generally regarded as a bad idea to have aliases and so Pascal, Modula-2 and Ada restrict the use of pointers. The only operations available with pointer variables in these languages are dereferencing, assignment and comparison for equality.

A pointer type can be declared in Pascal in the following way:

type *integerpt* = ↑ *integer*;

Variables may then be declared in the usual way:

var *pipoint, another* : *integerpt*;
  pi : *integer*;

As Pascal has no equivalent of the C language's & operator, neither *pipoint* nor *another* can be assigned the address of an existing integer variable such as *pi*.

In Pascal, new objects are created by calls of the predefined procedure *new*. The effect of executing the statement:

new(*pipoint*);

is to allocate space for a new integer variable and to assign its address to

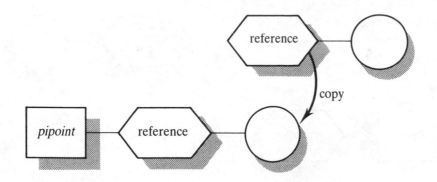

FIGURE 3.6
Effect of executing
new(pipoint).

pipoint. This is shown in Figure 3.6. Normally, declaration-reference binding occurs on block entry. However, in this case, it has occurred during
statement execution and is referred to as **dynamic storage allocation**. Other
languages use a similar approach although the syntax is different. For
example, in Ada, it is written:

> *pipoint* := **new** *integer*;

while in C and Modula-2 the amount of space required must be stated. In
Modula-2, this is written as:

> ALLOCATE(pipoint, SIZE(INTEGER))

However, as the amount of storage required is known from the pointer
type, this seems rather unnecessary.

The newly created object is known as a **dynamic variable** and can be
referred to in Pascal and Modula-2 as *pipoint* ↑ . This can be given a value
by writing:

> *pipoint* ↑ : = 17;

To summarize:

pipoint	is of type	pointer to *integer*
pipoint ↑	is of type	*integer*

However, aliasing is still possible because after the execution of:

> *another* := *pipoint*;

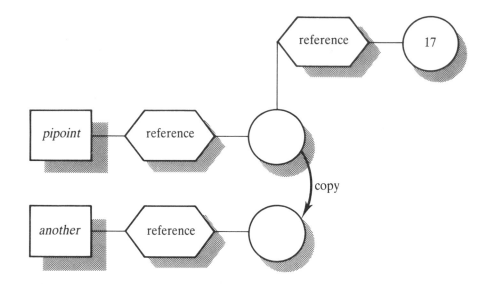

FIGURE 3.7

Effect of executing
another := pipoint.

the situation is as shown in Figure 3.7, where *pipoint* and *another* both
point to the same integer variable, although we at least have the security of
knowing that the aliasing is restricted to dynamic variables.

If *pipoint* is declared in a subprogram, then it is only allocated
storage while that subprogram is being executed. Consider what happens
when a dynamic variable is accessed via *pipoint* and in no other way. On
exit from the procedure in which *pipoint* is declared, the dynamic variable
will still exist, but it will no longer be possible to access it. In this case, it is
said to be **garbage**.

Another way that garbage can be created is by further calls of *new*.
After a second call of *new(pipoint)*, the situation will be as shown in Figure
3.8. As *another* is still pointing to the object created by the original call of
new(pipoint), no garbage has been created. However, if this is followed by
a call of *new(another)*, the situation shown in Figure 3.9 will arise and
garbage will have been created.

During the execution of a large program, the amount of garbage can
build up. To overcome this problem, languages like Pascal have a *dispose*
operation (DEALLOCATE in Modula-2). The effect of:

dispose(pipoint);

is to deallocate the space allocated to the dynamic variable pointed to by
pipoint, so that it can be reused in a later call of *new*. Thus, it appears that
the build up of garbage can be avoided by preceding each call of *new* by a

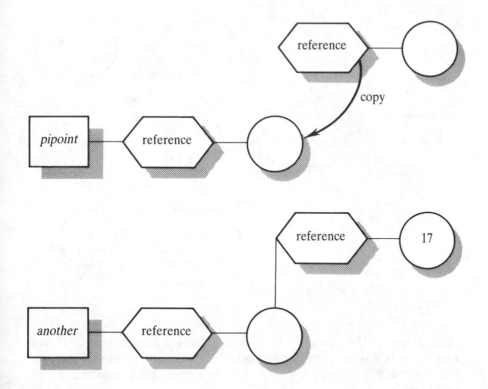

FIGURE 3.8

Effect of a second call
of *new(pipoint)*.

call of *dispose*. However, the problem with this is that there may be more
than one access path to the dynamic variable, as was shown in Figure 3.7. If
the call *dispose(pipoint)* had been executed in these circumstances, it
would have resulted in the pointer variable *another* pointing to an area of
store that had been returned to the system for reuse. This is known as a
dangling reference and will normally lead to a program either crashing or
giving the wrong results. The *dispose* operation must, therefore, be used
with great care.

The solution to the problem of garbage build-up is in fact to let the
system determine which dynamic variables can no longer be accessed and
for an automatic **garbage collector** to be invoked when the available space
runs low.

The space available for dynamic variables is usually organized in the
free space list. A call of *new(pipoint)*, for example, will remove the amount
of space required for the dynamic variable from the free space list and
assign its address to *pipoint*.

A garbage collector has two functions. It first determines those store
locations that have been allocated to dynamic variables and which can no
longer be accessed, and then it collects these store locations together and

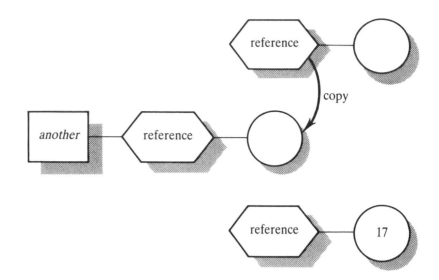

FIGURE 3.9

Effect of a subsequent
call of *new(another)*.

returns them to the free space list. This approach is used in languages like
LISP, but as it is time consuming and adds to the complexity of the run-
time system, it is virtually unheard of in the implementation of imperative
languages.

SUMMARY

- Associated with a variable are attributes such as its name, type, reference and current value.

- Early binding of an object's attributes leads to efficient programs while run-time binding leads to more flexibility.

- Static scope is when name-declaration binding occurs at compile time.

- The characteristics of a type are its allowed values and the set of operations that can be used to manipulate these values.

- When the type of all objects can be determined at compile time, a language is said to be strongly typed.

- The lifetime (or extent) of a variable is when, during the execution of a program, that variable has storage space allocated to it.

- Integer numbers are represented exactly in a computer while the representation of real numbers is only approximate.

- Enumeration types allow the programmer to express a solution in terms of the problem to be solved.

- Unlike C, the languages Pascal, Modula-2 and Ada restrict the use of pointers so that they can only refer to dynamic variables.

- Dynamic variables are created during statement execution.

- When a dynamic variable can no longer be accessed, it is said to be garbage. Inaccessible locations may be returned to the free space list either explicitly, by means of an operation such as *dispose*, or automatically by the system invoking a garbage collection routine.

- Most imperative languages use the *dispose* operation (or its equivalent) while functional languages use garbage collection.

EXERCISES

3.1 What is the difference between a constant and a variable?

3.2 In ALGOL 60, the identifiers *false*, *true*, *integer* and *real* are reserved words while in Pascal they are predefined identifiers and may be redefined. Which approach is preferable and why?

3.3 Although variables may be initialized as part of their declaration in Ada, this is not possible in Pascal. What advantages and disadvantages would result if a Pascal implementation gave all variables a default initial value? Suggest suitable default values for integer, character and real variables. What, if any, are the drawbacks of the choices you have made?

3.4 Distinguish between the lifetime and the scope of a variable.

3.5 What advantages result from being able to perform type checking at compile time?

3.6 Compare the facilities for declaring subrange variables in Pascal and PL/I.

3.7 Languages such as ALGOL 60, FORTRAN and PL/I do not have type declarations. What are the advantages of being able to declare new types in languages like Pascal?

3.8 Define an enumeration type for the months of a year and list a suitable set of operations on objects of type *month*.

3.9 List those situations in Pascal where values of a discrete type may be used, but not values of type *real*.

3.10 COBOL, PL/I and Ada have a predefined fixed-point type. Why is this type absent from the other widely used languages?

3.11 Why can the ability to refer to variables by more than one name (aliasing) lower the reliability of programs?

3.12 Section 3.8 showed how dangling references can be introduced by careless use of *dispose*. What other source of dangling references exist in languages that contain the equivalent of the C language's & operator?

Bibliography

The description in this chapter has been informal and is based to a large extent on how the features are implemented on present day computers. This is similar to the approach taken by Ghezzi (1982). A more theoretical approach is given in the book by Tennent (1981).

Barron, D. W. (1977), *An Introduction to the Study of Programming Languages*, Cambridge University Press.

Ghezzi, C. and Jazayeri, M. (1982), *Programming Language Concepts*, John Wiley.

Tennent, R. D. (1981), *Principles of Programming Languages*, Prentice-Hall.

CHAPTER 4

Expressions and Statements

The main components of an imperative language are declarations, expressions and statements. Declarations were the subject of the last chapter and this chapter now deals with expressions and statements. An expression yields a value, while a statement is a command to carry out some operation that normally alters the state. (Informally, the state can be considered to be the locations in store and their associated values.)

The order of evaluation of an expression depends on the precedence rules. With the exception of the logical operators, there is a broad agreement between different programming languages as to the order of precedence of the operators. There has also been a trend in language design towards compatibility of types in assignment statements and to impose restrictions on mixed-mode operations.

*Structured control statements are an important feature in language design. This chapter discusses such statements in detail with particular attention being given to the development of the **for** statement.*

Finally, the advantages of providing exception handling facilities in a language is discussed and a comparison made between the exception handling facilities of PL/I and Ada.

4.1   Expressions

Expressions are composed of one or more operands (that is, variable or constant objects) whose values may be combined by operators. For example, the expression:

$a * b + 4.0$

could be evaluated by substituting the values for the variables a and b, multiplying these values together and then adding 4.0 to the result. However, the evaluation of an expression is not as simple as it might appear at first sight, as there are many subtleties. For example, the above expression could also be evaluated by adding 4.0 to the value of b and multiplying the result by the value of a. Since these two methods will normally give different values, it is necessary to have precise rules, called the **precedence rules**, to govern the order in which an expression is evaluated. Pascal, which is typical of many languages, has the following evaluation rules:

(1)   Evaluate any expressions enclosed within brackets first, starting with the innermost brackets.

(2)   Apply the operator precedence shown in Table 4.1 within the brackets.

(3)   If the operators in (2) have the same precedence, apply them in order from left to right.

Rules somewhat similar to these also apply in many other languages – for example, FORTRAN, Ada, Modula-2, etc. However, some languages have completely different rules; for example, in APL all the operators have the same precedence and the expressions are evaluated from right to left.

Application of the precedence rules allows a tree structure to be constructed. The tree structure corresponding to the expression:

$a + b * c / d$

is shown in Figure 4.1. Here, the values of b and c are first multiplied

Table 4.1   Pascal operator precedence (highest at the top).

*, /, **div**, **mod**
+, −
=, <>, >, <, >=, <=

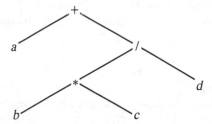

FIGURE 4.1

Tree structure.

together, the result is then divided by d and the result of that operation is added to a.

The evaluation of an expression should produce a value and nothing more; that is, it should not change the state of the program. However, if function calls are used in an expression, there is no guarantee that a side effect of the function will not change the state. This practice is bad programming style and should be strongly discouraged. (A further discussion of this topic is given in Chapter 5.)

The action of an operator and a function is very similar, indeed the syntax analyzer can treat them both the same except that an operator obeys precedence rules. This is illustrated by operations like *abs*, which finds the absolute value of the argument. In a language like Ada, *abs* is an operator while in Pascal *abs* is a standard function.

Most of the simple operators in expressions are **binary** (or **dyadic**); that is, they operate on two operands and produce a single result. A **unary** (or **monadic**) operator, on the other hand, operates on one operand and produces a single result. Some operators, like + and −, can be both unary and binary under different conditions. For example, consider the two expressions:

$$- a * b + c$$
$$+ x / y - z$$

In the first expression, − is used as a unary operator while * and + are binary; however, in the second expression, / and − are binary and + is unary.

Boolean expressions

So far, the expressions used in this chapter have been arithmetic expressions; that is, the operands have been of numeric type and the operators arithmetic. However, expressions can be of different types. One type that occurs in nearly every language is Boolean (sometimes known as logical). In a Boolean expression, the value returned must be either true or false. Boolean expressions usually involve relational operators, as in:

$$a + b > 0$$
$$x = y$$

However, a Boolean expression can also contain variables of type Boolean and Boolean operators. The common Boolean operators are **not**, **and**, **or**. Ada also includes exclusive or (**xor**) while ALGOL 60 has two extra Boolean operators for implies and equivalence. When using Boolean operators, programmers must be aware of both their effect and their order of precedence. Normally, **not** has the highest precedence, followed by **and**, and **or** has the lowest. However, as a Boolean expression such as:

$$a > b \text{ or } c < d + 4$$

can include Boolean operators as well as both arithmetic and relational operators, Table 4.1 needs to take into account the operators **not**, **and**, **or**. ALGOL 60 places such Boolean operators below the relational operators. Pascal, on the other hand, made a commendable attempt to reduce the number of levels of precedence by giving **not** the highest precedence, **and** the same precedence as * and **or** the same as +. However, as a result, the above Boolean expression is invalid in Pascal (assuming a, b, c and d are integer variables), because it would mean attempting to evaluate b **or** c. To achieve the same result as ALGOL 60, it is necessary to write, therefore:

$$(a > b) \text{ or } (c < d + 4)$$

Languages like Ada and C have adopted precedence strategies that avoid the need for extra brackets in such expressions although Modula-2 has followed the Pascal approach.

Boolean operators are often used in **if** and **while** statements to combine relational expressions; for example:

if $(i = 0)$ **or** $(a[i] > a[i + 1])$ **then** ...

However, in such a case, if $i = 0$ is true, $a[i]$ may not be inside the array bounds. Logically, of course, there is no need to evaluate the second relation if the first one is true because the result is bound to be true by the definition of the operator **or**. This is known as **short-circuit** evaluation and works as follows:

(1)   Given a **and** b where a is false, b is not evaluated.
(2)   Given a **or** b where a is true, b is not evaluated.

Some Pascal compilers take advantage of short-circuit evaluation while others do not, which is not a very satisfactory situation for the programmer. Modula-2 uses short-circuit evaluation but Ada provides distinct Boolean operators for cases where short-circuit evaluation is desired. Ada's method is to introduce two further logical operators (**and then**, **or else**) with the same precedence as **and** and **or**. These operators function as follows:

(1)   *a* **and then** *b*, where *b* is only evaluated if *a* is true.

(2)   *a* **or else** *b*, where *b* is only evaluated if *a* is false.

The C logical operators are && and ||. The && operator corresponds to the Ada **and then** operator while || corresponds to **or else**.

Mixed-mode expressions

A previous section showed how operators like + and − may be overloaded; that is, have different meanings depending on their operands. Such operators are also called **polymorphic**. The evaluation of *a* + *b* differs if *a* and *b* are real or *a* and *b* are integer. The advantage of overloading an operator is that it allows its normal use to continue. The alternative approach, which is to have a different operator for real addition and integer addition, would be clumsy.

A further problem of evaluating such an expression when the operands *a* and *b* are of different types is that languages differ in how they deal with such mixed-mode expressions. Three categories of language can be identified:

(1)   Languages such as Ada and Modula-2 that forbid mixed-mode expressions.

(2)   Languages like Pascal that allow 'sensible' combinations such as adding an integer to a real. The result of such an expression is, as would be expected, of type *real*.

(3)   Languages like PL/I and C that allow 'unusual' combinations such as the ability to add an integer to a character. A major problem with this approach is that it can lead to unexpected results.

Hence, to add an integer to a real in a language like Ada or Modula-2, the type conversion must be done explicitly. For example, if *a* and *b* are of type *integer* and type *real*, respectively, such an expression would have to be written as:

real(*a*) + *b*

in Ada. The only disadvantage of this approach is that more has to be written.

Strong typing

A language is strongly typed if all type checking can be done statically (that is, at compile time). There are many advantages in using such languages: it is easier to find errors because they are normally reported at compile time and efficiency is improved because run-time type checks are unnecessary. The trend towards strongly typed languages is, like the restrictions on mixed-mode operations, a move away from the free and easy methods of PL/I. In the strictest sense, Pascal is not strongly typed, but there are only a few minor areas where static type checking is not possible. Ada is strongly typed.

4.2   Statements

Statements are the commands in a language that perform actions and change the state. Typical statements are:

- Assignment statements, which change the values of variables.
- Conditional statements, which have alternative courses of action.
- Iterative statements, which loop through many statements until some condition is satisfied.

This section considers assignment statements while conditional statements are considered in Section 4.3 under the heading 'Sequencing and Control'. Iterative statements are the subject of Section 4.4.

A design aim of ALGOL 68 was that the number of independent language concepts should be reduced. One idea was that there should be no distinction between statements and expressions and so all statements in ALGOL 68 have a value. This idea has not been adopted in many later languages because, although it can lead to shorter and more efficient programs, it can also make programs much more difficult to read and understand, as it encourages the use of side effects within expressions.

Assignment statements

The general form of the assignment statement is:

$EL := ER$

where *EL* is the expression on the left-hand side of an assignment statement that gives a reference as its result and *ER* is the expression on the right-hand side of an assignment statement that gives a value as its result. The value of the right-hand expression is then assigned to the reference given by the left-hand expression. Assignment is, therefore, an operation on reference-value pairs.

In ALGOL 68, the value of an assignment statement is the value assigned to *EL*. In C, where the assignment operator is =, statements do not have a value, although an assignment such as:

$$EL = ER$$

is an expression and so can be used within other expressions in the same way as in ALGOL 68, with the same advantages and disadvantages.

In many languages, there are restrictions on the expressions *EL* and *ER*. For example, many languages only allow a variable name or indexed variable for *EL*. Languages may also have restrictions on the compatibility between the type of *EL* and the type of value given by *ER*. As an example, consider the typical Pascal or Ada assignment statement:

$$x := a + b * c;$$

If the type of *x* is the same as that of the result obtained by evaluating the expression on the right-hand side, then there are no problems. However, some languages state that if the two types are not the same, then it is a compile-time error. Such a strict interpretation of assignment compatibility is common in modern languages like Ada.

Languages such as ALGOL 68 and Pascal have adopted a different approach to assignment compatibility by allowing what is known as **widening**. If *x* is of type *real* and the right-hand expression has an integer value, then the assignment is valid as, essentially, there is no loss of information in making such an assignment. However, in the reverse situation, where *x* is of type *integer* and the right-hand expression has a real value, such an assignment causes a loss of information since the real value must be either truncated or 'rounded' to the integer type. Although such assignments are allowed in older languages (ALGOL 60 uses rounding while FORTRAN uses truncation), most later languages like Pascal do not allow assignment when information is lost. In such languages, the programmer is expected to decide what is required and program accordingly, using the standard conversion functions available. To assign the real *x* to the integer *i* in Pascal, either of the following statements can be written:

$$i := trunc(x)$$
$$i := round(x)$$

depending on whether truncation or rounding is required.

PL/I is far more flexible as regards assignment compatibility and will allow the assignment of what most languages would consider incompatible types; for example:

real → Boolean
character → integer

Although there are specific rules for the conversions, experience with the language shows that such obscure constructions are seldom required and that the looser assignment rules result in errors propagating from their inception, making debugging much more difficult.

C is more strongly typed than PL/I, but still allows conversions when the left-hand and right-hand expressions of the assignment statement have different types. However, not all of these conversions are consistent; for example, *float → int* causes truncation of the fractional part while *double → float* results in rounding.

Assignment operators

As statements of the form:

a := a + expression

occur frequently in computer programs, languages such as C, ALGOL 68 and Modula-2 provide a special short-hand notation. In C, this can be written:

a += expression;

in ALGOL 68:

a +:= expression

and in Modula-2 there is a special statement:

INC(a, expression)

Similar operators also exist in C (−=, *= and /=) and in ALGOL 68 (−:=, *:= and /:=). Although these assignment operators allow the compiler to generate efficient code without resorting to extensive optimization techniques, it is unclear whether such an advantage outweighs the added language complexity.

C also has increment (++) and decrement (−−) operators. They can be used in two ways. The effect of executing:

a = 1; b = ++a;

is to set *a* to 1, increment the value of *a* by 1 and then assign its value to *b*. The result is that *a* and *b* will both have the value 2. The effect of executing:

$$a = 1; b = a++;$$

is to assign the value of *a* to *b* before *a* has been incremented. Hence, *b* will have the value 1 and *a* the value 2. Although such operators allow very compact code to be written in C, the resulting programs are often difficult to understand.

Multiple assignment statements

Many languages allow multiple assignment statements. For example, in PL/I, the value of the expression in the statement:

A, B, C = *expression*;

is evaluated and then assigned to each one of the variables given in the list on the left-hand side. Similarly, in ALGOL 60, this is written:

$$a := b := c := expression;$$

In languages that allow assignments to have values, such as ALGOL 68 and C, the assignment operator has very low precedence and is evaluated from right to left. Multiple assignment then comes out naturally. The value of the C assignment:

$$a = expression;$$

is the value assigned to *a*. Hence, in the statement:

$$a = b = c = expression;$$

the expression is evaluated first and its value assigned to *c*. The value of the assignment:

$$c = expression;$$

is then assigned to *b* and that value is then assigned to *a*.

Compound statements

Languages usually have a facility to group several statements together so that they may be considered as one statement. In Pascal, for example, this is done by the use of the **begin** ... **end** construct, so:

> **begin** S1; S2; S3; ... **end**

can be treated like a single statement. This construct is derived from a similar construct in ALGOL 60 although ALGOL distinguishes between compound statements and blocks. The former are given as above while the latter contain at least one declaration; for example:

> **begin real** *x*; **integer** *i, j*;
> S1; S2; S3; ...
> **end**

The language C has a similar construction to the compound statement but uses the enclosing brackets { } to group statements together.

As will be seen in the next section, a construction such as the compound statement is vital in languages such as ALGOL 60, Pascal and C when constructing structured control statements. However, more recent languages, such as Ada and Modula-2, have used explicit terminators for conditional and iterative statements, and so the necessity for compound statements has disappeared. This is a welcome change to students who often forgot the **begin** ... **end** bracketing keywords and were then bemused when the flow of control did not meet their expectations.

4.3   Sequencing and Control

As the execution of statements is central to imperative languages, sequencing mechanisms are necessary for routing control from one statement to another and for separating individual statements. As was mentioned in Chapter 1, the end of a line terminates a statement in FORTRAN, BASIC and COBOL while a semicolon is used to either separate statements in Pascal and Modula-2 or terminate them in Ada and C. Conditional and iterative statements are necessary so that the flow of control can vary depending on a program's input data.

Selection

The earliest conditional statements were those used in FORTRAN and they had the form:

```
IF (C1) L1, L2, L3
```

This is the FORTRAN arithmetic IF statement and it allows the programmer to choose between three alternative paths. Hence, depending on whether the result of evaluating the expression C1 is negative, zero or positive, there is a branch to the statement with the integer label L1, L2 or L3. There is also a similar logical IF statement in FORTRAN 66 which has the syntax:

    IF (*logical expression*) *statement*

However, its use is limited as only a single statement can be obeyed when the logical expression is true and that statement cannot be a DO or another IF statement.

    Statements containing conditional jumps to statement labels tend not to appear in current languages, even in up-to-date versions of FORTRAN. Instead, most languages use the **if** statement introduced by ALGOL 60 as their basic conditional statement; for example:

    if C1 **then** S
    if C2 **then** S1 **else** S2

where C1 and C2 are conditions and S, S1 and S2 are statements. The structure of these two forms of **if** statement is shown diagrammatically in Figure 4.2.

    Often, in a program, a situation arises where several statements are to be obeyed after finding that a condition such as C1 is true. As the statements S, S1 and S2 above can be compound statements, this can be easily achieved in ALGOL 60 without having to resort to explicit jump instructions, as would be necessary in FORTRAN 66. Statements such as

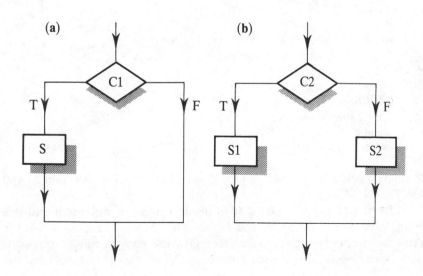

FIGURE 4.2

Structure of the two forms of an **if** statement.

the ALGOL **if** statement are called **structured statements** and have the important property that they have only one entry and one exit point. This property can prove very helpful when trying to reason about a program's effect.

Although ALGOL **if** statements have proved relatively straightforward and easy to use, they can result in a problem known as 'the dangling else' because both forms are allowed. For example, in the following statement:

>   **if** C1 **then if** C2 **then** S1 **else** S2

it is not clear whether the single **else** is associated with the first **if** ... **then** or the second **if** ... **then**. Therefore, two interpretations are possible:

>   **if** C1 **then begin if** C2 **then** S1 **end else** S2

or:

>   **if** C1 **then begin if** C2 **then** S1 **else** S2 **end**

Different languages have found different solutions to cope with this ambiguity. ALGOL 60 forbids conditional statements after a **then** and so extra **begin** ... **end** brackets must be used. Pascal and PL/I make the interpretation that the **else** is normally associated with the innermost **if**; when the other interpretation is required, **begin** ... **end** brackets are utilized. In Ada, each **if** is paired with a closing **end if**; for example:

>   **if** C1 **then**
>   **if** C2 **then** S1;
>   **end if**;
>   **else** S2;
>   **end if**;

or:

>   **if** C1 **then**
>   **if** C2 **then** S1; **else** S2;
>   **end if**;
>   **end if**;

A similar solution is also adopted in ALGOL 68, Modula-2 and FORTRAN 77.

An **if** statement can be nested inside another **if** statement and this nesting process can be continued as required. In such cases, it is usually better for the nested **if** statement to follow the **else**, as this corresponds much more closely with human processing. When the **if** statement follows the **then** part, the human mind must stack information for later processing and repeated operation will soon exhaust the stacking ability of most humans. Some languages, notably Ada and Modula-2, have an **elsif** construction to assist in the presentation and understanding of cascaded conditional statements.

When a selection from many statements is required another construction called the **case** statement is best used. This was first implemented in ALGOL W and has been adopted by most subsequent languages. The Pascal version is as follows:

```
case E of
   CL1 : S1;
   CL2 : S2;
      .
      .
      .
   CLn : Sn
end
```

where E is an expression, CL1, CL2, ..., CLn are case labels and S1, S2, ..., Sn are statements. The case labels must be constant values of the same type as the expression E.

The use of the **case** statement can be illustrated by writing down the number of days in a month as a Pascal **case** statement, where January is the integer 1, February 2, etc.

```
case month of
   1, 3, 5, 7, 8, 10, 12 : days := 31;
   4, 6, 9, 11 : days := 30;
   2 : if years mod 4 = 0 then
         days := 29
      else days := 28
end
```

The expression after the word **case** is often called the **selector** and must be of a discrete type.

More recent languages, notably Ada, have made two changes to the basic **case** statement. The first is the inclusion of a default condition. In Pascal, if the expression value is not one of the constant values in the case lists an error will occur; for example, if *month* has the value 0. Such a default case is covered in Ada by the compulsory inclusion of **others**, so the programmer must explicitly consider what action is required if an unspecified value is encountered. (Note that **others** is unnecessary if all the discrete type alternatives are covered in the **case** statement.) Secondly, Ada allows ranges of values to be used for each constant in the case list while in Pascal each value must be explicitly defined. The following Ada example illustrates these modifications:

```
case ch is
   when '0' .. '9' => put_line("digit");
   when 'A' .. 'Z' => put_line("letter");
   when others => put_line("special character");
end case;
```

Similar multi-selection statements are also included in languages such as ALGOL W, ALGOL 68, Modula-2 and C. However, S-ALGOL and some other experimental languages are unusual in that the selector in the **case** statement is allowed to be a string, as in:

```
case name of
   "Julia" : write "It was Julia"
   "Alan" : write "It was Alan"
   default : write "It was some-one else"
```

It is assumed that *name* is a string variable and that the S-ALGOL output statement is self-explanatory. Although such a **case** statement is a useful facility for the programmer, it does introduce problems for the implementor.

4.4   Iterative Statements

The essence of making use of the computer's extraordinary speed of operation is to have loops of statements. Such loops are terminated in one of two ways: either by a condition being fulfilled or by completing a fixed number of iterations.

while statement

This is the most common of the statements controlled by a condition. In its simplest Pascal form it is:

>   **while** C **do** S;

where C is a condition and S is a statement. Its structure is shown diagrammatically in Figure 4.3. This Pascal form grew out of the more complex but less satisfactory **for ... while** statement in ALGOL 60 which most later languages have split into separate **for** and **while** statements.

repeat statement

This was introduced by Pascal and is similar to the **while** statement except that the condition is tested at the end of the loop instead of at the

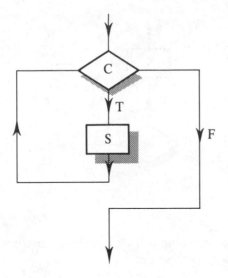

FIGURE 4.3
Structure of the **while** loop.

beginning. The Pascal form is:

> **repeat** *sequence of statements* **until** C;

Its structure is shown diagrammatically in Figure 4.4. The statements in the loop are always performed at least once, and this can have advantages, for example, when reading in data.

The language C has a traditional **while** statement in addition to a **do** ... **while** statement, which is similar to the **repeat** statement in that the test is at the end of the loop.

loop statement

This is a more general form of statement and includes both the **while** and **repeat** statements as special cases. In its Ada form it consists of:

> **loop**
>   *sequence of statements*
> **end loop**;

The sequence of statements can include an **exit** statement:

> **exit when** C;

Furthermore, it is possible to have more than one exit from a loop.

The following example shows how an **exit** statement can be used

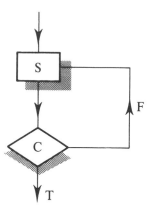

FIGURE 4.4

Structure of the **repeat** loop.

when reading and summing a list of positive numbers where the list is terminated by a negative number:

> *sum* := 0;
> **loop**
>   *get*(*number*);
>   **exit when** *number* < 0;
>   *sum* := *sum* + *number*;
> **end loop**;

This **loop** statement illustrates how a programmer can overcome a common problem in computing; that is, performing *n* and a half loops.

Figure 4.5 shows the structure of a loop with one exit, where S1 and S2 are sequences of zero or more statements. It can be seen from this figure that when S1 is null, it becomes a **while** statement and when S2 is null, a **repeat** statement. Hence, it is not necessary for Ada to include any iterative statement other than the **loop** statement. However, it does include a **while** statement, presumably on the grounds that it is part of most programmers armoury and that they would be lost without it.

for statement

This statement differs from the other **loop** statements in that it is used for an iteration that is to be performed a fixed number of times.

Pascal has two forms of the **for** statement:

> **for** *cv* := *low* **to** *high* **do** S
> **for** *cv* := *high* **downto** *low* **do** S

where *cv* is the control variable, *low* and *high* are discrete expressions and S is a statement. These two forms of the Pascal **for** statement are simplified

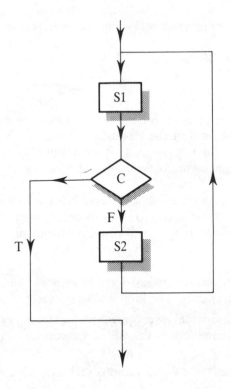

FIGURE 4.5

Structure of a **loop**
statement with one exit.

forms of the more general ALGOL 60 **for** statement:

    for *cv* := *initial* **step** *increment* **until** *final* **do** S

In the Pascal **for** statement there is an implicit increment. In the first
form it is +1 while in the second form it is −1. At first sight, this might appear a
major restriction; however, in practice, most **for** statements are used in
conjunction with arrays, the control variable being the same as the array
subscript. Thus, the majority of cases are covered by step lengths of +1 and
−1; the few unusual cases can be treated by special programming techniques.

Ada has adopted a similar approach to Pascal. The two forms of the
Ada **for** statement are:

    for *cv* **in** *low .. high* **loop**
      ...
    end loop;

and:

    for *cv* **in reverse** *low .. high* **loop**
      ...
    end loop;

Modula-2, on the other hand, allows an optional increment, as in:

```
FOR cv := initial TO final BY increment DO
    ...
END
```

The structure diagram for the **for** statement shown in Figure 4.6 is constructed on the lines of the Pascal/Ada statement so that the control variable does not go out of range. This is particularly necessary when *cv* is defined as a subrange variable whose values can be in the range *low* to *high*.

As the **for** statement has evolved from the looping statements of early languages, it is instructive to study its development to understand the advantages and disadvantages of the various forms provided by different languages.

- FORTRAN uses a very restricted DO loop with integer counting and positive increments. The loop is always executed at least once.

- ALGOL 60 provides a very powerful **for** statement. The initial, final and incremental values can all be expressions and can be of type **real**.

- COBOL uses PERFORM with variants such as:

```
PERFORM statement label n TIMES
PERFORM statement label VARYING cv FROM low BY increment
UNTIL cv GREATER THAN high
```

However, even more complicated variants are possible.

- PL/I has similarities to ALGOL 60.

- C has a very complex **for** statement. Its general form is:

      for (e1; e2; e3) S;

where each of the expressions e1, e2 and e3 are optional. This form is equivalent to:

      e1;
      while (e2) {S; e3;}

so if the traditional **for** statement is required, this can be written as:

      for ($i = 1$; $i <= n$; $i++$) S;

which is equivalent to:

      for $i := 1$ **to** n **do** S

in Pascal. But like the **while** statement it is not as obvious to the programmer.

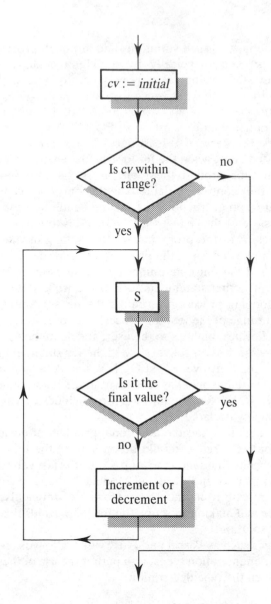

FIGURE 4.6

Structure of the Pascal/Ada **for** statement.

From the use of **for** statements in early languages, several conclusions seem to have been drawn. Firstly, using real values in a counting loop, as ALGOL 60 did, is likely to lead to error. For example:

> **for** $i := 0.0$ **step** 0.1 **until** 6.0 **do**

does not guarantee that the final value 6.0 will be considered within the loop. Its inclusion or non-inclusion depends on the rounding error and how the real numbers are represented in the particular computer. But programs should not be subject to such variations and although programmers could counter such problems (typically by adding a small fraction of the increment to the final value), it is now generally agreed that **for** loops should work with discrete types, since they are counting loops.

It is also better to allow **for** loops to do nothing in certain circumstances rather than to insist, as in FORTRAN, that the statements in the loop must be executed at least once. The increment and final value are best evaluated once, when the **for** loop is first encountered, and not re-evaluated each time around the loop, as is the case in ALGOL 60. Furthermore, the control variable should only be changed by the increment; that is, no instructions in S should be allowed to alter its value.

The purpose of the changes just outlined is to make the action of a **for** loop very clear to the programmer. By looking at the first line (no matter how complicated S is), the programmer can see the starting point, the increment and the finishing point. This is, in essence, the purpose of the **for** statement. Other statements such as the **while** statement can carry out the same looping process but, unlike the **for** statement, they do not make the exact range of the looping process, where it starts, what the step is and where it finishes, obvious to the user, and all in the first line of code.

The scope of the control variable in the **for** statement has also been the subject of some controversy. ALGOL W and Ada take the strong line that the control variable only has scope within the **for** statement and is not available outside it. In Ada, the **for** loop forms a block in which the control variable is implicitly declared.

Earlier languages had the additional problem of deciding what the value of the control variable should be on leaving the loop. The options were either the value that failed the loop test or the last value that was used in the loop statement S. In Pascal and Modula-2, the loop control variable is undefined on exit from the loop. However, implicitly defining the control variable and making its scope the **for** loop avoids this problem and seems the best solution.

Languages such as Pascal and Ada, which allow discrete types such as characters or enumeration types, also permit the use of these types in **for** statements. Given the type declaration:

> **type** *month* = (*Jan, Feb, Mar, Apr, May, Jun, Jul,*
> *Aug, Sep, Oct, Nov, Dec*);

the **for** statement:

> **for** $i := Jan$ **to** Dec **do** S

will iterate through the 12 values *Jan, Feb, ..., Dec*.

In the Pascal **for** statement:

> **for** $i := low$ **to** $high$ **do** S

the control variable i takes each value in the discrete range *low* to *high* in turn. In theory, this can be generalized so that the control variable can range over all the members of a structured data type such as a set, sequence, stack or tree. For example, given a set of names the meaning of the **for** loop:

    for x **in** d **do** S

would be to execute the statement S for each name x in the set d. The order in which the names x are selected from the set d is undefined, but this is not a problem. The requirement is to access each element in the set in turn; the precise order in which this is done is unimportant. **for** statements similar to this occur in CLU and Alphard, but both implementations are more complicated than the structure shown here.

4.5   *goto* Statement

Controversy has raged over the use of the **goto** statement since Dijkstra's letter to the *Communications of the ACM* entitled 'Goto Statement Considered Harmful' (1968). Most programmers in the early days of computing made widespread use of the conditional jump. Indeed, it was one of the most important features available for constructing the primitive loops of the 1950s and early 1960s. Of the early high-level languages, FORTRAN and COBOL encouraged the continued use of jumps (**goto** statements) with their associated labels. In ALGOL 60, with its somewhat better loop instructions, programs could be written with only a minimal use of **goto** statements, mainly to exit from **for** loops in failure situations. But ALGOL 60 allowed programmers to use loops and jumps as much as they wished, and even to the extent that they never needed to utilize **for** and **while** statements.

    Since the mid 1970s, however, the general consensus of opinion has swung strongly against the use of the **goto** statement. Overuse of such conditional jumps in complicated programs can lead to errors that are often obscure and difficult to locate. The reason many teachers argue against the use of BASIC and FORTRAN as the first language for programmers is that they encourage such bad habits.

    Modern high-level languages have usually compromised in their approach to the **goto** statement. With the exception of Modula-2, most such languages still include **goto** statements and labels while also providing loops by such methods as **for**, **while** and **repeat** statements.

    Languages such as Pascal, C and Ada have taken this line but have played down the use of the **goto** statement and have placed restrictions on its use. For example, ALGOL 60 permits jumps into and out of **if** statements but Pascal allows no jumps into any structured statement. PL/I, in contrast, went as far as allowing dynamic jumps where the label was considered to be a variable, and so it could be changed by the program. Scope problems in such situations are horrendous and make the ordinary static **goto** statement seem simple by comparison.

Newer languages do allow jumps although they are restricted. The **exit** statement in Ada and Modula-2 is a controlled jump to the end of a loop and Ada goes further than Pascal in not allowing jumps out of procedures. The break instruction in C is also a controlled exit from a loop. Given this current state of affairs, it is probably only a matter of time before the **goto** statement disappears altogether.

4.6   Exception Handling

During program execution, 'exceptional' events may occur making normal continuation undesirable or even impossible. Such exceptional occurrences can arise as a result of errors, such as attempted division by zero, arithmetic overflow or an array subscript going out of bounds, rare conditions like encountering the *end_of_file* marker or by the need for tracing and monitoring in program testing. Many programming languages leave the onus of dealing with such exceptional events completely with the programmer. It is then the responsibility of the programmer to test for such events and handle them as he or she sees fit. However, such a policy often leads to complex programs and can obscure the underlying structure of the program. Furthermore, some errors, such as attempted division by zero, are often impossible to handle as many systems merely report a run-time error and stop execution of the program.

An alternative strategy is to provide exception handling facilities as part of the language. The first language to do this in a systematic way was PL/I, by including features called ON-conditions. ALGOL 68 also included exception and default handling facilities but these were restricted to files and were not available for general program execution. Of the more recent languages, CLU and Ada are examples of those languages that have provided exception handling facilities of a reasonably general nature. Before examining the ON-conditions provided by PL/I and the exception handling facilities provided by Ada, contrasting the earlier methods used with the more sophisticated ideas of the 1980s, it is important to understand the nature of exception handling.

When an exceptional event occurs, an exception is said to be raised. Normal program execution is interrupted and control is transferred to a specially written part of the program, known as the **exception handler**.

Normally, different exception handlers exist for each kind of exception. A program written to handle the different exceptional events that might occur is called a **fault-tolerant program**.

As exception handling is in general a highly complicated operation, the discussion here will be confined to the following major issues:

- The facilities provided to recognize exceptions and their scope.
- How and when exceptions are raised.
- The specification of the exception handler and its relationship with that part of the program in which the exception occurs.
- What happens to the flow of control after execution of the exception handler has terminated.

PL/I *ON*-conditions

ON-conditions in PL/I are divided into three classes. The first class, which includes SUBSCRIPTRANGE, SIZE and CHECK, are ignored unless an ON-condition prefix has been set. The second class, which includes OVERFLOW, ZERODIVIDE and CONVERSION, are normally enabled but they can be disabled by a NO prefix. The third class, which includes ENDFILE, UNDEFINEDFILE and KEY, are always enabled and cannot be disabled.

ON-conditions are declared by statements such as:

```
ON OVERFLOW BEGIN; statements
            END;
```

The piece of code written between the BEGIN ... END brackets is, in effect, the exception handler. It can be used to give a sophisticated error message, to recover from the error or to perform the calculation that raised the exception in a different way. The programmer can choose to ignore an exception condition by including a piece of code such as:

```
ON ZERODIVIDE;
```

In this case, the exception handler is a null statement; therefore, the exception is trapped and then ignored. There are, of course, dangers in such an approach.

An exception can be raised by the statement:

```
SIGNAL CONDITION exception_name;
```

This will simulate an occurrence of the ON-condition.

ON-condition prefixes

As the ON-conditions in the first class are not normally enabled, a prefix must be placed in front of the appropriate procedure or block of code to invoke them; for example:

```
(SUBSCRIPTRANGE) : BEGIN; statements
                   END;
(CHECK(ROOT, A)) : GAUSS : PROCEDURE (X, Y, Z);
```

In the first example, the SUBSCRIPTRANGE is monitored throughout the statements between the BEGIN and END. If it is raised, the appropriate ON-condition is then obeyed. In the second example, the value of ROOT and A is printed out every time they are encountered in procedure GAUSS.

In the examples just given, the prefix was valid throughout the piece of code before which it appeared. However, the prefix can be turned off, called disabling the condition, by putting NO immediately in front of the prefix. For example:

```
(SIZE) : EXAMPLE : PROCEDURE (A, C);
                 .
                 .
                 .
(NOSIZE) : BEGIN; statements
                 END;
```

In this case, the prefix SIZE is valid throughout procedure EXAMPLE except in the inner block prefixed by (NOSIZE).

The ON-conditions in the second class do not require prefixes to enable them, although they can be turned off by a NO prefix.

ON-condition binding

When an ON-unit is encountered, it is bound to the block or procedure in which it occurs until either it is overridden by a new ON-unit for that condition or the block or procedure is left. When a condition is raised, the exception handler in the ON-unit is obeyed like a parameterless procedure and, when it is finished, control is either returned to the statement that raised the ON-condition or to the next statement, depending on the type of interrupt. However, as the exception handler in PL/I can include **goto** statements, control can be passed in a very arbitrary way, and more complex situations may arise.

Ada exception handling

The Ada exception handling mechanisms have, not surprisingly, benefitted from past experiences with PL/I ON-conditions. The principal idea in Ada is to provide each group of statements with an exception handling capability.

Exception handlers are associated with a statement sequence in what is called a **frame**, which always includes the structure:

```
begin
   statements
exception
   when overflow => ...;
   when help => ...;
end;
```

A frame can be a subprogram body, a package body or a block.

If, during the execution of the statements in a frame, an exception is raised, then control is passed to the appropriate handler at the end of the frame. When the actions in the exception handler have been completed, the frame is left. This is in contrast to PL/I where control is passed back to the point where the exception was raised.

If an exception is raised in a frame that does not have an exception handler for the condition, the exception is propagated to the next level. If the frame concerned is a subprogram body, the exception is passed to the frame containing the subprogram call. This is a dynamic process with the exception being raised again in the calling frame if it is not handled. A similar mechanism is used for blocks and package bodies.

In analogy with the Ada **case** construction, **others** can also be included in the exception handling mechanism to catch all the exceptions that are not specifically mentioned at the end of the frame.

Ada has both predefined and user-declared exceptions. The predefined exceptions – such as *constraint_error*, which is raised when, for example, subscripts exceed the declared bounds – are essential for an embedded language like Ada so that errors that cannot be checked at compile time are raised as an exception at run time. In contrast, user-declared exceptions, such as *overflow* and *help*, are activated only by the use of a raise statement. However, the raise statement can also be used to activate the predefined exceptions. Furthermore, the programmer is also provided with the facility to write exception handlers for the predefined exceptions.

Finally, Ada does not allow parameter passing to exception handlers. This is because exceptions are considered to be irregular conditions and the frame in which they occur should provide the appropriate exception handling operations before passing control back to the calling frame.

SUMMARY

- An expression yields a value while the execution of a statement alters the state.

- The order of evaluation of an expression depends on the precedence rules used in the language.

- Side effects in the evaluation of an expression should be avoided.

- The meaning of an operator can depend on its operands. Such an operator is said to be overloaded.

- Structured statements should have only one entry and one exit point. This helps when reasoning about a program's effect.

- There are two kinds of conditional statement in modern imperative languages: the **if** statement and the **case** statement.

- A default condition is not allowed in the Pascal **case** statement, but is permitted in C, Ada and Modula-2.

- There are three kinds of iterative statement in most modern imperative languages: the **while** statement, the **repeat** statement and the **for** statement.

- In Pascal and Ada, the **for** statement is restricted to unit steps.

- The control variable in an Ada **for** statement is implicitly declared. In Pascal and Modula-2, the control variable must be declared and its value is undefined on exit from the loop.

- When a run-time error occurs in PL/I or Ada, an exception is raised. Normal program execution is interrupted and control is passed to the appropriate exception handler.

- In PL/I, when the actions in the exception handler have been completed, control is passed back to the point where the exception was raised. In Ada, the frame in which the exception was raised is left.

- Exception handling is important in embedded systems as they have to be able to recover from errors that occur during program execution.

EXERCISES

4.1   Compare the precedence of the logical operators **and**, **or**, **not** in ALGOL 60, Pascal and Ada. List the drawbacks of the precedence rules adopted by each of these languages and outline your preferred solution.

4.2   Under what circumstances will short-circuit evaluation of logical operations lead to results that differ from those obtained from full evaluation?

4.3   In ALGOL 68, a statement has a value. What are the advantages and disadvantages of this?

4.4   As it is desirable for structured statements to have only one entry and one exit point, do you think that Ada should have been restricted so that **exit** statements were not allowed in **while** and **for** loops?

4.5   In Pascal, a positive decision was made not to include a default condition in the **case** statement. In contrast, in Ada, a default condition must be included unless the full range of the **case** expression is already covered by the case labels. Which approach leads to more reliable programs?

4.6   (a)   Describe how the **for** statement differs in ALGOL 60, Pascal and Ada.

   (b)   ALGOL 60 allowed the control variable to be changed within a loop. Why was that freedom removed in Pascal?

   (c)   What are the advantages of the control variable being implicitly declared, as it is in Ada?

4.7   Once an exception has been handled in PL/I, control is returned to the statement following the exception, while in Ada the frame containing the exception is left. Compare the effect of these two approaches.

Bibliography

Structured programming and the design of a suitable set of structured control statements was a major issue in language design in the late 1960s and early 1970s following Dijkstra's letter about the **goto** statement (1968). A special issue of the *ACM Computing Surveys* (1974) has an interesting series of articles on the topic.

ACM (1974), 'Special Issue: Programming', *ACM Computing Surveys*, **6**(4).

Dijkstra, E. W. (1968), 'Goto Statement Considered Harmful', *Comm. ACM*, **11**, pp. 147–148.

CHAPTER 5

Subprograms

One of the most important issues that has to be addressed in the design of a language is the support it gives to the control of complexity. This is achieved by hiding unwanted detail and is implemented by dividing programs into self-contained units that can only interact with one another through small strictly defined interfaces. This chapter looks at subprograms and how they form a satisfactory unit of decomposition for small programs. For larger programs, a means of grouping subprograms into larger units is needed and this is dealt with in Chapter 7.

Although the subprogram principle varies very little from one language to another, there are major differences in the way subprograms are combined to form complete programs. In FORTRAN, subprograms may be compiled independently. However, this is not possible in languages like Pascal as subprograms are declared within the main program and can be nested within other subprograms.

There are a number of diverse mechanisms for passing parameters. This chapter looks at and compares the main mechanisms used and at the effect they each have in promoting the reliability of programs.

The chapter also looks at the various methods of storage allocation and relates this to concepts such as the lifetime of a variable, discussed in earlier chapters.

5.1 Stepwise Refinement

The usual approach to program design, which the reader is assumed to be familiar with, is called **programming by stepwise refinement** or **top-down design**. The first step in this process is to produce a top-level algorithm expressed in terms of the problem to be solved. This approach allows the designer to concentrate on the organization and design of the solution without being distracted by implementation details. Although the statements in the top-level algorithm are not capable of being directly implemented on a computer, they can be regarded as the specifications of subproblems. Thus, the next step is to produce a solution to each of the subproblems by expanding the corresponding specification into a series of more detailed statements, each of which can in turn be considered as the specification of an even simpler problem. This stepwise refinement continues until the subproblems produced are simple enough for their solution to be written directly in a programming language.

The language feature that helps support this approach to design is the subprogram. Hence, instead of producing the solution to a subproblem by directly expanding a statement in the top-level algorithm, an appropriate subprogram can be defined and then used. In this way, the final main program will not be too different from the original top-level algorithm, since many of the top-level statements will have been implemented by subprogram calls. Furthermore, if meaningful identifiers are used for each of the subprograms, a reasonable idea of the intent of a program can be gained by reading the relatively short main program.

Subprograms are, therefore, a major abstraction mechanism. By using a subprogram, it is possible to concentrate on what the program does without having to bother about how it does it. This ability to hide unwanted detail is the main tool used to control complexity in programming languages.

Chapter 2 described how information hiding can be further promoted by the use of packages in Ada, modules in Modula-2 and classes in SIMULA. A more detailed description of these features is given in Chapter 7 which also shows that the stepwise refinement of data structures is at least as important as the stepwise refinement of commands.

As subprograms are central to the production of structured programs, virtually all programming languages include a mechanism for declaring and calling subprograms. Although there are major differences in what may be passed as parameters to or returned as the value of a function, there is general agreement among languages as to the form of both subprogram declarations and calls.

5.2 Using Subprograms

Two kinds of subprogram are commonly used in programming languages; namely, procedures (or subroutines) and functions. A procedure call is a statement in its own right, while a function call is part of an expression and returns a value.

A major idea behind language design is that there should be as few distinct concepts as possible. Hence, although languages such as FORTRAN, Pascal and Ada make a clear distinction between functions and procedures, others, such as ALGOL 68 and C, regard a procedure as a special case of a function in which the returned value is either void or is ignored.

The parameters in a subprogram declaration are referred to as formal parameters while the parameters in the call of a subprogram are referred to as actual parameters. When a subprogram is called, each actual parameter is associated with its corresponding formal parameter. To illustrate this, consider the following Pascal example. This swaps the values of two integer variables *higher* and *lower* and then swaps the values of the integer variables *his* and *hers*. It does this by declaring a procedure and having two procedure calls.

```
program exchange(input, output);
var higher, lower, his, hers : integer;

    procedure swap(var first, second : integer);
    var intermediate : integer;
    begin
      intermediate := first;
      first := second;
      second := intermediate
    end {swap};

begin
    ...
    swap(higher, lower);
    ...
    swap(his, hers);
    ...
end.
```

In Pascal, the types of the corresponding formal and actual parameters must match and this check is performed at compile time. In the first call of *swap*, the variable *higher* is associated with the formal parameter *first* and the variable *lower* is associated with the formal parameter *second*. The

EXAMPLE PROGRAMS – SUBPROGRAMS

FORTRAN 77

```
PROGRAM EXCHAN
INTEGER HIGHER, LOWER, HIS, HERS
...
CALL SWAP(HIGHER, LOWER)
...
CALL SWAP(HIS, HERS)
...
STOP
END


SUBROUTINE SWAP(FIRST, SECOND)
INTEGER FIRST, SECOND, INTERM
INTERM = FIRST
FIRST = SECOND
SECOND = INTERM
RETURN
END
```

C

```
main( )
{ int higher, lower, his, hers;
  ...
  swap(&higher, &lower);
  ...
  swap(&his, &hers);
  ...
}

void swap(first, second)
int *first, *second;
{ int intermediate;
  intermediate = *first;
  *first = *second;
  *second = intermediate;
}
```

Modula-2

```
MODULE exchange;
  VAR higher, lower, his, hers : INTEGER;


  PROCEDURE swap(VAR first, second : INTEGER);
  VAR intermediate : INTEGER;
  BEGIN
    intermediate := first;
    first := second;
    second := intermediate
  END swap;


BEGIN
  ...
  swap(higher, lower);
  ...
  swap(his, hers);
  ...
END exchange.
```

Ada

```
procedure exchange is
  ...
  higher, lower, his, hers : integer;


  procedure swap(first, second : in out integer) is
    intermediate : integer;
  begin
    intermediate := first;
    first := second;
    second := first;
  end swap;


begin
  ...
  swap(higher, lower);
  ...
  swap(his, hers);
  ...
end exchange;
```

effect of executing the procedure body is therefore to swap the values of *higher* and *lower*.

Subprograms allow the user to think at a more abstract level. Thus, once a *swap* procedure has been declared, it is no longer necessary to think about how to swap two integer variables (or the need for an intermediate). Such a procedure, in effect, adds a new operation to the language. If a collection of such subprograms is created, it is not necessary for a programmer to have to start from scratch when writing a new program; instead, the subprograms, which have already been written and tested, can simply be incorporated.

The outline programs given on pages 122 and 123 show how the declaration and call of a *swap* subprogram are achieved in several different languages. Although the mechanisms used to pass parameters differ considerably, all the subprograms can clearly be seen to be performing the same operation.

In FORTRAN and C, the types of the actual and formal parameters are not checked to ensure that they match while in Modula-2 and Ada they are checked at compile time. The different parameter-passing mechanisms are described in Section 5.4.

In most languages, the structure of a subprogram and the structure of the main program are very similar. However, instead of the words procedure or subroutine, Pascal and FORTRAN 77 use the word **program/** PROGRAM to denote the main program and Modula-2 the word MODULE. C uses a subprogram called *main* while Ada allows an ordinary procedure such as *exchange* to be the main program.

Finally, declarations can be made within a subprogram in the same way as they can in a main program. They are then called **local declarations**.

5.3   Program Structure

As well as using parameters, subprograms can communicate with one another by sharing access to non-local information. The way in which this is done depends on the program structure adopted by the language.

FORTRAN

In FORTRAN, a program consists of a main program in addition to a series of independent subprograms. The structure of a FORTRAN 77 program is shown in Figure 5.1. Note that the local variable R is only in scope within the main program while S and T are only in scope in the subroutines in which they are declared.

```
PROGRAM MAIN
COMMON X, Y, Z
INTEGER R

   .
   .
   .

STOP
END
```

```
SUBROUTINE A ...
COMMON U, V, W
INTEGER S

   .
   .
   .

RETURN
END
```

```
SUBROUTINE B ...
COMMON E, F, G
INTEGER T

   .
   .
   .

RETURN
END
```

FIGURE 5.1

Structure of a
FORTRAN program.

Subprograms in FORTRAN can interact with one another via parameters or through a list of COMMON variables. Although the COMMON list must be repeated in each subprogram, the identifiers do not have to be the same in each case, and the lists do not have to be of the same length. Variables in corresponding positions in each of the COMMON lists share the same locations in store. Hence, any change to the variable U in subroutine A of Figure 5.1

automatically changes the value of the variable X in the main program and the value of the variable E in subroutine B.

As well as allowing subprograms to communicate with one another, COMMON lists are sometimes used to reduce a program's storage requirements. They do this by enabling variables that have no connection with one another to share the same storage locations. This is called **overlaying** and it was an important feature of FORTRAN when it was first designed as then the main stores of computers were small and space was often at a premium. However, such a concept does not aid the understanding or improve the reliability of programs!

Independent compilation

As FORTRAN subprograms do not depend on one another, they can be compiled independently and held in libraries of pre-compiled routines. Such an approach allows programmers to incorporate tried and tested routines in their programs. Furthermore, if changes need to be made to a subprogram, then only that subprogram has to be recompiled, which is a major advantage when modifications have to be made to large programs containing many subprograms. However, the drawback of this approach is that full type checking across subprogram boundaries is not possible: as each subprogram is compiled independently, it is not possible to check that the type of the actual parameters in a subprogram call matches the type of the formal parameters in the subprogram declaration. This presents a major problem when trying to produce large, reliable systems consisting of many subprograms. (The difference between independent and separate compilation is discussed in Section 7.3.)

ALGOL-like languages

In ALGOL 60 and its many successors (for example, Pascal), an alternative approach has been adopted. Such languages have one monolithic program and subprograms can either be declared within the main program or nested within other subprograms. This is illustrated by the Pascal program skeleton given in Figure 5.2.

Languages that allow the nesting of subprograms are said to be **block structured**. As was described in Section 3.2, each subprogram in Pascal can be regarded as a block and subprograms inherit all the declarations made in enclosing blocks. ALGOL 60, Modula-2 and Ada also allow the declarations of subprograms to be nested in this manner while FORTRAN and C do not.

The rules governing the visibility of identifiers are called the scope rules and they were described in Chapter 3. The rule that an identifier is always bound to its most local declaration means that a programmer can

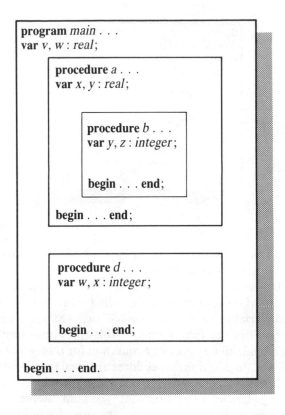

```
program main . . .
var v, w : real;

    procedure a . . .
    var x, y : real;

            procedure b . . .
            var y, z : integer;

            begin . . . end;

    begin . . . end;


    procedure d . . .
    var w, x : integer;

        begin . . . end;

begin . . . end.
```

FIGURE 5.2

Pascal program
skeleton.

concentrate on one procedure at a time and choose the most suitable identifiers without worrying if these identifiers are used elsewhere in the program. Hence, within procedure *b* of Figure 5.2, the integer variable *y* can be declared and used without worrying that a real variable *y* has already been declared in an enclosing block.

If identifiers are declared as locally as possible, the number in scope at any particular time is kept to a minimum. To help promote this condition, ALGOL 60, ALGOL 68, C and Ada allow the nesting of blocks that are not subprograms. This is illustrated in the Ada program segment shown in Figure 5.3 where one block is nested within another. As the usual scope rules apply, the integer variable *a* and the real variables *b* and *d* are visible in the inner block while the integer variable *b* is hidden.

In a block-structured language, subprograms are declared in an environment created by the enclosing blocks. Although this rules out independent compilation, it does make full type checking possible across subprogram boundaries. (Note that several implementations of Pascal do allow independent compilation, but this is usually accomplished in a way that involves the drawbacks found with FORTRAN.)

Reconciling the advantages of being able to pre-compile parts of a program and yet be able to have full type checking has been a major

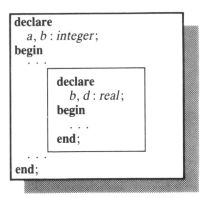

FIGURE 5.3

Nested blocks in Ada.

concern of language designers. The way in which this has been achieved in Ada and Modula-2 is described in Section 7.3.

Variables used in a subprogram can be declared in an enclosing block. However, when a subprogram is called there is no indication that such non-local variables may be accessed or, what is worse, may be changed as a result of the call. To be reliable, programs must be easy to read and understand, and a necessary condition for this is that there are no hidden side effects. In addition, procedures are used to support the decomposition of a problem into a series of smaller subproblems, each of which can be tackled independently. Procedures should therefore be as self-contained as possible. For these reasons, the use of non-local variables is now generally frowned upon.

As an example, the language Alphard has retained block structure, but subprograms cannot inherit the names of variables declared in enclosing blocks, although they do inherit the names of types. The language Euclid, which was derived from Pascal, has gone even further. In Euclid, subprograms have a **closed scope**. (Another name for the usual scope rules is **open scope**.) In closed scope, declarations are not normally inherited from an enclosing block. Instead, each subprogram has an import list indicating which identifiers in the enclosing blocks may be used in the subprogram. To prevent the import lists becoming too long, constant, subprogram and type identifiers, but not variable identifiers, may be declared to be **pervasive**. Identifiers thus declared are then automatically available in inner blocks without having to be imported.

The C language

The structure of a C program can be thought of as being intermediate between that of FORTRAN and the ALGOL-like languages. A large C program is usually divided into separate parts with each part being held in a separate file. The contents of each file, which may hold several subprograms, may be compiled independently of the rest of the program. Variables, constants and types can be declared outside subprograms in what can be considered as an outer block, but their visibility is restricted to the subprograms in the current file. A file containing part of a program could have the following outline contents:

```
int a

y()
{  ... /* a is visible and can be used */ ...
}

z()
{  ... /* a is visible and can be used */ ...
}
```

If a subprogram in a part of the program declared in another file needs to access the integer variable a, a must be declared to be an external identifier, as in:

```
w()
{  ... /* a is not visible */ ...
}

x()
{  extern int a;
   ... /* a is visible and can be used */ ...
}
```

C therefore manages to support independent compilation by ensuring that global identifiers are re-declared when they are needed in files other than the one in which they were originally declared. No type checking takes place, however, to ensure that the different declarations match.

5.4 Parameters

Parameters can be classified into three groups or modes. They can be used to:

- pass information to a subprogram,

Table 5.1 Parameter-passing mechanisms.

Language	Mechanism						
	value	constant-value	reference-constant	result	reference	value-result	name
ALGOL 60	*						*
FORTRAN					?	?	
PL/I					?	?	
ALGOL 68		*			*		
Pascal	*				?		
C	*				*		
Modula-2	*				?		
Ada (scalars)		*		*		*	
Ada (others)		?	?	?	?	?	
Alphard		*	*		*		

- receive information from a subprogram, or
- pass information to a subprogram where it is to be updated before being returned.

Ada has three different parameter modes called **in**, **out** and **in out**, corresponding to each of the three cases, but most other languages manage with fewer modes.

To complicate matters further, each mode can be implemented in different ways. In addition, some languages define the mechanism to be used while others leave it up to the compiler writer. This section considers the following mechanisms:

- Passing information in: call by value, constant-value and reference-constant.
- Passing information out: call by result.
- Updating information: call by value-result, reference and name.

Table 5.1 shows the methods used in several different languages. An asterisk in the table indicates that the mechanism is specified by the language and a question mark that it is a possible mechanism.

Passing information in

In **call by value**, the formal parameter acts as a local variable, which is initialized with the value of the actual parameter. Consider the Pascal procedure:

```
procedure readandwrite(total : integer);
var symbol : char;
begin
  while total > 0 do
  begin
    read(symbol); write(symbol);
    total := total − 1
  end
end {readandwrite};
```

If *length* is an integer variable that has been given the value 10, the effect of the procedure call:

```
readandwrite(length);
```

will be to pass a copy of the value of *length* to the formal parameter *total*. Within the procedure, the changes made to *total* are to this local copy, and so they have no effect on the actual parameter *length*. Thus, when the program returns from the procedure, after having read and written 10 characters, the actual parameter *length* will still have the value 10.

In **call by constant-value**, the formal parameter is a local constant rather than a local variable. The following Ada version of the foregoing procedure requires a local variable as the value of *total* may not be changed:

```
procedure read_and_write(total : in integer) is
  symbol : character;
  count : integer := total;
begin
  while count > 0 loop
    get(symbol); put(symbol);
    count := count − 1;
  end loop;
end read_and_write;
```

It is now clearer that the actual parameter is not affected by the procedure call. In both call by value and call by constant-value the actual parameter may be a constant or an expression as only the value of the actual parameter is passed.

A major drawback of these two methods is that when the parameter is a structured object, such as an array, a copy of the complete structure is created, which is expensive in space and time. To overcome this inefficiency, Pascal and Modula-2 programmers often pass array or record parameters by reference rather than by value, even when the structure is not being updated. In **call by reference**, it is the address of the actual parameter that is passed. However, this method does not have the advantage of call by value: when only a copy is passed to a subprogram, this guarantees that any change to the formal parameter has no effect on the actual parameter.

In Ada, the passing of structured parameters of mode **in** may be implemented by **reference-constant** instead of by constant-value. The difference between call by reference-constant and call by reference is that the formal parameter is a local constant. As a constant cannot be updated, there is no reduction in security.

Figure 5.4 illustrates the three methods discussed here for passing information into a procedure.

Passing information out

Call by result is used in Ada to implement **out** mode parameters for scalar types. The formal parameter acts as an uninitialized local variable which is given a value during execution of the procedure. On leaving the procedure, the value of the formal parameter is assigned to the actual parameter, which must be a variable. This is shown in the following Ada procedure:

```
procedure read_negative(neg_number : out integer) is
  number : integer;
begin
  get(number);
  while number >= 0 loop
    put_line("number not negative, try again");
    get(number);
  end loop;
  neg_number := number;
end read_negative;
```

As an **out** parameter may not appear within an expression, it is necessary to have a local variable called *number*. In the call:

```
read_negative(amount);
```

the value of the integer variable *amount* is not updated to the value of *neg_number* until procedure *read_negative* is left.

Call by result was originally used in ALGOL W, but with a subtle difference from the mechanism described here. In Ada, the address of the actual parameter is computed on subprogram entry while in ALGOL W it is not computed until subprogram exit. These two approaches only give different answers in rather contrived situations, as will be seen later in this section.

As call by result means that a local copy must be created within the procedure, it suffers from the efficiency drawbacks that occur with structured parameters, as already discussed. For this reason, Ada allows structured **out** parameters to be passed by reference. As languages such as (a)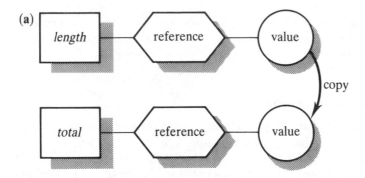

(b)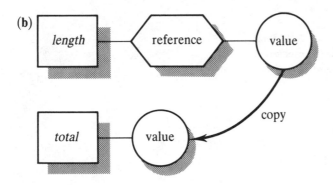

(c)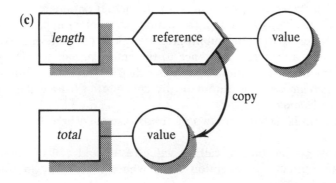

FIGURE 5.4

Passing information into a procedure: (a) call by value; (b) call by constant-value; (c) call by reference-constant.

Pascal and Modula-2 do not have a special parameter mode corresponding to the **out** mode of Ada, they use the same mechanism as that for updating information.

Updating information

Call by value-result is, as might be expected from its name, an amalgamation of call by value and call by result. The formal parameter acts as a local variable which is initialized to the value of the actual parameter. Within the procedure, changes to the formal parameter only affect the local copy. It is only when the subprogram is left that the actual parameter is updated to the final value of the formal parameter. For example, given the following Ada procedure to update a bank account by reading and then adding on the next 10 transactions:

```
procedure update(balance : in out integer) is
   transaction : integer;
begin
   for j in 1 .. 10 loop
      get(transaction);
      balance := balance + transaction;
   end loop;
end update;
```

then in the call:

```
update(currentaccount);
```

the actual parameter *currentaccount* is only updated when the procedure is left.

In Ada, **in out** scalar parameters must be passed by value-result although structured parameters may be passed by reference. The definitions of Pascal and Modula-2 do not specify the mechanism to be used for variable parameters, but call by reference is always chosen.

In **call by reference**, the address of the actual parameter (that is, a pointer to the location containing the actual parameter) is passed to the formal parameter. Within the subprogram, any use of the formal parameter is treated as an indirect reference to the actual parameter. Hence, if the **var** parameter in procedure *update* is called by reference, the actual parameter *currentaccount* is automatically changed each time there is an assignment to *balance*.

Figure 5.5 illustrates the two methods discussed here for updating information.

In most circumstances, call by value-result and call by reference have the same effect, an exception being where there is an interaction

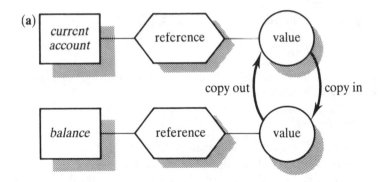

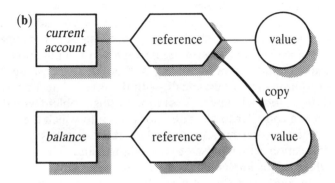

FIGURE 5.5

Updating information:
(a) call by value-result;
(b) call by reference.

between the parameters and non-local variables. Programs should be written in such a way that they do not depend on the mechanism used.

Call by value-result has the same disadvantages with structured objects as call by value and so in such circumstances call by reference would seem to be the better choice. Call by value-result, on the other hand, has the advantage that all references within the subprogram are to local variables, which is faster than the indirect references to non-locals used in call by reference.

Being able to reference variables indirectly introduces the possibility of **aliasing**. If the actual parameter is in scope within the body of the called procedure, it can be accessed in two ways: either directly as a non-local variable or indirectly through the formal parameter. This can lead to errors which are very difficult to find and correct. An example of aliasing is shown on page 138 in the call of procedure *whichmode*.

Another form of aliasing is when the same actual parameter is passed to two different reference formal parameters. This could happen, for example, with the *swap* procedure with the call:

>   *swap*(*this*, *this*);

Languages such as Pascal have outlawed such subprogram calls, but it is not clear how calls such as:

>   *swap*(*a*[*i*], *a*[*j*]);

should be treated. This call is legal unless the values of *i* and *j* are equal and so erroneous calls can only be detected at run time.

To avoid the problems raised by aliasing, a variable in Euclid may not be passed as a **var** parameter to a subprogram in whose import list it appears. This has the consequence that call by reference and call by value-result always have the same effect.

In Pascal, Modula-2 and Ada, actual parameters passed by reference or by value-result must be variables, but FORTRAN and PL/I allow them to be constants or expressions. At first glance, this does not appear to be possible as the actual parameter must be capable of being updated. In some early implementations of FORTRAN this led to constants being changed as a result of a subprogram call, with the effect that the resulting errors were difficult to track down. A solution to this problem with call by reference is for the compiler to allocate a location into which the value of the constant or expression may be put when the call takes place. The address of this location is then passed to the subprogram. When parameter passing in FORTRAN is implemented as call by value-result, the solution is not to generate code for the result part when the actual parameter is not a variable.

Parameters in C

Arrays in C are called by reference while all other parameter types are passed by value. The effect of call by reference for scalar objects can be achieved by having formal parameters of a pointer type and passing the address of a variable as the actual parameter. Hence, in procedure *swap*, shown in the previous section:

```
void swap(first, second)
int *first, *second;
{  int intermediate;
   intermediate = *first;
   *first = *second;
   *second = intermediate;
}
```

the parameters *first* and *second* are both value parameters, but the * in their declaration indicates that their type is 'pointer to integer'. The assignment:

> *first = *second;

should be read as 'the value held in the location pointed to by *second* is assigned to the location pointed to by *first*'. A possible procedure call is:

> swap(&*higher*, &*lower*);

The & operator means that it is not the values of *higher* and *lower* that are passed, but their addresses. The effect is exactly the same as call by reference, the difference being that the C programmer needs to be more aware of what is going on and how parameter passing is being implemented. It can be argued that one of the aims of high-level languages is to hide implementation details so that the programmer can concentrate on the problem to be solved. Thus, this example shows how C is a lower level language than Pascal or Modula-2.

Call by name

ALGOL 60 uses call by name as the mechanism for updating information. This involves the equivalent of textual substitution of the actual parameter for each occurrence of the formal parameter. In call by reference, the address of the actual parameter is calculated at the point of call. In call by name, on the other hand, the actual parameter is passed unevaluated and its address is recalculated each time the formal parameter is used during the execution of the subprogram. Although this method introduces the possibility of a different address being produced for different uses of the same formal parameter, it does in fact only lead to different results from call by reference when the programmer is being 'overclever'. Thus, as call by name is much more expensive to implement than call by reference, it has not been used in recent languages.

Overloading

Ada allows more than one subprogram with the same identifier to be declared in the same scope, but they must have a different parameter profile so that they can be differentiated from one another. Hence, the following declarations are allowed:

> **procedure** *swap*(*a*, *b* : **in** *real*) **is**
> **begin** ... **end** *swap*;
> **procedure** *swap*(*a*, *b* : **in** *integer*) **is**
> **begin** ... **end** *swap*;

COMPARISON OF METHODS

In the following rather contrived example, the effect of the call *whichmode(a[element])* on *a* and *element* depends on how the parameter is passed. It must be emphasized that this example is only given to highlight the differences between the various methods; such tricky programming is not encouraged.

```
...
var element : integer;
    a : array [1 .. 2] of integer;

procedure whichmode(x : ? mode integer);
begin
  a[1] := 6;
  element := 2;
  x := x + 3
end;

begin
  a[1] := 1; a[2] := 2;
  element := 1;
  whichmode(a[element]);
...
```

If the parameter is passed by result, an error will occur as the value of x in the expression $x + 3$ is undefined. If x was an **out** mode parameter in Ada, this use of x would give a syntax error. The other possibilities are given in Table 5.2.

When the parameter is called by reference, elements of the array *a* can be accessed in two different ways: either directly as in:

```
a[1] := 6;
```

or, because the actual parameter is *a[element]*, indirectly as in:

```
x := x + 3
```

This is an example of aliasing and is the cause of call by value-result and call by reference giving different answers. The reason that call by name gives a different answer from call by reference is that the address of *a[element]* on procedure entry is different from its address when the statement:

```
x := x + 3
```

is executed. Similarly, as the address of *a[element]* computed on procedure entry is different from that on procedure exit, the two variants of call by value-result give different answers.

Table 5.2 Results of different parameter-passing mechanisms.

Mechanism	Result		
	$a[1]$	$a[2]$	*element*
call by value	6	2	2
call by value-result (ALGOL W)	6	4	2
call by value-result	4	2	2
call by reference	9	2	2
call by name	6	5	2

The call *swap*(2.0, 5.0) is a call of the first procedure while the call *swap*(2, 5) is a call of the second. If it is not possible to tell from the actual parameters which procedure is being called, then a compile-time error results.

A use of this feature is in the library of input/output routines where, for example, different *put* procedures write out values of different types. For example, there is one *put* routine for type *integer*, one for type *real* and one for type *character*. Thus, in the call *put*(*item*), the procedure used will depend on the type of the variable *item*. Overloading therefore gives a simple straightforward interface for the input/output routines, which is easy for novices to learn and use.

To achieve a similar effect, Pascal 'cheats'. The *read* and *write* routines in Pascal appear to be ordinary Pascal procedures, but as they may have parameters of different types (and a variable number of parameters), they do not follow the standard Pascal rules.

Input/output routines in Modula-2 do follow the normal rules for procedures, but as overloading is not allowed, separate routines are required for each parameter type: WriteInt is used to write the value of an integer, Write the value of a character and WriteReal the value of a real. However, this is less convenient and more error prone than the Ada approach.

Named parameters

The usual mechanism for pairing actual and formal parameters is by position, with the first actual parameter corresponding to the first formal parameter, and so on. An alternative mechanism, available in PL/I and Ada, is to have **named association**. For example, consider the following Ada procedure:

```
procedure increment(item : in out integer;
                    by : in integer) is
begin
   item := item + by;
end increment;
```

If *number* is a variable of type *integer*, then a possible call is:

> *increment*(*number*, 2);

Using named association, the procedure call could be written in one of the three following ways:

> *increment*(*number*, *by* => 2);
> *increment*(*item* => *number*, *by* => 2);
> *increment*(*by* => 2, *item* => *number*);

As can be seen, the names of the formal parameters are repeated in the procedure call to indicate the association between the actual and formal parameters. Positional and named associations may be mixed, but in such cases all the positional associations must come first. When the formal parameter identifiers are carefully chosen, named association can lead to clearer code, especially when there are a large number of parameters whose relative positions have no intrinsic meaning.

Default parameters

Another feature of Ada is that **in** mode parameters may be given a default initial value. Hence, the *increment* procedure could be written as:

```
procedure increment(item : in out integer;
                    by : in integer := 1) is
begin
  item := item + by;
end increment;
```

A call such as:

> *increment*(*number*, 2);

will increment *number* by 2, but if a second actual parameter is not given, as in the call:

> *increment*(*number*);

by is given the default value of 1.

Named association and default parameters are most useful when used together. For example, when real values are written in Ada, parameters are needed to specify the format; that is, the number of digits before the decimal point (*fore*), the number after the decimal point (*aft*) and the number in the exponent (*exp*). A possible statement to write out the value of the real variable *size* is:

put(*size*, *fore* => 2, *aft* => 5, *exp* => 3);

which is more understandable than:

put(*size*, 2, 5, 3);

as there is then nothing in the procedure call to indicate which actual parameter corresponds to *fore*, which to *aft* and which to *exp*. It is quite easy, on the other hand, to remember that the first parameter represents the value being written. As *fore*, *aft* and *exp* have default values, they do not have to be explicitly mentioned in a call of *put*. This allows calls such as:

put(*size*, *aft* => 5);

where two of the format parameters are given their default value. In an earlier use of *put* in procedure *read_and_write*, all three format parameters were in fact given their default values. An advantage of this feature is that a novice user does not have to know about the existence of these extra parameters until he or she becomes more experienced.

5.5   Functions

A function differs from a procedure in that it returns a value. The type of the returned value is usually given in the function heading, as can be seen from the example functions given on page 142 which return the sum of the values of their two integer parameters.

The value to be returned is given in FORTRAN, ALGOL 60 and Pascal by assigning a value to the name of the function, but this approach has been replaced in more recent languages by the use of an explicit **return** statement. Execution of a **return** statement causes immediate exit from a function, thereby making multiple exit points possible. In contrast, assignment to the name of a function does not cause an exit; such functions are left once their final statement has been executed. Ada, C and FORTRAN also allow the use of a **return** statement with procedures.

Function calls occur as part of an expression, as in the statement:

j := 3 * *add*(7, 11);

EXAMPLE PROGRAMS – FUNCTIONS

FORTRAN

```
INTEGER FUNCTION ADD(A, B)
INTEGER A, B
ADD = A + B
RETURN
END
```

ALGOL 60

```
integer procedure add(a, b);
   value a, b; integer a, b;
   add := a + b
```

Pascal

```
function add(a, b : integer) : integer;
begin
   add := a + b
end {add};
```

C

```
int add(a, b)
int a, b;
{  return (a + b);
}
```

Modula-2

```
PROCEDURE add(a, b : INTEGER) : INTEGER;
BEGIN
   RETURN a + b
END add
```

Ada

```
function add(a, b : in integer) return integer is
begin
   return a + b;
end add;
```

which assigns the value 54 to j. The value returned by a function can be regarded as an extra **out** parameter. Languages differ in what can be returned. ALGOL 60, FORTRAN, Pascal, C and Modula-2 do not allow structured values to be returned while Ada and ALGOL 68 do. (Languages that allow functions to be returned as the value of a function are discussed in Chapter 9.)

The exact order of evaluation of the operands in an expression is often not specified in the definition of a language so that the compiler writers have a free hand in producing optimal code. Evaluation of the expression:

$$a + b * c$$

in Pascal or Ada, for example, will cause the values of b and c to be multiplied together and the result added to a. However, when a, b and c are functions, the user has no knowledge of the order in which the three function calls will take place. It is, therefore, even more important than with procedures that functions have no side effects.

Good programming practice suggests that information should only be passed into a function via its parameters and that the only effect of the function on the rest of the program should be through the returned value. Ada, in fact, does not allow **out** or **in out** parameters with functions, although both it and most other languages (with the exception of experimental languages such as Euclid) do still allow access to, and modification of, non-local variables. Programmers should not normally indulge in this latter freedom.

Operators

Most languages have a set of built-in infix operators such as $+$, $-$ and $*$ while functions correspond to prefix operators. Thus, a call of *add* is written as:

   $c := add(2, 3);$

while the corresponding infix form is:

   $c := 2 + 3;$

To illustrate the use of these two forms of operators, consider an enumeration type called *day* which is declared as:

   type *day* **is** (*sun, mon, tues, wed, thurs, fri, sat*);

Consider also a function with two parameters – *today* of type *day* and *n* of type *integer* – that will return the day which is '*n* days after *today*'. In Ada, the names of functions are not restricted to identifiers. The operators can be redefined, as in:

```
function "+"(today : in day; n : in integer) return day is
begin
  return day'val((day'pos(today) + n) rem 7);
  --day'pos converts a day to the corresponding integer in
  --the range 0 .. 6 while day'val converts an integer in
  --the range 0 .. 6 to the corresponding day
end "+";
```

Assuming that *newday* has been defined to be of type *day*, a possible call of the function is:

  newday := "+" (*tues*, 6);

although the more natural approach:

  newday := *tues* + 6;

shows more clearly that a new operator has been defined and would normally be used. In both cases, *newday* will be given the value *mon*. This new definition of + does not replace the existing definitions, but extends it. It is the overloading property of Ada that determines, from the type of the parameters (that is, the operands), which of the + operators is intended. If this cannot be decided unambiguously, a compile-time error occurs. All the + operators have the same precedence.

  Most languages overload operators like +, − and * thereby allowing them to represent either integer or floating-point operations. What Ada has done is to incorporate this feature into the language and to use it as the basis for extending the available operations in a natural way. This topic will be discussed further in Chapter 7 when abstract data types are dealt with.

5.6   Storage Management

Modern languages are usually implemented in such a way that storage for program code and storage for data items are allocated separately. The area of store set aside to hold the data items used in a call of a subprogram is called its **data area** or **activation record**.

There are two main storage strategies for allocating data areas: static and block-structured dynamic.

Static storage allocation

This method requires that the maximum size of each data item is known at compile time and that no data item can have multiple simultaneous occurrences. As this second requirement rules out languages that allow recursive subprograms – that is, subprograms that can call themselves – FORTRAN is the only language of the languages discussed in this chapter that can make use of this method.

FORTRAN subprograms are compiled independently and are then linked together when the program is loaded into store for execution. With static storage allocation, declaration-reference binding – that is, the allocation of data items to their final storage locations – occurs at load time. Although this method is straightforward and allows data items to be accessed efficiently, it does have the drawback that local variables occupy storage locations even when the subprogram in which they are declared has not been called. When a subprogram is entered for a second or subsequent time, all the local variables have the values they had on the previous exit. Programmers should not make use of this effect, for although FORTRAN allows such a storage mechanism, the definition of the language does not insist on it. As an alternative, a more complicated approach such as stack storage management may be used.

Stack storage management

In most modern languages, as was outlined in Section 3.2, declaration-reference binding occurs on block entry. This means that the declaration of a local variable is bound to a different storage location each time a block (that is, a subprogram) is entered. The storage mechanism that is usually used to implement this type of binding is called **stack storage management**. Using this mechanism, storage is allocated to the main program's data area at load time, while storage for a subprogram's data area is only allocated when the subprogram is called. On return from the subprogram, this storage is de-allocated.

To illustrate block-structured storage allocation, consider the following skeleton Pascal program:

```pascal
program main(output);
var b, d : integer;

  procedure z;
  var e, f : integer;
  begin
    ...
  end {z};

  procedure y;
  var g, h : integer;
  begin
    ...
    z;
    ...
  end {y};

begin
  ...
  y;
  ...
  z;
  ...
end.
```

The changes that occur in the allocation of storage to the data areas as the execution of this program progresses are shown in Figure 5.6. When execution begins, space is allocated to the data area of *main*. It is only when procedure *y* is called that space is allocated to its data area – that is, to the variables *g* and *h*. In procedure *y*, there is a call of procedure *z*. On entry to *z*, space is allocated to its data area. On exit from procedure *z* and return to *y*, space for *z*'s data area is de-allocated; at this point, the local variables *e* and *f* cease to exist in the sense that they no longer have storage locations allocated. On return from *y* to the main program, the local variables in *y* cease to exist in the same way.

There is now a second call of *z*, this time from the main program. This call results in space being allocated once again to *z*'s data area. However, as the storage locations allocated are different this time, when *z* is entered for this second time, its local variables do not inherit their previous values.

The mechanism just outlined results in a stack of data areas called the **run-time stack**. When a subprogram is entered, space for its data area is allocated; on exit from the subprogram, the data area is popped from the stack. Thus, the lifetime of the variables *b* and *d* declared in the main program extends throughout the execution of the whole program, while the lifetime of, for example, *g* and *h* starts when procedure *y* is called and ends when it is left.

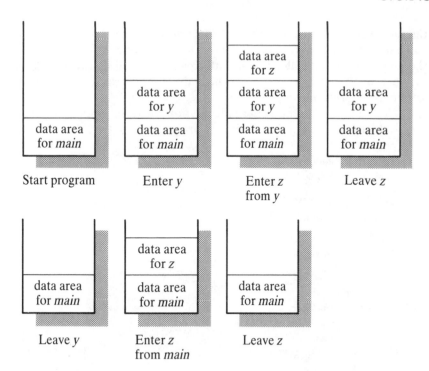

FIGURE 5.6
Stack storage allocation.

An advantage of this type of storage allocation is that space is only allocated when it is needed, which is in contrast to static storage allocation where storage for all data items is allocated at load time. A drawback is that, as the locations allocated to local variables are not fixed, the code generated by the compiler to access them is more complex than in the case of static allocation. However, this approach is so useful that modern computers have special hardware instructions to ease access to variables allocated storage on the run-time stack.

Provided that the size of all local variables is constant, the relative position of an item within a data area is known at compile time and is called its **offset**. The position of the data area, on the other hand, is unknown until the subprogram is entered at run time. When a data area is added to the run-time stack, its base address can be stored in a register as a pointer to the current data area. Local variables may then be accessed using this base address plus the offset determined at compile time.

Data areas

In addition to parameters and local variables, data areas need to hold certain system information, such as the address of the instruction that must be returned to on leaving the subprogram. Also, on leaving a subprogram, the run-time stack must be restored to its position before the subprogram was entered and so each data area must hold a pointer to the data area of the subprogram that called it. This information, which links the data areas together in the reverse order in which the subprograms were called, is known as the **dynamic chain**.

To understand how the information held in the data areas is accessed, consider the following Pascal program:

```
program main(output);
var b, d : integer;

    procedure z;
    var e, f : integer;
    begin
      ...
    end {z};

    procedure y;
    var g, h : integer;

        procedure x;
        var j, k : integer;
        begin
          ...
        end {x};

    begin
      ... z; ... x; ...
    end {y};

begin
  ... z; ... y; ...
end.
```

In the main program, only variables b and d can be accessed. When executing procedure z, the local variables e and f and the non-local variables b and d can be accessed. When y is being executed, the local variables g and h and the non-local variables b and d can be accessed. When x is executed, the non-local variables g, h, b and d can be accessed as well as the local variables j and k.

When procedure z is called from procedure y, three data areas will be on the run-time stack (z, y and *main*), but variables in only two of the data areas will be accessible (z and *main*). When procedure x is called from y, three data areas will again be on the run-time stack, but this time variables in all three data areas will be accessible. Thus, a mechanism is needed that allows access to certain non-local items, but which restricts access to others.

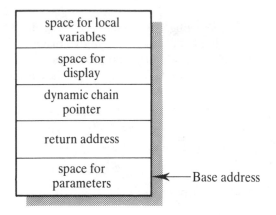

FIGURE 5.7

Possible data area structure.

The rules governing which data areas may be accessed and which cannot are the scope rules, and so this information is known at compile time. A solution is to hold in each data area a table of the base addresses of all the data areas that can be accessed. This table is known as a **display**. Items can be accessed using their offset from the relevant base address held in the table. The information in a display is called the **static chain** as it links together the accessible data areas using the static scope rules.

Returning to the example program, the display for procedure z will contain pointers to the data areas of the main program and z itself. The display for procedure y will contain pointers to the data areas of the main program and y itself, while the display for procedure x will contain pointers to the data areas of the main program and y as well as to x's own data area. The size of the display for each data area depends on the textual depth at which the procedure is nested and is known at compile time.

The structure of a typical data area is shown in Figure 5.7.

Space is allocated for parameters in the data area in the same way as for local variables. For value parameters, the value of the actual parameter is copied into the appropriate location in the data area on procedure entry. With reference parameters, it is the address of the actual parameter that is held in the data area.

5.7 Recursion

Stack storage management is capable of dealing with recursive subprograms – that is, subprograms that may call themselves. Each time a subprogram is called, its data area is added to the run-time stack. With a recursive subprogram, this means that there will be several data areas in existence simultaneously, one for each recursive call. This can best be illustrated by considering the following recursive program which calculates factorials. It is written in Pascal, although programs written in ALGOL 60, ALGOL 68, C, Ada and Modula-2 all behave in essentially the same way.

```
program fact(input, output);
var number : integer;

    function factorial(n : integer) : integer;
    begin
      if n > 1 then
        factorial := n * factorial(n − 1)
      else
        factorial := 1
    end {factorial};

begin
  read(number);
  if number < 0 then
    writeln('error: negative number')
  else
    writeln('factorial is', factorial(number))
end.
```

Before looking at the execution of this program, it is important to note that the definition of the factorial function in the program uses the property that factorials can be defined in terms of a simpler version of themselves. In general, $n!$ is $n * (n − 1)!$. This can be illustrated by considering the value of four factorial (written as 4!), which is $4 * 3 * 2 * 1$ or, to put it another way, $4 * 3!$.

Consider now the execution of program *fact* when *number* has been given the value 3. This leads to the call *factorial*(3). The function *factorial* is entered and, as *n* has been given the value 3, the expression:

$3 * factorial(2)$

is to be evaluated. This involves a recursive call of function *factorial*. In this second call of *factorial*, *n* has the value 2 and this leads to evaluation of the expression:

$2 * factorial(1)$

Function *factorial* is entered for a third time, but as *n* has the value 1, the execution of this call is completed, returning with the value 1. The program now completes execution of:

$2 * factorial(1)$

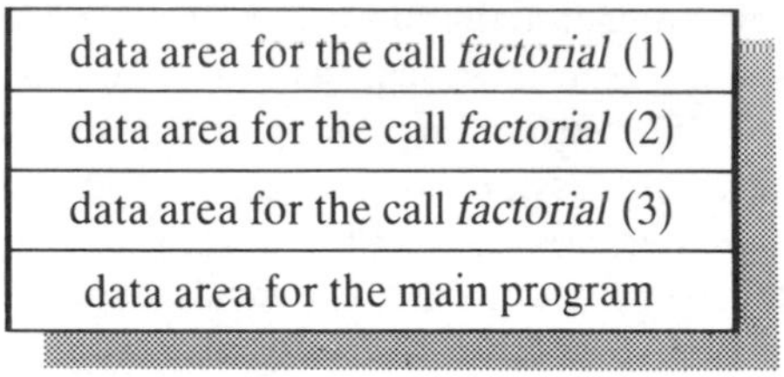

| data area for the call *factorial* (1) |
| data area for the call *factorial* (2) |
| data area for the call *factorial* (3) |
| data area for the main program |

FIGURE 5.8

Data areas for a recursive function.

and so returns from the call *factorial*(2) with the value 2. Finally, the program completes execution of:

   3 * *factorial*(2)

and returns to the main program with the answer 6.

The structure of the data areas for the recursive function *factorial* is shown in Figure 5.8. In each data area, a location is set aside for the value parameter *n*. When function *factorial* is entered for the third time, three data areas for *factorial* are in existence simultaneously. Therefore, three 'incarnations' of *n* can be considered to be in existence simultaneously with the respective values of 3, 2 and 1. (Note that such a situation does not cause any problems as any reference to *n* is always to the one in the current data area.) When the program returns from the function calls, the data areas are removed from the stack in the reverse order to that in which they were added.

Recursive subprograms are most effective when the solution to a problem can be expressed in terms of a simpler version of itself. Such solutions often involve data structures such as linked lists and trees, which can also be defined recursively. This class of problem will be treated in Chapters 9 and 10 when functional and logic programming are discussed.

5.8   Forward References

Pascal has been designed so that it can be translated by a one-pass compiler. To make this possible, the scope of an identifier extends from its declaration to the end of the block in which it is declared, rather than throughout the whole block. As a consequence, all identifiers, including subprogram identifiers, must be declared before they can be used. However, this is not always possible when two subprograms are **mutually**

recursive – that is, when each calls the other. To get round this problem, **forward declarations** are used in Pascal, as illustrated in the following two procedures S and F. The effect of calling procedure S is to read and validate an arithmetic expression consisting of a series of zero or more additions where the operands are either a or are bracketed arithmetic expressions with the same form as the overall expression. An example valid expression is:

$$a+(a+(a)+((a+a)+a))$$

Procedure S calls procedure F which in turn may call procedure S.

```
procedure F(var ca : char); forward;

procedure S(var cb : char);
begin
  F(cb);
  while cb = '+' do F(cb)
end {S};

procedure F;
begin
  read(ca);
  if ca = '(' then
  begin
    S(ca);
    if ca <> ')' then writeln('missing bracket')
  end else
  if ca <> 'a' then writeln('missing operand');
  read(ca)
end {F};
```

The compiler can deal with the call of procedure F from within procedure S as it knows the number and type of the parameters of F from the forward declaration. The actual body of F is given later in the program although the parameters are not repeated.

In C, any subprogram called before it has been declared is assumed to be an integer function. When this is not the case a declaration such as:

float a( );

must be given before the first call of a.

In ALGOL 60, ALGOL 68, FORTRAN and Modula-2 the order of declaration of the subprograms does not matter whereas in Ada it does. Ada differentiates between the specification and the body of a subprogram. The declaration:

function a(b : integer) **return** real;

is of a function specification while:

> **function** $a(b : integer)$ **return** $real$ **is**
> **begin** ... **end** a;

is a function body. Normally, only a subprogram body is declared, although it is always possible for a subprogram specification to be declared as well. This allows subprogram specifications to be used in the same way as forward subprogram declarations in Pascal. The one difference is that the parameters are given in the forward declaration in Pascal, and are not repeated in the actual body, while with Ada they must be given in both situations. Although this requires more writing, it makes programs easier to read.

5.9 Subprograms as Parameters

So far, this chapter has shown how constants, expressions and variables can be passed as subprogram parameters. In most languages, it is also possible to pass functions and procedures as parameters. These are referred to as **formal functions** or **formal procedures**.

The ability to pass subprograms as parameters is of central importance in functional languages and is discussed in Chapter 9. It is less widely used in imperative languages, although it is useful in numerical analysis where it allows general mathematical routines to be written. For example, to calculate the value of:

$$\frac{f(x2) - f(x1)}{x2 - x1}$$

for any function f and any value of $x1$ and $x2$, the following Pascal function could be used:

> **function** $slope(f(y : real) : real; x1, x2 : real) : real$;
> **begin**
>   **if** $x1 = x2$ **then**
> $slope := 0$
>   **else**
> $slope := (f(x2) - f(x1))/(x2 - x1)$
> **end** $\{slope\}$;

A call of this function requires three parameters, the first of which is a real function with one real parameter. Given the functions:

```
function straight(x : real) : real;
begin
  straight := 2 * x + 1
end {straight};

function tan(x : real) : real;
begin
  tan := sin(x)/cos(x)
end {tan};
```

then possible calls of *slope* might be *slope*(*straight*, 3.8, 3.85) and *slope*(*tan*, 3.8, 3.85). Both of these calls will return real values.

In FORTRAN, ALGOL 60, C and the original definition of Pascal, the type of the parameters in the formal subprograms do not have to be specified and this leads to a loophole in the type checking rules. This omission was rectified for Pascal when its ISO and ANSI standards were produced.

Modula-2 goes further than Pascal and allows procedure types and procedure variables. Thus, it is possible, for example, to have the type declaration:

```
TYPE realfunc = PROCEDURE(REAL) : REAL;
```

and the variable declaration:

```
VAR fx : realfunc;
```

The variable fx can take as values functions that have one real value parameter and which return a real value. Given a function similar to *straight*, the assignment can then be:

```
fx := straight;
```

The function *slope* would be written in Modula-2 as:

```
PROCEDURE slope(f : realfunc; x1, x2 : REAL) : REAL;
BEGIN
  IF x1 = x2 THEN
    RETURN 0
  ELSE
    RETURN (f(x2) − f(x1))/(x2 − x1)
  END
END slope;
```

The call *slope*(*straight*, 3.8, 3.85) is still possible in this case, but it is also possible to have the call *slope*(*fx*, 3.8, 3.85) where the function passed depends on the current value of *fx*. In Modula-2, therefore, subprograms are much closer to becoming first-class objects which can be manipulated in the same way as variables. It is permissible, for example, to have arrays of subprograms. ALGOL 68 and the functional languages go further than Modula-2 and allow functions to be returned as the value of a function.

A general topic of interest to language designers is that if all objects are first class, then the definition of a language will be simplified, as there will be fewer special cases. There is, however, no guarantee that the implementation of the language will be less complicated.

Subprograms may not be passed as parameters in Ada, although a similar effect is achieved by what are called **generics**. Instead of *slope* having three parameters, one of which is a formal function, the Ada equivalent is a **generic subprogram** with two parameters. First, the generic subprogram specification is declared:

```
generic
   with function f(y : real) return real;
function slope(x1, x2 : real) return real;
```

and then the subprogram body:

```
function slope(x1, x2 : real) return real is
begin
   if x1 = x2 then
      return 0;
   else
      return (f(x2) − f(x1))/(x2 − x1);
end slope;
```

A generic subprogram is a **template** from which an actual subprogram may be obtained by what is called **instantiation**. If two Ada functions *straight* and *tan* are assumed, two possible instances of the generic function *slope* are one in which calls of *f* are replaced by calls of *straight* and one in which they are replaced by calls of *tan*. These instances may be produced by the two generic instantiations:

```
function straight_slope is new slope(f => straight);
function tan_slope is new slope(f => tan);
```

Generic instantiation occurs at compile time and results in two completely different *slope* functions being created: one called *straight_slope* and the other called *tan_slope*. In the case of Pascal, on the other hand, there will only be a single *slope* function. The equivalent of the Pascal calls of *slope* (*straight*, 3.8, 3.85) and *slope*(*tan*, 3.8, 3.85) are *straight_slope*(3.8, 3.85) and *tan_slope*(3.8, 3.85). The subject of generics will be discussed further in Section 7.6.

SUMMARY

- The ability to hide unwanted detail is the main tool for controlling complexity. By using a subprogram, it is possible to concentrate on what the program does rather than on how it does it.

- A procedure call is a statement in its own right, while a function call is part of an expression and returns a value.

- A FORTRAN program consists of a main program in addition to a series of independent subprograms.

- In a block-structured language such as Pascal, subprograms are declared in an environment created by the enclosing blocks.

- In Pascal, C and Modula-2, the parameter-passing mechanism of call by value is used to pass information into a subprogram.

- In call by value, the formal parameter acts as a local variable, while in call by constant-value (used in Ada) it acts as a local constant.

- Call by value can be expensive in terms of space and time when the parameter is a structured object.

- In the absence of aliases, call by reference and call by value-result have the same effect.

- The only effect of a function call on the rest of a program should be through its returned value.

- Ada allows the redefinition of operators such as "+".

- Stack storage management is required to support recursive subprograms.

- If the amount of storage required by all local objects can be determined at compile time, it is possible to implement a language so that the relative position of each object within a data area is known at compile time. This was a major goal in the design of Pascal.

- Pascal was designed so that it can be translated by a one-pass compiler.

- Subprograms can be passed as parameters in Pascal and in Modula-2, but not in Ada. Ada uses generic subprograms to achieve a similar effect.

EXERCISES

5.1 Subprograms in FORTRAN may not be nested and can be compiled independently of one another. Pascal procedures and functions may be nested, but cannot be compiled independently. Discuss the advantages and disadvantages of these two approaches and any possible compromises between the two.

5.2 Compare the approach to type checking across subprogram boundaries adopted in FORTRAN, Pascal, C and Ada.

5.3 Compare the program structure of C with that of Pascal and FORTRAN. Which features do you consider are closer to FORTRAN and which are closer to Pascal?

5.4 Ada is unusual in having **out** parameters. Is the addition of this extra concept worthwhile or are **in out** parameters sufficient to cover this case?

5.5 Compare the parameter-passing mechanisms call by value, call by constant-value and call by reference-constant for both simple and structured parameters.

5.6 Find out if your local implementation of Pascal uses call by reference or call by value-result to implement variable parameters.

5.7 Assuming that j has the value 1, $a[1]$ the value 2 and $a[2]$ the value 3, what would be the effect of the call $swap(j, a[j])$ when the parameters are passed (a) by value-result, (b) by value-result (ALGOL W), (c) by reference and (d) by name? Would any of the parameter-passing mechanisms give a different answer if the call was $swap(a[j], j)$?

5.8 Ada is based on Pascal, but is much larger. Compare the parameter-passing facilities in the two languages with particular regard to the question of whether the introduction of default parameters and named association is worth the added complexity.

5.9 Good programming practice indicates that procedures should be free from side effects. Why is this even more important with functions? As it is generally agreed that changing non-local variables is undesirable, why is this feature permitted in almost all languages including those that have only recently been defined?

5.10 In Exercise 3.8 of Chapter 3, you were asked to list a suitable set of operations on objects of type *month*. Give implementations of these operations in Pascal and in Ada.

Bibliography

The bibliography at the end of this book gives a list of textbooks on the main programming languages. They all give further information on the structure of subprograms and how parameters are passed in their particular language. A discussion of parameter passing in several languages has been given by Tai (1982). Details of the implementation of subprograms, parameter passing and data areas are given in books on compiling by Aho (1986) and Bornat (1979) while a more general description is given by Pratt (1984).

Aho, A. V., Sethi, R. and Ullman, J. D. (1986), *Compilers: Principles, Techniques and Tools*, Addison-Wesley.

Bornat, R. (1979), *Understanding and Writing Compilers*, Macmillan.

Pratt, T. W. (1984), *Programming Languages: Design and Implementation* (Second Edition), Prentice-Hall.

Tai, K. C. (1982), 'Comments on Parameter Passing Techniques in Programming Languages', *ACM SIGPLAN Notices*, **17**(2), pp. 24–27.

CHAPTER 6

Data Structures

Chapter 3 looked at simple types. This chapter now looks at structured types, which have simpler types as components. The two basic data structures of modern languages are the array and the record.

All the components (elements) of an array have the same type and the elements are accessed using a computable index. The components (fields) of a record may have different types and are referred to by name. An important use of records is in the construction of dynamic structures, such as linked lists and trees, where one or more of the fields of the record are of a pointer type.

Strings in many imperative languages are implemented as arrays of characters, which restricts the available set of string operations. In SNOBOL4, on the other hand, the character string is a basic type in the language and a full set of string operations are available.

Pascal is unusual in having a set data type. Pascal also introduced a file data type which has been used as the basis for files in Modula-2 and Ada.

6.1   Introduction

A data object that is constructed from other data objects is called a **data structure** (or, more rarely, a structured data object). The objects from which it is composed are called components and they may be simple data objects or other structured objects.

The early languages, FORTRAN and ALGOL 60, had only one kind of data structure, called the **array**, whereas most modern languages have both arrays and records. (The latter are called *structures* in PL/I and *structs* in C.) Figures 6.1 and 6.2 show the major features of arrays and records, respectively. The richness of data structures in most languages is obtained by combining these two basic data structures in various ways. At the simplest level, such combinations are arrays of records and records some of whose fields are arrays. Both these combinations are useful in computing applications, but probably the most interesting and useful extension of the basic data structures is that in which records are used in conjunction with pointers to form **dynamic data structures**.

The judicious selection of the appropriate data structures is as important as top-down design in the production of a well-structured program.

6.2   Arrays

Arrays have been widely used as data structures since the earliest programming languages. To specify an array, its attributes must be known, which are:

- The name given to the array.

- The type of its elements: this is a single type since all elements are of the same type.

- The number of components: usually this is given as the number of dimensions with an upper and lower bound for each dimension.

- The type of the subscripts: in early languages this was always integer.

In imperative languages, the specification of the attributes of an array are given in the declaration. In Pascal, this declaration might be:

```
type matrix = array [1 .. 10, 0 .. 15] of real;
var   a : matrix;
```

Example

type *list* = **array** [1 . . 20] **of** *real*;
var *a* : *list*;

Component type

Homogeneous – all elements are of the same type.

Access to components

This is accomplished by knowing the position of the components in the array; for example, the fourth element in the array given above is referred to as *a* [4]. The array index may be an expression.

Efficiency

Efficient access at run time although not as efficient as simple variables due to the computable index.

Use

If the position of the required components (elements) of a structure has to be computed at run time, then arrays are an appropriate data structure. They are usually used in conjunction with loops and are very important in the solution of scientific and engineering problems.

FIGURE 6.1
Array features.

The name of this array is *a*, its elements are all of type *real*, it is two dimensional with bounds 1 and 10 for the first dimension and 0 and 15 for the second dimension, and the subscripts are of type *integer*. The elements of an array are accessed using a computable index – that is, by evaluating the subscripts that can, in general, be expressions. Hence if *i* and *j* are integer variables with values 3 and 5 respectively, $a[i - 1, j + 1]$ refers to the element at position row 2, column 6.

Array elements can normally be used in a language wherever a variable of that type is allowed. The only major exception to this rule is that most languages do not allow a subscripted variable as the control variable of a **for** statement.

Example

type *person* =
  record
    name : *string*;
    age : 0 . . 99;
    sex : (*male, female*)
  end;
var *john* : *person*;

Component type

Heterogeneous – mixed types.

Access to components

Access is by the name of the component field of the record; for
example, *john.age*.

Efficiency

As the field selectors are fixed at compile time, the components
of a record may be accessed as efficiently as simple variables.

Use

They are used to group together data items, which are components of
a single item in the problem domain.

FIGURE 6.2

Record features.

Implementation

An array is normally implemented as a **descriptor** followed by the array
elements in contiguous storage locations. It is not normally necessary for
the programmer using a high-level language to know details of the array
storage, but to illustrate the general idea Figure 6.3 shows a typical way in
which the Pascal array *a* could be implemented. (Note that the type is not
usually stored but checked at compile time, as is the amount of storage
needed for each component.)

As the elements of an array are normally referred to frequently,
they need to be accessed quickly and easily, as otherwise a considerable
inefficiency will result. There are several ways in which this can be
achieved, but the commonest is the **mapping function**. This is a formula

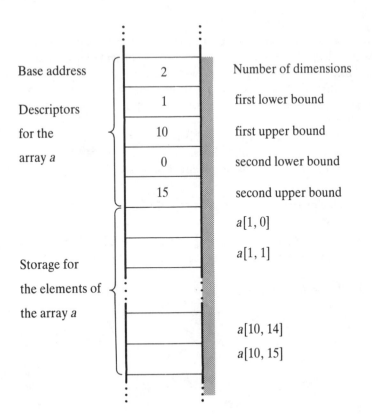

Base address	2	Number of dimensions
Descriptors	1	first lower bound
for the	10	first upper bound
array *a*	0	second lower bound
	15	second upper bound
		$a[1, 0]$
		$a[1, 1]$
Storage for		
the elements of		
the array *a*		
		$a[10, 14]$
		$a[10, 15]$

FIGURE 6.3

Possible storage representation for the array *a*.

that allows a direct calculation of the address of the element required. For the example of Figure 6.3, the array elements are stored in row order, and so the address of element $a[i, j]$ is:

Base address + 5 + component_size
    *(row_length * (i − first_lower_bound) + j − second_lower_bound)
                = Base address + 5 + 1 * (16 * (i − 1) + j − 0)

Name-size binding

More important than the details of the storage of an array is the time at which the required amount of storage is determined. The binding of the name of an array to its required amount of storage is referred to here as **name-size binding**, and there are three possibilities.

Static arrays (compile-time binding)

In this case, the size is fixed when the array variable is declared and it cannot change at run time. The major languages using this method are FORTRAN, Pascal, Modula-2 and C. It is simple to compile and is fast at run time. This method is used in Pascal as, for reasons of efficiency, a design decision was made that the size of all objects should be known at compile time. Chapter 5 showed how storage can be allocated to data areas on block entry and how it is important that the relative position of all items within the data area is known at compile time. With static arrays, this is indeed the situation.

There are disadvantages of this method however: it is inflexible and arrays must be declared to be the maximum size they can ever attain, which can lead to considerable wastage in storage space.

Semi-dynamic arrays (binding on block entry)

In this case, the size of an array is not determined until block entry. As this method was introduced into language design in ALGOL 60, a typical piece of code from that language will be used to illustrate the idea.

```
begin integer m, n;
  read(m, n);
  begin real array x[1 : m, 1 : n];
    .
    .
    .
  end;
    .
    .
    .
end
```

With this method, the relative position of all of the items in a data area is no longer known at compile time as the size of x is not known until values for m and n are read at run time. This situation complicates the process of accessing the array elements. However, it does not affect storage allocation as this takes place on block entry, at which time the size of the array is known.

Many other languages, such as SIMULA 67, ALGOL W, ALGOL 68 and Ada, have followed ALGOL 60 in allowing semi-dynamic arrays. The advantage of using this method is that arrays can be created to exactly the size required by the particular problem.

Dynamic arrays (binding during statement execution)

The amount of storage used by a dynamic array can be changed at any time during the array's lifetime. This is a very flexible arrangement for the programmer and is ideally suited to interactive languages where it may be required to add new array elements at any time. It is not surprising, therefore, that an interactive language like APL should feature such arrays. Another language that makes use of dynamic arrays is SNOBOL4 and, as will be seen in Section 6.5, there is a close connection between dynamic arrays and strings of variable length. Dynamic arrays also occur in ALGOL 68 which has, in addition to semi-dynamic arrays, a construction called a **flex**. In ALGOL 68, a dynamic integer array d with initially no space can be declared by:

> **flex** $[1 : 0]$ **int** d;

The assignment:

> $d := (1, 2, 5, 9)$;

then makes the bounds from 1 to 4 and puts the four values into the elements $d[1]$, $d[2]$, $d[3]$ and $d[4]$.

The flexibility of dynamic arrays has to be set against both their lack of any bound checking (it is not possible to check bounds and at the same time allow them to be dynamically changed) and their slow run-time performance. This effect on performance is caused by the need to use inefficient storage methods, like linked lists, for dynamic arrays.

Array parameters

Consider the problem of finding the sum of the elements of an array of 20 reals. In Pascal, this could be declared as:

> **type** *list* = **array** $[1 .. 20]$ **of** *real*;

and a suitable function would be:

```
function sum(a : list) : real;
var i : integer;
    total : real;
begin
  total := 0.0;
  for i := 1 to 20 do
    total := total + a[i];
  sum := total
end {sum};
```

However, if the problem is extended to find the sum of the elements in an array of 40 reals, a completely new function must be written as the size of an array is part of its type. This was a major problem in early versions of Pascal although it did not occur in earlier languages such as FORTRAN and ALGOL 60 where the size of the array could be passed as a parameter.

The ISO Pascal standard has solved this problem by introducing what are known as **conformant array parameters**. Function *sum* now becomes:

```
function sum(a : array [low .. high : integer] of real) : real;
var i : integer;
    total : real;
begin
  total := 0.0;
  for i := low to high do
    total := total + a[i];
  sum := total
end {sum};
```

If *b* is of type *list*, the function call *sum(b)* will cause *low* and *high* to be given the values 1 and 20, respectively. The function *sum* is, therefore, now able to accept one-dimensional arrays of reals of any size.

Ada has **constrained** and **unconstrained** array types. The declaration:

```
type list is array (integer range <>) of real;
```

declares an unconstrained array type *list*. An array variable *b* can then be declared as:

```
b : list(1 .. 20);
```

The size of a particular array can be found by using what are called its attributes. Hence, *b'first* is 1, *b'last* is 20 and *b'range* is the range 1 .. 20. These attributes can be used in the body of a function so that arrays of differing sizes can be dealt with. The Ada function for *sum* is:

```
function sum(a : list) return real is
  total : real := 0.0;
begin
  for i in a'range loop
    total := total + a(i);
  end loop;
  return total;
end sum;
```

Type equality

Chapter 5 explained that when a function or procedure is called, the types of the actual and formal parameters must match. This leads to the question of when two arrays are of the same type. Consider the following Pascal declarations:

```
type first = array [1 .. 10] of integer;
     second = array [1 .. 10] of integer;
var  a : first;
     b : second;
     c : array [1 .. 10] of integer;
     d, e : array [1 .. 10] of integer;
     f : first;
```

As can be seen, there are six array variables all of which have 10 elements of *type* integer. Structurally, these six array variables are all the same, but are they all of the same type? In the original definition of Pascal, this problem was not addressed and so the answer was left up to the compiler writers.

Two approaches can be taken to this problem. If **structural equivalence** is assumed, then all six variables are of the same type. An alternative approach, known as **name equivalence**, assumes that two variables only have the same type if they have the same type name. The ISO Pascal standard adopts name equivalence as the criterion and so *a*, *b*, *c* and *d* all have different types while *a* and *f* are of the same type as are *d* and *e*.

Name equivalence is also used in Ada, but as the Ada declaration:

```
d, e : array (1 .. 10) of integer;
```

is equivalent to:

```
d : array (1 .. 10) of integer;
e : array (1 .. 10) of integer;
```

the variables *d* and *e* are of different types, which seems rather counter-intuitive.

The question of name and structural equivalence was first discussed in a paper by Welsh (1977) and interested readers might like to consult this document.

Operations on complete arrays or slices of arrays

With the exception of some operations on strings and array assignment, Pascal does not allow operations on complete arrays although other languages, notably PL/I and APL, do. Thus, in PL/I, it is possible to write:

```
X = 0;
```

which will make all the elements of the array X zero.

Similar operations on complete arrays are available in APL although there are problems when assignment is to the array that is being altered. For example, consider:

```
X = X/X(I, J);      in PL/I
X <- X ÷ X[I, J]    in APL
```

Both of these statements seem to be carrying out the same operations, but the question is what happens when X(I, J) itself is altered. Is the new value immediately used as the divisor or not? In PL/I, as soon as X(I, J) is changed, the new value is used as the divisor. In APL, on the other hand, the operation is carried out on a copy of X and so the same value of X[I, J] is used throughout the operation.

Ada allows the specification of array values, called **array aggregates**, which are especially useful in cases where it is necessary to initialize an array. Given the Ada declaration:

type *vector* **is array** (1 .. 6) **of** *integer*;
a : *vector*;

the following assignments are allowed, each having the same effect:

a := (7, 0, 7, 0, 0, 0);
a := (1 => 7, 2 => 0, 3 => 7, 4 .. 6 => 0);
a := (1|3 => 7, **others** => 0);

Many languages allow operations on **slices** of an array. The commonest situation of this is in a two-dimensional array where a row or a column is to be used as the slice. Again, the notation varies somewhat between languages: for example, the third row of a two-dimensional array would be denoted A(3, *) in PL/I and A[3;] in APL, while the fourth column would be A(*, 4) in PL/I and A[;4] in APL. These slices may also be used as one-dimensional arrays in a quite natural way. It is particularly convenient to use such a slice as an actual parameter of a procedure whose equivalent formal parameter is a one-dimensional array.

In Pascal and Ada, a two-dimensional array is an array of arrays and so the concept of a row slice is a natural one. A row of a two-dimensional array can be passed as a one-dimensional array parameter to a procedure or function, but it is not possible to treat a column as a slice. In Ada, a slice can be part of a one-dimensional array. For example, given the declaration:

a, b : *vector*;

an assignment such as:

$a(1 .. 3) := b(4 .. 6);$

is possible which sets the first three elements of a to the values of the fourth, fifth and sixth elements of b, respectively.

In Pascal, C and Modula-2, functions may only return scalar values or pointers. In Ada, arrays or records may also be returned. As an example, consider the problem of adding two vectors together. In Ada, this can be accomplished by the function:

```
function add(left, right : vector) return vector is
   total : vector;
begin
   for i in left'range loop
      total(i) := left(i) + right(i);
   end loop;
   return total;
end add;
```

If a, b and c are all of type *vector*, a possible function call is:

$c := add(a, b);$

However, if the function is called "+" instead of *add*, the following statement could be written:

$c := a + b;$

which gives a much more natural way of dealing with vector arithmetic than is possible in most other languages.

Array notation

Languages vary in their notation for array elements. In FORTRAN, the subscripts are contained in round brackets as in A(I), while other languages such as Pascal, Modula-2 and C have followed ALGOL 60's lead and have used square brackets as in $a[i]$. The argument in favour of square brackets is that arrays and their subscripts can clearly be distinguished from those parts of a program that use round brackets – that is, in expressions and function calls. The counter argument for round brackets is that they make arrays look like functions, and this is not unreasonable as they are both mapping functions: an array selects a particular element from a table whereas a function performs the same process using an algorithm. This argument for round brackets is far from convincing and could possibly be biased by the fact that a restricted character set often does not allow square brackets! Nevertheless, the designers of Ada made a positive decision to use round brackets for arrays, since square brackets are also available in its character set.

6.3   Records

A **record** type is a structured type that is composed of heterogeneous elements of data – in fact, in languages such as PL/I and ALGOL 68 it was called a structure. The declaration of a record type specifies the name of the record and the name and the type of the various fields of the record. Implicit in the declaration of a record is its tree structure. This is because the fields of a record can themselves be records and this introduces a hierarchical structure similar to that of a tree.

A typical example of how a record can be used in data processing is given in Figure 6.4(a) for a PL/I structure and in Figure 6.4(b) for the equivalent Pascal record. The equivalent tree structure is shown in Figure 6.4(c). There are 10 different elements in this record and the type of each needs to be declared. This must be done explicitly in languages like Pascal but in PL/I it can be done explicitly or by default. These 10 different elements are the terminal nodes (or leaves) of the equivalent tree structure in Figure 6.4(c).

The tree structure of the record is perhaps clearer in the declarations in languages like PL/I (which was based on COBOL records) where the level numbers are given and these can conveniently be made the same as the level numbers of the equivalent tree. Languages like Pascal, on the other hand, use records and subrecords, and this makes the tree structure less evident.

Complicated records are not commonly used in Pascal where the prime use of records is not in the solution of data processing problems, but to allow logically related data items to be grouped together as one structured variable.

The individual items in a record or structure are referred to by name and not by computable index as in an array. The name needs to be qualified. For example, in the PL/I structure given in Figure 6.4(a), the name:

```
STUDENT.DEPARTMENT.ADVISOR.SURNAME
```

could be used to refer to one particular element. This is a fully qualified name but it can be abbreviated, provided it is not ambiguous. The problem of very long names is common to records in most languages. Another method of reducing their length is to use, as in Pascal and Modula-2, the

(a)
```
DECLARE
  01 STUDENT,
     02 NUMBER FIXED,
     02 NAME,
        03 FIRST NAME CHARACTER(10),
        03 INITIAL CHARACTER(4),
        03 SURNAME CHARACTER(10),
     02 DEGREE,
        03 COURSE CHARACTER(4),
        03 YEAR DEC FIXED(1),
     02 DEPARTMENT,
        03 DEPT NAME CHARACTER(10),
        03 ADVISOR LIKE NAME;
```

(b)
```
type string = packed array [1 . . 10] of char;
     shortstring = packed array [1 . . 4] of char;
     namestring =
       record
         firstname : string;
         initial : shortstring;
         surname : string
       end;
     degreetype =
       record
         course : shortstring;
         year = 1 . . 4
       end;
     dept =
       record
         deptname : string;
         advisor : namestring
       end;
     student =
       record
         number : integer;
         name : namestring;
         degree : degreetype;
         department : dept
       end
```

(c)
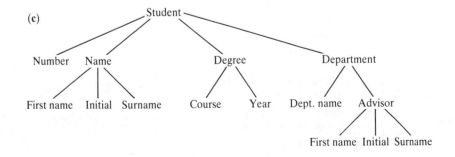

FIGURE 6.4

(a) A PL/I structure.
(b) A Pascal record.
(c) The equivalent tree structure.

with statement. Assuming that *st* has been declared to be of type *student*, the Pascal code:

```
read(st.degree.year);
if st.degree.year = 4 then
  writeln('Final year student')
else
  st.degree.year := st.degree.year + 1;
```

can be written as:

```
with st.degree do
begin
  read(year);
  if year = 4 then
    writeln('Final year student')
  else
    year := year + 1
end;
```

Ada has **record aggregates** and so values can be assigned to complete records. Given an Ada record variable *person* with the same structure as the Pascal record *namestring* of Figure 6.4(b), this can be written:

```
person := (firstname => "Alan       ",
           initial  => "P   ",
           surname  => "Clark      ");
```

Variant records

In some languages, such as Pascal, Modula-2 and Ada, a facility is provided where a single record can have several **variants**. In Pascal, this is accomplished by having a fixed part, with fields as in a normal record, followed by a variant part, in which there are alternative fields. For example:

```
type student =
  record
    {fixed part}
    name : string;
    studentno : integer;
    {variant part}
    case undergraduate : boolean of
      true : (advisor : string);
      false : (course : string;
               supervisor : string)
  end;
```

The field *undergraduate* is called the **tag field** and in this example there are two alternatives. The tag field determines whether there is a single field, *advisor*, in the variant part or two fields, *course* and *supervisor*. Pascal's method of using variant records can unfortunately lead to insecurities and inconsistencies. These arise if the tag field is changed without changing the variant fields that depend on the tag.

Ada allows similar variant records, although with some syntactic differences, and the insecurities of the Pascal construction are removed by not allowing the tag field to be changed independently of the dependent fields in the variant part.

Other languages such as ALGOL 68 and SIMULA 67 have completely different ways of achieving the same objective as the variant record. In ALGOL 68, a separate type is used to define a **discriminated union** while in SIMULA 67 the feature is provided by means of a **concatenated class**.

Arrays and records combined

As was shown in the example of a record in Figure 6.4, it is quite legitimate in most languages to have fields of an array type. In the example given, this was simply to provide strings, but it often has more sophisticated uses. Consider, for example, the problem of providing a simple stack structure in Pascal. This can be done as follows:

```
type stacklist =
   record
      a : array [1 .. 20] of real;
      head : 0 .. 20
   end;
var  stack : stacklist;
```

The two fields of the record *stacklist* represent the elements of the stack in the array *a* and the pointer to the top of the stack in the integer *head*. Thus, the representation of the stack is contained wholly within the record. More complex representations of tree and graph structures can be similarly contained within a single record.

Returning to the Pascal definition of *stacklist*, the stack must be initialized before items can be added to it. Thus, after the assignment:

```
stack.head := 0
```

the stack is initialized and is empty. In Ada, on the other hand, default initial values can be specified in type definitions and so a separate initialization stage is not required. The Ada definition of type *stacklist* would be:

```
type reallist is array (1 .. 20) of real;
type stacklist is
  record
    a : reallist;
    head : integer range 0 .. 20 := 0;
  end record;
```

The alternative way of combining data structures – that is, of having arrays of records – is also a useful feature. An example in Pascal is:

```
studentlist : array [1 .. 3000] of student;
```

where *student* is defined by the record given in Figure 6.4(b). An individual field in any of the 3000 student records can be picked out. For example, *studentlist[i].number* selects the student number of the *i*th student in the array of student records.

6.4   Dynamic Data Structures

A very different kind of data structure is obtained by using records in conjunction with pointer variables. Fields in a record can be specified to be of pointer type and data structures in which individual records are linked to others can be built up by means of pointer fields. Thus, in Pascal, a simple linear-linked list can be written as follows:

```
type ptr =  ↑ node;
     node =
        record
           data : char;
           next : ptr
        end;
var  p, listhead : ptr;
     ch : char;
```

Note that the above type declaration is one of the few places in Pascal where an object (*node*) can be used before it has been declared.

Procedure *new* was introduced in Chapter 3. The effect of a call of *new(p)* is to create a record of type *node* which is pointed at by the pointer variable *p*. This is shown in Figure 6.5. The value 'A' can be assigned to the *data* field and **nil** to the *next* field by writing:

```
p ↑ .data := 'A'; p ↑ .next := nil
```

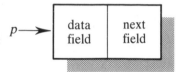

FIGURE 6.5
Creating a record.

A list can be read in and linked as follows:

```
listhead := nil;
read(ch);
while ch <> ' ' do
begin
  new(p); p ↑ .data := ch;
  p ↑ .next := listhead;
  listhead := p;
  read(ch)
end;
```

Figure 6.6 shows the state of the linked list after each cycle round the loop as the characters A, B and C followed by a space are read in.

Languages differ in the restrictions they put on pointers. Pascal is quite rigid in this respect and a pointer variable may only point to an object of one particular type. In the example just given, *listhead* is of type *ptr* and therefore can only be used to point to objects of type *node*.

PL/I has a much looser system as regards pointers, allowing them to be used with different record types (called **areas** in PL/I). However, this makes it difficult to do any type checking of records at compile time.

Ada follows much the same pattern as Pascal although the syntax is different. As a name cannot be used before it has been declared in Ada, it is necessary to write:

```
type node;
type ptr is access node;
type node is
  record
    data : character;
    next : ptr;
  end record;
```

Dynamic variables in Ada can be given initial values when they are created. Thus, instead of the Pascal:

```
new(p); p ↑ .data := ch; p ↑ .next := listhead
```

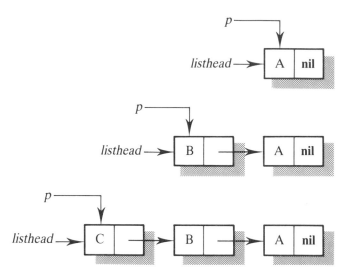

FIGURE 6.6

Stages in building a linked list.

the following can be written:

$p := \textbf{new } node'(data => ch, next => listhead);$

Dynamic data structures can be considerably more complicated than simple linked lists. One structure that they model in a particularly appropriate way is the tree. In a tree structure there is more than one pointer field in each record. A type declaration in Pascal for a binary tree could be:

```
type ptr =  ↑ node;
     node =
        record
          data : char;
          left, right : ptr
        end;
```

The effect of *new(root)*, where *root* is of type *ptr*, is shown in Figure 6.7.

Both lists and trees can be conveniently defined recursively. For example, a binary tree can be defined as follows:

A binary tree is either null or it consists of a special node, called the root, which has a value and two descendants, called the left subtree and the right subtree. The left subtree and the right subtree are themselves binary trees.

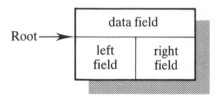

Root

FIGURE 6.7
Creating a node.

As trees can be defined recursively, they are most easily manipulated using recursive procedures. To illustrate how this may be done, consider the problem of printing out a binary tree representing an algebraic expression in what is known as **reverse Polish notation** where an operator follows its two operands. This can be achieved by using the following recursive Pascal procedure:

```
procedure revPolish(p : ptr);
begin
  if p <> nil then
  begin
    revPolish(p ↑ .left);
    revPolish(p ↑ .right);
    write(p ↑ .data)
  end
end;
```

Assuming that *root* points to the tree shown in Figure 6.8, the procedure call *revPolish(root)* will cause the contents of the tree to be printed out in the order:

*a b c + / d ***

Tracing through the execution of *revPolish(root)* is left as an exercise for the reader.

The use of records and pointers does entail a great deal of detailed programming on the part of the programmer. Some of this can be reduced by the judicious use of modules or packages with their associated data structures, procedures and functions. The detailed building of dynamic data structures from records and pointers is a feature of the more sophisticated imperative languages, such as ALGOL 68, Pascal, PL/I, Ada and Modula-2. The alternative method of approaching such dynamic data structures is with functional languages and this issue is taken up again in Chapter 9.

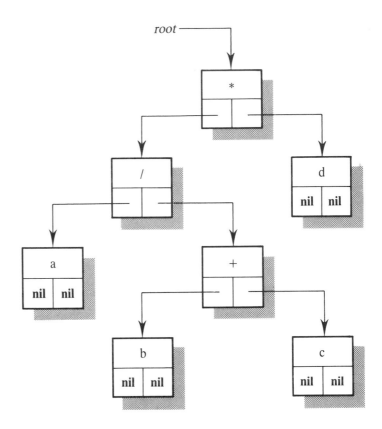

FIGURE 6.8
A binary tree.

6.5 Strings

Character strings and their manipulation only played a very minor role in the early scientific languages and it was SNOBOL4 that actually showed how character strings could be manipulated in a programming language. However, it was soon realized that the unrestricted manipulation of strings brings with it considerable penalties in the slowness of the run-time program.

String operations are best divided into two categories. The first category consists of string comparisons, the selection of a component (a character or group of characters) and the moving of strings. The second category of operations includes the construction of new strings, the concatenation of strings (joining two strings together), the replacement of substrings within a string and the decomposition of a string into substrings.

The operations in the first category cause few problems for the compiler writer as the strings remain the same length throughout. Operations in the second category, on the other hand, have the potential of altering the length of the strings or giving strings whose length cannot be predicted at compile time, and thus require linked lists for their implementation.

In Pascal, Ada, Modula-2 and C, strings are simply arrays of characters and since arrays are not dynamic in these languages, the length of a string cannot be changed once it has been declared. In Pascal, a string is typically declared as:

type *name* = **packed array** [1 .. 8] **of** *char*;

The reserved word **packed** used in this declaration indicates that the compiler should allocate the minimum amount of space possible for objects of type *name*, even though this may increase the time required to access individual array elements. The need to declare this requirement explicitly has not been carried over into Modula-2 and Ada.

In Pascal, the length of an array is part of the type and so any attempt to assign or compare strings of different lengths gives an error at compile time. This means that trailing blanks must always be inserted in string constants. Hence, if *person* is of type *name*, four trailing blanks are required in the assignment:

person := 'Alan   '

A similar assignment is necessary in Ada although strings of different length may be compared. Hence, the expression:

person < "James"

is legal in Ada while in Pascal three trailing blanks are needed, as in:

person < 'James   '

Trailing blanks do not have to be inserted in Modula-2 string assignments and so:

person := 'Alan'

is legal. A null character is automatically inserted after the four characters of 'Alan'. When the string constant fits exactly, as in:

person := 'Margaret'

no null character is inserted. Although string assignment has been made easier to use, it is not possible in Modula-2 to use the relational operators to compare strings, as it is in Pascal and Ada.

The language C also uses the null character as an explicit string terminator but, unlike Modula-2, space must be set aside for it in all strings. The null character is represented in a C program as the character '\0'. Assuming *str* has been defined as an array of characters, *ch* as a character and *i* as an integer, a line of characters could be read in by the C statements:

```
i = 0;
while ((ch = getchar ()) != '\n')
   str[i++] = ch;
```

This reads characters into the array *str* until the newline character is encountered, when it is then necessary to add the statement:

```
str[i] = '\0';
```

to append the null character to the end of the string. The null character can be used to recognize the end of the string and so C strings are in effect variable up to a maximum defined length.

In C, there is a distinction between character constants and string constants. For example, 'x' is a character constant but "x" is a string of length two, the first character of which is x and the second is the null character. Similarly, 'x' and "x" in Ada are character and string constants, respectively. As Pascal uses single quotes for both characters and strings, string constants of length one are not possible.

COBOL also has strings of fixed declared length and the Pascal string given at the beginning of this section would be declared in COBOL as:

```
NAME    PIC X(8)
```

This gives a character string variable called NAME containing exactly eight characters. However, in contrast to Pascal, a string value can be adjusted during assignment either by truncating the excess characters or by padding out the string with additional blanks on the right, if it is not long enough.

Since these languages have fixed declared length strings, only the first category of string operations is allowed, although Ada does permit some second category operations provided that the length of the string is not changed. Examples are:

```
person := "James    ";
person(2 .. 5) := "immy";
```

Ada also has the concatenation operator &. This can be useful in constructing a string with a constant and a variable part, as in:

> *put_line*("Hello " & *person*);

At the other extreme are languages such as SNOBOL4 that have the character string as a basic type and it can vary arbitrarily in length. No bounds are placed on the string's length and so, if strings get longer, extra storage has to be allocated. ALGOL 68 is another language that allows strings to have a dynamic length. As was seen in Section 6.2, it does this by having the mode *string* predefined as a flexible array of characters, as in:

> **mode** *string* := **flex** $[1 : 0]$ *char*;

This is an array with dynamic bounds that will automatically expand or contract to accommodate the length of string required.

All the string operations in the first and second category are potentially available to languages such as SNOBOL4 and ALGOL 68 although, of course, the methods vary. In ALGOL 68, for example, substrings are selected by subscripting whereas in SNOBOL4 this is done by pattern matching. The SNOBOL4 statement:

```
TEXT 'programme' = 'program'
```

will find the first occurrence of 'programme' in the string TEXT and replace it by 'program'. To replace all occurrences, the statement could be written:

```
LAB1 TEXT 'programme' = 'program' :S(LAB1)
```

The S here stands for success and so if a successful replacement is made in TEXT, a jump is made to the statement labelled LAB1. The statement:

```
TEXT 'programme' = 'program'
```

is therefore repeated until no more replacements can be made.

Between the two extremes of fixed declared length strings and variable strings is a compromise position adopted by PL/I; that is, to have a variable length up to a declared upper bound. PL/I does this by the following declaration:

```
DECLARE NAME CHARACTER VARYING(15);
```

The variable NAME will hold a character string up to a maximum length of 15 characters. However, unlike COBOL, if the string is less than 15 characters in length, PL/I holds exactly the correct number of characters and does not need to add trailing blanks. PL/I also allows fixed length strings and these are declared in a similar way, although the word VARYING is omitted.

Strings of the PL/I type can be represented in Pascal, Ada or Modula-2 as a record. An example in Pascal is:

```
type varstring =
  record
    string : packed array [1 .. 80] of char;
    currentlength : 0 .. 80
  end;
```

To manipulate such varying strings and to convert to and from ordinary strings, a series of procedures and functions is needed. Ada and Modula-2 have better facilities for doing this than Pascal, as will be seen in the next chapter, although some dialects of Pascal have such a string type built in.

PL/I allows concatenation of strings by means of the operator ||. It also has several built-in string facilities, such as SUBSTR and LENGTH, which can be used for further string manipulation. The SUBSTR function can appear on the left-hand side of an assignment statement, as in:

```
SUBSTR(S, 4, 3) = "BASIC";
```

where the three-character string starting at the fourth character is replaced by the five-character string BASIC. This contrasts with the corresponding Ada construct where the two strings must have the same length.

Most languages, an exception being Modula-2, allow relational operations to apply to strings; thus, operators such as equal, not equal and greater than can be used with string variables. A collating sequence is used to decide the outcome of a comparison of two strings. For example, to evaluate $a > b$, where a and b are two character string variables, the collating sequence starts with the leftmost characters of a and b and compares them. If a decision can be made, the sequence stops and no more comparisons are made. If a decision cannot be made – for example, if the first character of a is the same as the first character of b – then the sequence proceeds to compare the second characters of a and b. This sequence continues in this manner until either a decision is reached or both strings are exhausted. Normally, if the strings being compared are not the same length, the shorter one is padded out with null characters on the right. In Pascal, when the strings are not the same length, a syntax error results.

(a)

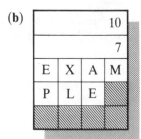

In Pascal this reflects the declaration:

    st : **packed array** [1 . . 10] **of** *char* ;

(b)

This reflects the PL/I declaration:

    `DECLARE ST CHARACTER VARYING(10);`

(c)

This assumes that a pointer uses one word.

FIGURE 6.9

String storage implementation:
(a) fixed declaration length;
(b) variable length up to a maximum bound;
(c) unbounded length (SNOBOL4 method).

String implementation

The implementation of strings depends on which of the three methods of string handling has been adopted. The easiest method to implement is the fixed length method, where each character is normally held in a byte, with four characters per 32-bit word. The PL/I method requires in addition two integer descriptors, one for the maximum length and the other for the current length. There is no need in this case for trailing characters to be made blank.

    The least efficient implementation is that involving dynamic strings of unbounded length. In this implementation an integer descriptor is needed for the current length in addition to a linked list of characters. The inefficiency arises because of the slowness of operations on dynamic data structures as opposed to those on arrays. The various storage implementations are shown diagrammatically in Figure 6.9 where each character occupies a byte and a word is four bytes or 32 bits.

6.6   Sets

A **set** is an unordered collection of distinct elements (objects) of the same type. This is in contrast to both lists and arrays which are ordered collections of possibly non-distinct elements.

Very few of the major languages have included the set as a standard data structure. The notable exceptions are Pascal and Modula-2, where sets are basically implemented as a packed array of *Boolean*. This is, in essence, the bit string method of implementing sets. If a set consists of days of the week, the following declarations can be written in Pascal:

> **type** *day* = (*sun, mon, tues, wed, thur, fri, sat*);
> 　　　 *weekset* = **set of** *day*;
> **var**　*w*1, *w*2 : *weekset*;
> 　　　 *d* : *day*;

At some stage, the set *w*1 might be [*mon, thur, sat*]. This could be represented as the bit string 0100101.

To illustrate the Pascal set operations, suppose that *w*2 = [*mon .. fri*]. (Similar operations are available in Modula-2.)

- Membership: is the value *d* a member of set *w*1?

    if *d* **in** *w*1 **then** ...

- Insertion: the expression *w*1 + [*mon*] inserts *mon* into the set *w*1 unless it is already present.

- Deletion: the expression *w*1 − [*mon*] deletes *mon* from the set *w*1 if it is a member of that set.

- Union: the expression *w*1 + *w*2 gives the set [*mon .. sat*]; that is, the set of those values that are in either *w*1 or *w*2, or in both.

- Intersection: the expression *w*1 * *w*2 gives the set [*mon, thur*]; that is, the set of those values that are members of both *w*1 and *w*2.

- Difference: the expression *w*1 − *w*2 gives the set [*sat*]; that is, the set of those values in *w*1 which are not also in *w*2.

- Inclusion: the expression *w*1 <= *w*2 is true if *w*1 is a subset of *w*2. As *sat* is a member of the set *w*1, but not of *w*2, the expression *w*1 <= *w*2 gives the value false. The set operations >=, <> and = are also available and have their obvious meanings.

In addition to these operations, there is also straightforward assignment, as in:

$w2 := [mon, thur, sat];$

The empty set is represented by [].

The bit string method of implementing sets is satisfactory if the number of possible elements in the set is small, as in the Pascal example given at the beginning of this section where it was 7. This usually implies in Pascal implementations a restriction on the overall set size, which often is hardware dependent.

When this is not the case, more elaborate storage methods such as hashing have to be resorted to. This is particularly necessary when a set can contain a large number of different integers or character strings. Nevertheless, some of the set operations can be performed very efficiently using hashing methods. Membership, insertion and deletion can all be done quickly provided the amount of storage for the hashing table is sufficient. Problems arise when the number of elements in the set approaches the size of the scatter storage table used by the hashing method. The operations of union, intersection and difference are not carried out as efficiently by hashing as they are by bit string methods.

Pascal is unusual in having sets although several languages allow bit strings and operations on bit strings. In essence, such bit strings (with their operations) can be manipulated like sets. Systems programming languages are prime examples of languages that need to be able to manipulate bit patterns. In Modula-2, sets are primarily used for this purpose. Of the earlier languages, PL/I and ALGOL 68 had similar types with names like BIT and *bits*. The approach taken in Ada is to represent a bit pattern as a *Boolean* array. The Boolean operators **and**, **or** and **xor** can be applied to such arrays. For example, given the declarations:

type *bytestring* **is array** $(1 .. 8)$ **of** *Boolean*;
a, b, c : *bytestring*;
t : **constant** *Boolean* := *true*;
f : **constant** *Boolean* := *false*;

the execution of the statements:

$a := (f, f, f, t, t, t, t, t);$
$b := (t, f, t, f, t, f, t, f);$
$c := a$ **and** $b;$

will result in c being assigned the value (f, f, f, f, t, f, t, f), which can be used to represent the bit string 00001010.

6.7   Files

Files are large collections of data that are kept on secondary storage devices. They are liable to have an extensive lifetime, which will normally be longer than the run of the computer program that created them. Generally, files of this nature are not explicitly represented in early high-level languages. As the physical structure of a file depends on the operating system, it is not easy to define a set of language constructs that are both machine independent and that give sufficient control over file operations.

Pascal was, therefore, unusual in having a file type defined in the language, although this approach has been followed by most of its successors. A file in Pascal can be thought of as an ordered collection of homogeneous data. A typical Pascal file definition is:

type *stream* = **file of** *entities*;

where entities can be of any type except another file.

There are two main differences between a Pascal array and a Pascal file. Firstly, the size of an array is given as part of its declaration while a file is unbounded. Secondly, the access to arrays is random – that is, the time to access an element in an array is independent of its position – whereas with Pascal files the access is sequential, mirroring the way that sequential files are accessed on backing store.

In Pascal, file variables usually correspond to external disk files. In such cases, the variable must be listed as a parameter in the program heading as well as being declared as a variable, as in:

program *ex*(*old*, *new*);
   type *stream* = **file of** ...;
   var *old*, *new* : *stream*;

Local files may also be declared both within the main program and within a procedure. The normal rules governing the lifetime of an object apply to files and so a file declared within a procedure will come into existence when the procedure is entered and will cease to exist when the procedure is left. The main use of local files is in the temporary storage of information of unknown size. When the maximum size is known an array is more commonly used.

Operations on files are usually given by a set of predefined functions and procedures. Operations are required to open files for reading and writing, to determine the current position within a file, and to read and write information. As files are, therefore, primarily associated with the input and output of data, a detailed discussion of files is delayed until Chapter 11, which discusses input and output.

SUMMARY

- The judicious selection of appropriate data structures is as important as top-down design in the production of a well-structured program.

- All components of an array have the same type and are accessed using a computable index.

- In Pascal and Modula-2, the size of an array is fixed at compile time. In Ada, fixing the size of an array can be delayed until block entry.

- In Pascal and its derivatives, a two-dimensional array is an array of arrays.

- The components of a record can have different types and are accessed by name.

- Pascal is strongly typed except in the case of variant records. This problem is overcome in Ada.

- Dynamic data structures are built from records that have one or more fields of a pointer type.

- The representation and manipulation of strings is determined by whether the language design allows operations that can potentially increase the string length.

- Sets and files are rarely included in languages as first-class objects.

EXERCISES

6.1 Arrays and records are both aggregates of data. How do they differ? What information would you expect in the declaration of (a) an array and (b) a record?

6.2 Describe how a mapping function can be used to find the storage location of an array element. What is meant by the base address in such a situation and how is it used by the compiler? Given the following Pascal array declarations, what would be suitable mapping functions?

> **var** x : **array** [2 .. 10] **of** *real*;
> a : **array** [1 .. 7, 0 .. 5] **of** *integer*;

In what locations, relative to the base address, would you expect to find $x[7]$ and $a[3, 2]$?

6.3 Discuss the concept of dynamic bounds in an array explaining the meaning of the terms static array, semi-dynamic array and dynamic array. Give examples of languages that implement arrays in each of these ways. What are the advantages and disadvantages of each method to the programmer and to the implementor?

6.4 In Pascal, a two-dimensional array can be regarded as a one-dimensional array, each of whose elements is itself a one-dimensional array. What advantages does this give? How is the concept extended to three and higher dimensional arrays?

6.5 Give an example of a Pascal procedure with a one-dimensional array as a formal parameter together with a call of the procedure in which the corresponding actual parameter is a slice of a two-dimensional array. Definitions of appropriate one- and two-dimensional array types should also be given.

6.6 What additional information must be available at run time in the implementation of semi-dynamic arrays, as compared with static arrays?

6.7 How do variant records allow programmers in Pascal and Ada to overcome the drawbacks of compile-time type checking? How could the definition of Pascal variant records be improved so that type insecurity does not arise?

6.8 Show how a queue can be represented by a record with three fields, one of which is an array whose elements are the items in the queue and the other two are used to indicate the front and rear of the queue. Use this structure to define two operations, one to add a new element to the rear of the queue and the other to delete an element from the front of the queue.

6.9 Lists may be implemented as arrays or as linked lists. Which is to be preferred when solving:

(a) a problem that requires the elements of the list to be accessed in a random order,

(b) a problem that requires the elements of the list to be accessed sequentially,

(c) a problem that requires the ordering of a list of ordered elements to be retained during the insertion and deletion of elements.

6.10 Modify procedure *revPolish*, given in Section 6.4, so that it will print the algebraic expression in forward Polish notation, where the operator precedes its two operands.

6.11 Why are recursive algorithms particularly appropriate for the manipulation of structures such as lists and trees?

6.12 Given the Ada declaration:

a : **array** $(1 .. 7)$ **of** *character*;

the effect of the assignment:

$a(4 .. 6) := a(3 .. 5)$;

is to make a copy of the value of $a(3 .. 5)$ before the assignment takes place. If a initially has the value 'CORECAT', what will its value be after the assignment?

6.13 (a) Discuss the facilities that programming languages have provided for string handling. Contrast a language like Pascal, which has relatively primitive string operations, with a language like SNOBOL.

(b) Why are string handling operations divided into two categories and what are the operations in each category? How did PL/I try to reach a compromise between primitive and sophisticated string handling?

6.14 Describe how a linked list could be used in the implementation of a set. Outline procedure declarations for the insert and delete operations.

Bibliography

There are a large number of textbooks on the representation and manipulation of data structures, several of which are listed below. The first volume of Knuth's *The Art of Computer Programming* (1968) was the earliest book to make a systematic approach to data structures. It is a pity that only three volumes of this monumental series were published.

Another influential book was *Algorithms + Data Structures = Programs* by Wirth (1976) which emphasized that data structures are at least as important as algorithms in the construction of programs.

Many recent books take all their examples from one particular language, usually Pascal. The other recent trend is to emphasize the importance of data abstraction as is done, for example, in the book by Lings (1986).

Aho, A. V., Hopcroft, J. E. and Ullman, J. D. (1983), *Data Structures and Algorithms*, Addison-Wesley.

Hoare, C. A. R. (1972), 'Notes on Data Structuring' in *Structured Programming*, Academic Press, pp. 83–174.

Knuth, D. E. (1968), *The Art of Computer Programming, Volume 1: Fundamental Algorithms*, Addison-Wesley.

Lings, B. J. (1986), *Information Structures: A Uniform Approach Using Pascal*, Chapman & Hall.

Page, E. S. and Wilson, L. B. (1983), *Information Representation and Manipulation Using Pascal*, Cambridge University Press.

Standish, T. A. (1980), *Data Structure Techniques*, Addison-Wesley.

Welsh, J., Sneeringer, M. J. and Hoare, C. A. R. (1977), 'Ambiguities and Insecurities in Pascal', *Software Practice and Experience*, **7**, pp. 685–696.

Wirth, N. (1976), *Algorithms + Data Structures = Programs*, Prentice-Hall.

CHAPTER 7

Modules

As was discussed in Chapter 5, complex problems are best solved by decomposition into smaller subproblems. Similarly, the design, implementation and maintenance of complex programs is usually handled by dividing such programs into self-contained units called modules, where each module is itself divided into two parts: a small strictly defined interface through which it can interact with other modules and a hidden implementation part.

This chapter looks at the way in which modules are implemented in Modula-2 and Ada, which allow both full type checking across module boundaries and separate compilation. As long as the specification part of a module is unaffected, recompiling the implementation part of a module does not require the recompilation of any other modules.

Modules enable type and subprogram declarations to be grouped together, and this forms the basis for the implementation of what are known as abstract data types. It is shown how the full implementation of abstract data types requires facilities such as the generic packages which are available in Ada, but not in Modula-2. The properties of abstract data types leads naturally to a discussion of the ideas behind object-oriented design. These ideas are illustrated by comparing the object-oriented features of Ada with those of Smalltalk and C++.

7.1   Large Programs

As a result of their size and complexity, large problems must be solved by a team of programmers rather than by a single individual. Each member of the team is set a well-defined task by a team leader, who alone may know the overall design of the system. For this approach to be possible, there must be some mechanism for dividing the problem into separate parts which only interact with one another through small strictly defined interfaces.

Large systems, by their nature, are usually in use for many years and during this time they may undergo substantial modification. Some of the changes will be due to the discovery of errors, but others will be due to changes in the system requirements, which could not be foreseen when the original system was designed. As it is not practicable to redesign large systems from scratch, due to their high cost and the time involved, the programs should be designed and written so that they can be easily modified. The best way of achieving this is for the programs to be written in such a way that the effect of any change is localized. This again points to a solution where the program is designed and implemented in separate parts (modules), each with a clearly defined external interface.

As solutions to different large problems often require solutions to similar subproblems, modules should be capable of being reused. In this way, a library of software components can be made available 'off the shelf' for use in the construction of new programs. Modules allow a large system to be designed by specifying what each module is to do and what its interface to the rest of the system is to be. Once this has been done, different users may implement each of the modules without any need for consultation.

Chapter 5 discussed how problems can be solved using stepwise refinement and how subprograms can be used to hide detail, so the user need only be concerned with 'what' a subprogram does and not 'how' it does it. Subprograms can be considered to be modules that can be joined together to form complete programs. Their parameters act as small well-defined interfaces. However, as will be seen in Section 7.2, this type of module has a limitation on its ability to hide information. Newer programming languages such as Modula-2, Ada, Euclid, Alphard and CLU use a more powerful form of module. Instead of a single subprogram, such a module consists of a collection of related subprograms, types and objects. It is possible to decide what information is to be visible from outside the collection and what information is to be kept hidden. This can be achieved in several ways. One method is to have an **export list**; for example, in a Euclid module, information is hidden unless explicitly listed for export.

Another method is to divide a module into two parts. The part that tells the user 'what' the module does then acts as the interface with the user while the part containing the details of 'how' the operations are carried out is hidden from the user. An Ada module is called a **package**. The interface with the outside world is called the **package specification** and the implementation details are held in a separate **package body**. In Modula-2, these two parts are known as the **definition module** and the **implementation module**, respectively. Package specifications and definition modules should always be as small as possible, since they form the interfaces between what are otherwise self-contained units. A large interface is often a sign that the decomposition of the problem could be improved.

As an example of a module, consider the following Ada package:

```
package days_in_week is
    type day is (sun, mon, tues, wed, thurs, fri, sat);
    function next_day(today : day) return day;
    function day_before(today : day) return day;
end days_in_week;

package body days_in_week is

    function next_day(today : day) return day is
    begin
      if today = sat then
        return sun;
      else
        return day'succ(today);
      end if;
    end next_day;

    function day_before(today : day) return day is
    begin
      if today = sun then
        return sat;
      else
        return day'pred(today);
      end if;
    end day_before;

end days_in_week;
```

As identifiers declared in a package specification are visible from outside the package, users of this module can declare objects of type *day* and call the functions *next_day* and *day_before*. The only information about *next_day* and *day_before* that is given in the package specification is that needed by the user to call the subprograms properly; namely, the number and type of the parameters and the type of the returned function values. Details of the implementation of the subprograms (the subprogram bodies) are hidden in the package body, since there is no need for the user to have access to this information.

A package specification is an example of an Ada **program unit** while its corresponding body is called a **secondary unit**. An Ada program consists of a series of program and secondary units. One of the program units, the main program, must be a procedure. Variables declared in a program or secondary unit are allocated space at load time, which allows the separation of the scope and extent of a variable in a way not possible in languages such as Pascal.

To make the items in the visible part of a package available to another program or secondary unit, the unit is prefixed with what is called a **context clause**, as in:

```
with days_in_week; use days_in_week;
procedure main is
    ...
    holiday, working_day : day;
    ...
begin
    ...
    holiday := sat;
    working_day := day_before(holiday);
    ...
end main;
```

The context clause:

```
with days_in_week; use days_in_week;
```

enables the user to refer to type *day* and to the functions *next_day* and *day_before* within procedure *main*. A context clause consists of a **with** clause and an optional **use** clause. If the optional **use** clause is omitted, as in:

```
with days_in_week;
```

it would still be possible to use the visible information from package *days_in_week*, but the objects would have to be referred to by their full names: *days_in_week.day*, *days_in_week.next_day* and *days_in_week.day_before*. The structure of this simple Ada program is shown in Figure 7.1.

The Modula-2 definition and implementation modules corresponding to the Ada package are as follows:

```
DEFINITION MODULE DaysInWeek;
    EXPORT QUALIFIED Day, NextDay, DayBefore;

    TYPE Day = (Sun, Mon, Tues, Wed, Thurs, Fri, Sat);
    PROCEDURE NextDay(Today : Day) : Day;
    PROCEDURE DayBefore(Today : Day) : Day;
END DaysInWeek.
```

```
package days_in_week is
  -- visible information that may
  -- be accessed by other units
end days_in_week;

package body days_in_week is
  -- hidden implementation details
end days_in_week;
```

```
with days_in_week;
procedure main is
  -- information exported by
  -- days_in_week is accessible
end main;
```

FIGURE 7.1

Structure of a simple Ada program.

```
IMPLEMENTATION MODULE DaysInWeek;

  PROCEDURE NextDay(Today : Day) : Day;
  BEGIN ... END NextDay;

  PROCEDURE DayBefore(Today : Day) : Day;
  BEGIN ... END DayBefore;

END DaysInWeek.
```

As with Ada, all identifiers in a definition module are automatically available in the corresponding implementation module, but unlike Ada, where identifiers in a package specification are visible by default outside the package, identifiers in a definition module must be explicitly exported by means of an export list. Also, like Ada, the contents of the implementation module are hidden and cannot be accessed by users of the module. Information on how to call a subprogram is given in the definition part while the implementation of the subprogram is hidden in the implementation part.

In the definition module just given, the reserved word QUALIFIED indicates that Day, NextDay and DayBefore must be referred to as DaysInWeek.Day, and so on, outside module DaysInWeek although, as will be seen later, this requirement can be superseded in an importing module by the use of a FROM clause. As qualified export is virtually always used, it really should be the default.

A possible Modula-2 main program is:

```
MODULE main;
    FROM DaysInWeek IMPORT
            Day, NextDay, DayBefore;
    ...
    VAR Holiday, WorkingDay : Day;
BEGIN
    ...
    Holiday := Sat;
    WorkingDay := DayBefore(Holiday);
    ...
END main.
```

The identifiers declared in the definition module DaysInWeek that are to be used in main are given in the import list. As it is normal for all identifiers in a definition module to be exported, the export list is usually redundant, and it is not clear whether it adds much to the understanding or clarity of programs. In contrast, the import list serves an important function: only the identifiers actually used in *main* are imported and the import list clearly states what they are and where they have come from.

Such a useful checklist is not given by an Ada context clause as all identifiers in a specification are automatically imported. As a procedure or package can import variables and types from several different packages, it can be far from clear where a particular identifier has been declared. It is therefore advisable to give the full name of infrequently used identifiers rather than the abbreviated form, made possible by a **use** clause.

7.2 Information Hiding

In large programs, it is often desirable for information to be visible to several subprograms and yet be hidden from the rest of the program. As an example, suppose that part of the solution to a problem required a table of 100 elements, a procedure *insert* to add new items to the table and a function *lookup* to search the table for an item, either returning its position if it is in the table or zero if it is not. In Pascal, this might be written:

```
program ...
type item = ...
     table = array [1 .. 100] of item;
...
var data : table;
```

```
procedure insert(x : item; var info : table);
begin ... end {insert};

procedure lookup(x : item; info : table) : integer;
begin ... end {lookup};

...

begin ... end.
```

To ensure the integrity of the data table, all access should be through *insert* or *lookup*. Unfortunately, for the table to be accessed by both subprograms, it must be declared in the main program, which means that it could be accessed or even changed by commands elsewhere in the program. A possible Ada package specification to deal with this problem is:

```
package retrieve is
    type item is ...
    type table is private;
    procedure insert(x : item; info : in out table);
    function lookup(x : item; info : table) return integer;
private
    type table is array (1 .. 100) of item;
end retrieve;
```

while the associated outline package body is:

```
package body retrieve is

    procedure insert(x : item; info : in out table) is
    begin ... end insert;

    function lookup(x : item; info : table) return integer is
    begin ... end lookup;

end retrieve;
```

The identifiers *item*, *table*, *insert* and *lookup* declared in the package specification of *retrieve* are visible outside the package. Type *table* has however been declared to be what is called a **private type** and information about its structure is given in what is called the **private part** of the package specification. This means that no information about the structure of *table* is available to users of the package. The only built-in operations available with a private type are equality and assignment.

Consider now how *retrieve* can be used in the program:

```
with retrieve; use retrieve;
procedure main is
   ...
   data : table;
   ...
begin
   ...
end main;
```

As the type identifier *table* is visible, objects of type *table* can be declared in procedure *main*, but as the structure of *table* is private, and therefore hidden, nothing is known in *main* about the structure of *data*. Hence, it can only be accessed through the subprograms *insert* and *lookup*.

A reasonable question to ask at this point is why Ada package specifications have a private part. Why, for example, can *table* not be declared private in the specification and its structure given in the package body? The reason is that an Ada package specification and the units that depend on it may be compiled without the compiler having any knowledge of the package body, but to achieve this the compiler must know from the specification alone how much space is required for each visible object and type.

The disadvantage of this set-up is that to change the implementation of *table*, both the package specification and the body must be modified. This problem can be overcome by the following alternative specification for *retrieve* in which table is an access (pointer) type rather than an array:

```
package retrieve is
   type item is ...
   type table is private;
   procedure insert(x : item; info : in out table);
   function lookup(x : item; info : table) return integer;
private
   type actual_table;
   type table is access actual_table;
end retrieve;
```

As the size of all access values (pointers) is the same, the compiler knows how much space to reserve for objects of type *table*. The structure of *actual_table* can be hidden in the package body as knowledge about its size is not required either in the specification of *retrieve* or by any program unit that depends on *retrieve*.

A definition module in Modula-2 may be compiled separately from its implementation module, but as there is no equivalent of a private part in a definition module, the only way a type such as *table* can be exported, while keeping its structure hidden, is to give the type name in the definition module and put the full declaration in the implementation module. For the reason just given, this is only possible with pointer types. This leads to the following outline Modula-2 program:

```
DEFINITION MODULE Retrieve;
   EXPORT QUALIFIED Item, Table, Insert, Lookup;


   TYPE Item = ...
        Table;
   PROCEDURE Insert(x : Item; VAR info : Table);
   PROCEDURE Lookup(x : Item; info : Table) : INTEGER;
END Retrieve.


IMPLEMENTATION MODULE Retrieve;


   TYPE ActualTable = ARRAY [1 .. 100] OF Item;
        Table = POINTER TO ActualTable;


   PROCEDURE Insert(x : Item; VAR info : Table);
   BEGIN ... END Insert;


   PROCEDURE Lookup(x : Item; info : Table) : INTEGER;
   BEGIN ... END Lookup;


END Retrieve.


MODULE main;
   FROM Retrieve IMPORT
           Item, Table, Insert, Lookup;
   ...
   VAR Data : Table;
   ...
BEGIN
   ...
END main.
```

The module structure developed so far allows more than one table to be declared. However, if only one table is required, there is no need for type *table* to be visible. Both *data* and *table* could be hidden in the package body or implementation module, respectively. A possible Ada package is, therefore:

```
package retrieve_2 is
   type item is ...
   procedure insert(x : item);
   function lookup(x : item) return integer;
end retrieve_2;

package body retrieve_2 is
   type table is array (1 .. 100) of item;
   data : table;

   procedure insert(x : item) is
   begin ... end insert;

   function lookup(x : item) return integer is
   begin ... end lookup;

begin
   --possible code to initialize the data table
end retrieve_2;
```

Normally, the use of non-local variables is discouraged so that a subprogram can be regarded as a black box and does not produce unexpected side effects. In this example, *lookup* accesses *data* as a non-local variable while *insert* changes its value. A parameter of type *table* cannot be passed to these subprograms because the type *table* would not then be hidden from users of the package. The hiding of information has thus taken precedence over the usual advice on the use of non-local variables. But this does not, in fact, conflict with the general view of side effects since the variable *data* is hidden within the package, and so changes to it are not visible from outside. The subprograms *insert* and *lookup* therefore remain black boxes to users of the package.

Moving the declaration of *data* from the main program to the body of package *retrieve_2* has had the effect of providing a straightforward solution to the earlier problem with static variables: the scope of *data* is now restricted to the package body while its extent is unchanged and extends throughout the execution of the program. A module with the same effect as *retrieve_2* can also be written in Modula-2 and this is left as an exercise for the reader.

A package body in Ada or an implementation module in Modula-2 may contain an optional sequence of statements that is executed as soon as space has been allocated to the variables in the module. This is indicated in the body of *retrieve_2*. If the table *data* always had to contain certain initial values, this optional statement sequence could be used to insert them into the table.

7.3 Separate Compilation

The discussion on modules has so far concentrated on the logical subdivision of a program into its components. Another important feature of programs is their physical decomposition into separate files whose contents may be compiled separately. Chapter 5 showed how FORTRAN programs are organized so that each subprogram can be compiled independently. The disadvantage of this approach is that it is not possible to check that the types of the actual parameters in a subprogram call match the type of the formal parameters in the subprogram declaration. Block-structured languages such as Pascal, on the other hand, allow full type checking, but not independent compilation.

When dealing with large systems composed of hundreds of subprograms, it is important to ensure that a change in one subprogram does not necessitate the recompilation of all other subprograms while, if the system is to be secure and reliable, it is important to have full type checking. Ada and Modula-2 solve this problem by replacing *independent* compilation by *separate* compilation. As an example, consider the following outline Ada program:

```
package low is
  ...
end low;

package middle is
  ...
end middle;

with low;
package body middle is
  ...
end middle;

with middle;
package high is
  ...
end high;

package body high is
  ...
end high;

with high, middle;
procedure main is
begin ... end main;
```

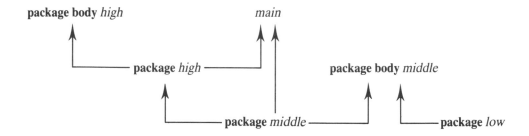

FIGURE 7.2

Package dependencies.

The packages *low*, *middle* and *high*, the package bodies *middle* and *high*, and the procedure *main* can all be compiled separately and, together with their context clauses, are called **compilation units**. These units are not totally independent, since some depend on information specified in others, and their interdependence is given by the context clauses. A package body is always dependent on its specification as identifiers declared in a specification are available in the corresponding body. Similarly, items in package *middle* imported into the specification of *high* are also imported into the body of *high*. The dependencies are shown diagrammatically in Figure 7.2 where the arrows show the direction in which information is passed.

No unit may be compiled before any of the units on which it depends. As the package specifications of *middle* and *low* do not depend on the others, they may be compiled first. The body of *middle* cannot be compiled until both its specification and the specification of *low* have been compiled. Note that the package body of *middle* depends on *low* while the specification of *middle* does not. This is quite a common occurrence as an implementation often requires more facilities than its specification.

Associated with each Ada program is a library file, called the **program library**, which contains information on the compilation units, including the time at which they were compiled. The compilation of the specification of package *high*, for example, is not done independently, but 'in the context of package *middle*' and the compiler uses the information in the library file to ensure strict type checking across the package boundaries.

To illustrate the effect of program modifications on compilation, consider the effect of changing and then recompiling the specification of package *middle*. In this case, the body of *middle*, the specification and body of *high*, and procedure *main* all have to be recompiled, since they all depend on *middle* either directly or indirectly. This is shown in Figure 7.3. Not much has therefore been gained.

If, on the other hand, it was the body of *middle* that was changed and recompiled, then no other unit would need to be recompiled, as units only depend on the specification of a package, not on the body. As most errors and modifications occur in the package bodies, with the

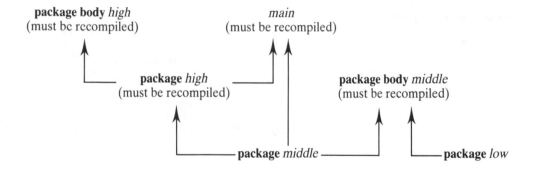

FIGURE 7.3

Effect of recompiling
package *middle*.

specifications being fixed at the design stage, the amount of recompilation required in practice is kept to a minimum. This also means that the implementation of a module can be completely changed without affecting the program units that use the module, as long as the interface stays the same. Localizing the effects of changes in this way is of paramount importance in the maintenance and enhancement of large programs. As an example, the effect of recompiling package *low* is shown in Figure 7.4. As it is only used by the body of *middle*, the effect is localized.

The approach taken in Modula-2 is essentially the same as that just outlined for Ada. Information can only be imported from a definition module and so an implementation module may be recompiled without requiring further recompilations. The amount of recompilation required in languages such as Euclid where the visible and hidden components are not physically separated is, however, much greater.

7.4 Local Modules

Modules in Ada and Modula-2 may be nested within other modules or subprograms. As an example, consider the following Ada procedure:

```
procedure main is
   a, b : integer;

   package inner is
      c, d : integer;
      ...
   end inner;
```

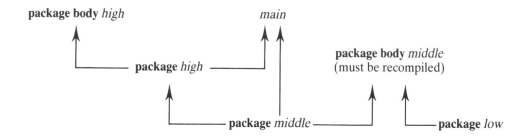

FIGURE 7.4

Effect of recompiling
package *low*.

```
use inner;

package body inner is
    e : integer;
    ...
end inner;

begin
    ...
end main;
```

Variables local to a subprogram only come into existence when the
subprogram is called and cease to exist when the subprogram is left.
Variables declared in a local module have the same extent as variables
declared in the enclosing block. Thus, when procedure *main* is entered,
space is allocated to the variables *c*, *d* and *e* as well as to *a* and *b*. The
identifiers *a* and *b* are visible within package *inner* in accord with the
conventional scope rules. The identifiers *c* and *d*, declared in the package
specification, are visible outside the package in *main*, although *e* remains
hidden as it is declared in the package body. The effect of the **use** clause is
so that the full names *inner.c* and *inner.d* do not have to be used within
main; it has no other effect.

Local modules in Modula-2 are not divided into definition and
implementation modules. The Modula-2 equivalent of the Ada program is:

```
MODULE main;
    VAR a, b : INTEGER;

    MODULE Inner;
        IMPORT a, b;
        EXPORT c, d;

        VAR c, d, e : INTEGER;
        ...
    END inner;
```

```
BEGIN
    ...
END main.
```

The visibility of identifiers is controlled by the import and export lists. The identifiers c and d are exported to the enclosing scope while, as e is not exported, it is hidden within Inner. Identifiers may be selectively imported by some modules and not others, although it is not clear whether the gains are worth the added complexity.

In Ada, the visible part of a package specification is clearly used as the module interface while in Modula-2 the situation is not so clear cut. With compilation units, it is normally intended that all identifiers in the definition module are to be visible, although they must also be given in the export list. With local modules, on the other hand, there is no equivalent of the definition module and the export list is the sole mechanism used to control visibility. Rather than half-heartedly using both definition modules and export lists, it would have been better if one mechanism had been chosen to control visibility.

7.5   Abstract Data Types

Most programming languages have a set of built-in or primitive types such as *integer*, *real*, *character* and *Boolean*, each of which is characterized by an allowed range of values together with a set of operations. Calculations with integers, for example, take place in terms of arithmetic operators ($+$, $-$, $*$, etc.), relational operators ($<$, $=$, $>$, etc.) and the assignment operator. When solving a problem involving integers, it does not usually help to consider how integers are represented on a computer (for example, in two's complement notation) or how operations such as addition are implemented. In fact, for most purposes, it would be a positive hindrance, as it would introduce unwanted detail.

Problems whose solutions are easily expressed in terms of the built-in types can be tackled in a straightforward manner. Hence, most conventional imperative languages are good at carrying out scientific calculations involving integer and real arithmetic while they are less good at, for example, list processing. LISP, on the other hand, is excellent at list processing because lists and operations on lists are part of the language. This suggests that the power of a language can be enhanced by extending the number of primitive types. Unfortunately, the number of types required for all possible problems is open ended, and so a better approach is to have a mechanism through which new types can be created.

Such a mechanism must provide the facilities to:

- declare a new type, give it a name and specify which operations are available to manipulate objects of the type, and
- hide the details of how the objects and the operations on the objects are to be implemented.

By clearly distinguishing between how an object may be used and how it is implemented, users can consider the object from an abstract point of view.

To illustrate this concept, consider a stack of items. It does not really matter what the items are, but for the moment assume that they are characters. The aim is to be able to declare stack variables and to define operations for pushing items on, and popping items off, a stack and for examining the top item. Once this has been done, the stack can be regarded as an abstraction and so it is possible to declare stack objects and perform stack operations without considering implementation details.

Conventional languages such as Pascal allow the definition of new types and the declaration of procedures and functions to perform operations on objects of these types. However, such languages do not have a mechanism, like the Ada package or Modula-2 module, that allows types and operations to be declared together as a unit and that enables the representation of a type and the implementation of the operations to be hidden while allowing the type name and the specifications of the operations to remain visible. It is only when the implementation of a type is hidden that it is possible to guarantee that it will only be manipulated through the defined operations, and that users will not take 'efficient' short cuts by manipulating internal details.

To define a stack type in Ada a package specification is required to give the type name and the specification of the associated operations. How the stack is to be represented is hidden in the private part. The following package specification declares a new type called *char_stack* together with the three operations *push*, *pop* and *top*. How objects of type *char_stack* are to be represented is private information not available to users of the type.

```
package stacks is
  type char_stack is private;
  procedure push(x : character; st : in out char_stack);
  procedure pop(x : out character; st : in out char_stack);
  function top(st : char_stack) return character;
private
  type values is array (1 .. 100) of character;
  type char_stack is
    record
      val : values;
      top_of_stack_ptr : natural := 0;
    end record;
end stacks;
```

The implementations of *push*, *pop* and *top* are given in the package body. An abstraction of a stack has thus been created. Such user-defined types are usually referred to as **abstract data types** or **encapsulated data types**.

As the name of the type is visible to users of the package, objects of type *char_stack* may be declared. However, as the type is private, the only way such objects may be examined or changed is through the defined operations, as in:

```
with stacks; use stacks;
procedure main is
    a, b : char_stack;
    ch : character;
begin
    ...
    push('f', a); push('g', b);
    pop(ch, a);
    ...
end main;
```

As the value of *top_of_stack_ptr* is set to zero by default, both *a* and *b* initially represent empty stacks.

As *char_stack* is a private type, the only built-in operations available on objects of type *char_stack* are equality and assignment. However, the predefined equality operator cannot be used to compare two stacks for equality as it would compare elements beyond the current top of stack pointer, as well as the elements that are currently on the stack. To deal with such situations, Ada has **limited private types**. When a variable such as *char_stack* is declared to be limited private, neither predefined equality nor assignment is available. If required, a new function =, which only compares the relevant elements in the array of characters, can be defined, but the assignment operator := cannot be redefined, and so if assignment is still required a special *assign* procedure must be declared.

The Modula-2 implementation of a stack abstract data type requires the use of a pointer type in the definition module as there is no equivalent of the Ada private part. This gives:

```
DEFINITION MODULE Stacks;
    EXPORT CharStack, Push, Pop, Top;


    TYPE CharStack;
    PROCEDURE Push(x : CHAR; VAR St : CharStack);
    PROCEDURE Pop(VAR x : CHAR; VAR St : CharStack);
    PROCEDURE Top(St : CharStack) : CHAR;
END Stacks.
```

```
IMPLEMENTATION MODULE Stacks;

TYPE Values = ARRAY [1 .. 100] OF CHAR;
     CharStack = POINTER TO ActualStack;
     ActualStack =
       RECORD
         Val : Values;
         TopOfStackPtr : INTEGER
       END;
  ...
  (*Declarations of Push, Pop and Top*)
  ...
END Stacks.
```

An Ada implementation along these lines is also possible.

In this example, the stack has been represented as an array. An alternative representation would be a linked list. This can be achieved by changing the implementation module in the following way:

```
IMPLEMENTATION MODULE Stacks;
  TYPE CharStack = POINTER TO Element;
       Element =
         RECORD
           Val : CHAR;
           Next : CharStack
         END;
  ...
  (*Revised declarations of Push, Pop and Top*)
  ...
END Stacks.
```

The definition module is unaltered and does not have to be recompiled. Users of the package see the stack abstract data type in exactly the same way as before and do not even have to be aware that the representation has been changed.

In the languages Euclid, CLU and Alphard, a module is a type. This fits in very well with the notion of an abstract data type. An outline Euclid module for type *char_stack* is:

```
type char_stack = module
  exports(push, pop, top)
  type the_stack =
    record
      var val : array 1 .. 100 of char
      var top_of_stack_ptr : unsigned_int := 0
    end the_stack
  var actual_stack : the_stack
```

```
    procedure push(x : char) =
        imports(var actual_stack)
    begin ... end push

    procedure pop(var x : char) =
        imports (var actual_stack)
    begin ... end pop

    function top(var x : char) returns char =
        imports (actual_stack)
    begin ... end top

end char_stack
```

The variable *actual_stack* used to hold the stack values is hidden in the module. New instances of this object are created each time a variable of type *char_stack* is declared, as in the following Euclid program fragment:

```
begin
    var a, b : char_stack
    var ch : char
    ...
    a.push('f'); b.push('g');
    a.pop(ch);
    ...
end
```

As a second example of an abstract data type, consider the complex numbers. Complex arithmetic is available in FORTRAN, PL/I and ALGOL 68, but not in most other languages. A complex number has a real and an imaginary part. In the number:

$$2.7 + 5.6i$$

2.7 is the real part, i is the square root of minus one and 5.6 is the imaginary part. The following statements are legal FORTRAN:

```
        COMPLEX X, Y
        X = (2.7, 5.6)
        Y = X + (0.1, 2.1)
C       Y HAS THE VALUE 2.8 + 7.7I
        X = X * Y
```

Type *complex* can be introduced into Ada through the following package.

```
package complex_type is
   type complex is private;
   function "+"(a, b : complex) return complex;
   function "−"(a, b : complex) return complex;
   function "*"(a, b : complex) return complex;
   function make_complex(rea, ima : float) return complex;
   function real_part(a : complex) return float;
   function imagin_part(a : complex) return float;
private
   type complex is
      record
         re, im : float;
      end record;
end complex_type;

package body complex_type is

   function "+"(a, b : complex) return complex is
   begin
      return (a.re + b.re, a.im + b.im);
   end "+";

   function "−"(a, b : complex) return complex is
   begin
      return (a.re − b.re, a.im − b.im);
   end "−";

   function "*"(a, b : complex) return complex is
   begin
      return (a.re * b.re − a.im * b.im,
              a.re * b.im + a.im * b.re);
   end "*";

   function make_complex(rea, ima : float) return complex is
   begin
      return (rea, ima);
   end make_complex;

   function real_part(a : complex) return float is
   begin
      return a.re;
   end real_part;

   function imagin_part(a : complex) return float is
   begin
      return a.im;
   end imagin_part;

end complex_type;
```

The functions *make_complex*, *real_part* and *imagin_part* are necessary as users of package *complex_type* have no knowledge of how type *complex* has been implemented. They can be regarded as type conversion functions. As the operators + , − and * have been redefined and overloaded, complex arithmetic can now be used as naturally in Ada as in FORTRAN, where it is part of the language. Thus:

```
with complex_type; use complex_type;
procedure main is
  ...
  x, y : complex;
  ...
begin
  ...
  x := make_complex(2.7, 5.6);
  y := x + make_complex(0.1, 2.1);
  -- y has the value 2.8 + 7.7i
  x := x * y;
  ...
end main;
```

Abstract data types such as *complex* cannot be defined as cleanly in languages such as Modula-2, which do not allow the redefinition of operators.

It would have been possible to have defined other operators in package *complex_type* such as:

```
function "+"(a : complex; b : float) return complex;
```

Although this would have allowed expressions such as:

```
x + 0.1
```

as a shorthand for:

```
x + make_complex(0.1, 0.0)
```

it would have been against the normal use of the + operator in Ada, where both operands have to be of the same type. Abstract data types should always be defined so that their use is compatible with the use of the primitive types.

7.6 Generics

Algorithms for the stack operations do not depend on the type of the stack elements. A package that implements a stack of characters is essentially the same as a package that implements a stack of integers or some other type. To implement stacks of different types in Modula-2, it is necessary to declare separate modules that are essentially copies of one another. In Ada, however, a single **generic package** can be defined which has the type of the stack element as a parameter. Such a generic package gives an abstraction of a stack that is independent of the element type. This has the advantage of making the program text shorter and hence easier to read. Also, as the stack operations are independent of the type of the element, once the package has been shown to be correct for an element of one type, it can be guaranteed to work for elements of any other type.

Generic subprograms were discussed briefly in Chapter 5. Generic subprograms and packages are templates that have to be instantiated to produce actual subprograms or packages. As an example, consider the following generic Ada stack package:

```
generic
   type item is private;
package stacks is
   type stack is limited private;
   procedure push(x : item; st : in out stack);
   procedure pop(x : out item; st : in out stack);
   function top(st : stack) return item;
private
   type values is array (1 .. 100) of item;
   type stack is
      record
         val : values;
         top_of_stack : natural := 0;
      end record;
end stacks;
```

The implementations of *push*, *pop* and *top* are given in the package body in the normal way. Package *stacks* has a generic parameter that gives the element type. Hence, a package with the properties of the earlier stack of characters can be produced by the following instantiation:

```
package stk_char is new stacks(item => character);
```

while a stack of integers would be produced by:

```
package stk_int is new stacks(item => integer);
```

As instantiation takes place at compile time, strong type checking is not compromised in any way.

Packages *stk_char* and *stk_int* may now be used as follows:

```
with stk_char, stk_int;
use stk_char, stk_int;
procedure main is
    a, b : stk_char.stack;
    d : stk_int.stack;
    ch : character;
begin
    ...
    push('f', a); push('g', b);
    pop(ch, a);
    push(42, d);
    ...
end main;
```

The identifiers *push* and *pop* are overloaded, but their parameters make it clear which version is being employed.

In this example, the size of the stack was fixed. To have stacks of differing sizes, a second generic parameter can be introduced, as in:

```
generic
    type item is private;
    size : integer;
package stacks is
    type stack is limited private;
    ...
private
    type values is array (1 .. size) of item;
    ...
end stacks;
```

An integer stack with, say, 50 elements can then be created by writing:

```
package stk_int is new stacks(item => integer, size => 50);
```

7.7 Object-Oriented Design

When tackling a large problem, an important question is to decide how to identify the components into which the problem is to be divided. The approach taken in **object-oriented design** is to build a model. This is accomplished by identifying the real-world objects involved and then designing a high-level solution, expressed in terms of these objects and their associated operations. Although there is seldom a simple correspondence between the real-world objects and the objects of the types built into a programming language, it is possible to model the objects by means of suitable abstract data types. These abstract data types are the components into which the problem is to be decomposed. To illustrate how such a model can be built up, consider the example of automating a library catalogue. The objects might be the books (represented by their title, author's name, library catalogue number, ISBN number and publisher) and the catalogue, which would be a list of books. The catalogue operations would include the ability to add a book to the catalogue together with the ability to search the catalogue with different book attributes as the key. Note that the abstract data type for the catalogue has the abstract data type for a book as a component. This approach separates the problems of writing programs to use the catalogue from the more difficult task of implementing the catalogue and its operations, and so allows these two parts of the problem to be tackled independently.

An Ada package specification for a book might be:

```
package books is
    type book is private;
    function mk_volume(ti, au, cat_no, isbn_no, pub : string)
        return book;
    function title(bk : book) return string;
    function author(bk : book) return string;
    function catalog_no(bk : book) return string;
    function isbn(bk : book) return string;
    function publisher(bk : book) return string;
private
    type book is ...
end books;
```

Type *book* and the necessary operations on *book* objects are exported by the package while the representation of a *book* and the implementation of the operations are hidden.

Consider now the library catalogue. If the catalogue is to be held on a computer, it might be decided that only a single copy of the current catalogue need be held. The catalogue package will therefore not export a catalogue type, but export operations that can examine or modify a hidden variable representing the catalogue object. This is similar to the hiding of the variable *data* and the type *table* in package *retrieve_2*. Part of a possible package specification is:

```
with books; use books;
package catalog is
    procedure add_to_catalog(bk : book);
    procedure del_from_catalog(bk : book);
    function item_in_catalog(bk : book) return Boolean;
    function item_with_title(ti : string) return book;
    ...
end catalog;
```

The procedures *add_to_catalog* and *del_from_catalog* modify the *catalog* object by adding or deleting a *book* while the functions *item_in_catalog* and *item_with_title* examine its current state.

As a library is likely to hold journals as well as books, a *journal* abstract data type needs to be defined and the package *catalog* extended with operations to add, delete and inspect journals. A *journal* could be declared as:

```
package journals is
   type journal is private;
   function mk_volume(ti, cat_no, pub : string;
                              vol, part : integer) return journal;
   function title(jour : journal) return string;
   function publisher(jour : journal) return string;
   function catalog_no(jour : journal) return string;
   function volume(jour : journal) return integer;
   function part_no(jour : journal) return integer;
private
   type journal is ...
end journals;
```

As books and journals have many features in common, as well as differences, it would be beneficial to define a package called *publications*, containing the common attributes, rather than defining a completely new package for each kind of object in the library. Package *books* and package *journals* could then be constructed from package *publications* by the addition of different sets of more specialized operations.

The representation of type *publication* could be given as a variant record with a tag field indicating whether a *book* or a *journal* was being represented. However, this approach is rather messy and, if it was later decided that a third kind of publication was to be held in the catalogue, the definition of type *publication* would have to be modified and the package *publications*, in addition to all the packages that depend on it, would have to be recompiled. There is, therefore, a lack of language support in Ada for the idea that different abstract data types can inherit information from a common ancestor. The next section, which looks at object-oriented languages, shows how inheritance can be handled.

7.8   Object-Oriented Languages

Object-oriented design as used in a language like Ada is a useful approach to the decomposition of a large problem into meaningful smaller components. It uses the powerful data abstraction, information hiding and operation overloading facilities of the language, but, as was shown at the end of the last section, there are drawbacks when it comes to defining objects that inherit features from a common ancestor.

The object-oriented approach has been taken much further in a group of languages that have the object as their central concept. The best known of these languages is Smalltalk. Smalltalk is not just a language; it is a complete system designed to support **object-oriented programming**. Rather than look at the Smalltalk system in detail, this section considers the additional features found in object-oriented languages and shows how they relate to concepts in conventional languages.

Both the package concept in Ada and the *object* in Smalltalk have as their origin the SIMULA *class*, but whereas a language like Ada has simplified the class concept, Smalltalk has extended it. Programming in an object-oriented style requires a different approach to problem solving. The learning process is, however, not made any easier by the introduction in the object-oriented community of almost an entirely new vocabulary.

Instead of abstract data types, there are **classes**. In the catalogue example of the previous section, *book*, *publication*, *journal* and *catalog* would be classes. Objects are **instances** of a class. The Ada example allows many instances of class *book*, *publication* and *journal*, but only one instance of class *catalog*. Associated with an object are **private instance variables**, which hold its current state. This corresponds to the value of a variable of a type such as *book* or to the value of the hidden variable in package *catalog*. Information hiding means that the current state of an object may only be changed or examined through one of its exported operations.

The main difference between Ada and object-oriented languages is the point at which name-declaration binding takes place. In Ada, to remove a journal *j* from the catalogue, the procedure call would be:

  catalog.del_from_catalog(j);

while to remove a book *bk*, the call would be:

  catalog.del_from_catalog(bk);

As Ada uses static binding, the particular *del_from_catalog* procedure to be used is determined at compile time.

In object-oriented languages, in contrast, the binding is dynamic. Hence, the name of an object is not bound to a particular class until run time. The operations available on instances of a class are called **methods**, and instead of calling a procedure or function, a **message** is sent to an object. The syntax:

  object_name : message_name(parameters)

will be used here to represent the sending of a message. Thus, to delete a book or a journal the message *del_from_catalog* would be sent to an object of class *catalog*. The message would have a single parameter *j_or_bk* which could be of class *journal*, *book* or *publication*. This is written as:

> *catalog* : *del_from_catalog(j_or_bk)*

Sending a message is obviously very similar to calling a procedure or function. The difference is that when a message is received by an object, it is the object that decides which method is to be executed. Associated with each class is a table of available methods. Selection of the appropriate method by an object takes place at run time and the method selected depends on the message name and the number and class of the parameters. In the example, therefore, the particular *del_from_catalog* method chosen depends on the class of *j_or_bk*.

Consider now the problem of deleting an item whose title is held in string *name* but it is unknown whether the title refers to a book or to a journal. If it is assumed that there is a function *kind_of_item* whose returned value is some enumeration type that indicates the type of the object found, the following Ada code could be written:

```
case kind_of_item(name) is
   when bk_typ =>
      del_from_catalog(book'(item_with_title(name)));
   when jnl_typ =>
      del_from_catalog(journal'(item_with_title(name)));
   ...
end case;
```

The operations *item_with_title* and *del_from_catalog* are overloaded and so each occurrence of the expression *item_with_title(name)* must be qualified so that its type is known at compile time. With dynamic binding, the same effect can be achieved with the single statement:

> *catalog* : *del_from_catalog(catalog* : *item_with_title(name))*

In this case, the message *item_with_title* with parameter *name* is sent to the *catalog* object and results in the appropriate object being returned. It is only at this point that the class of the returned object is known. The message *del_from_catalog* is now sent to *catalog*, which uses the type of the message parameter to select the appropriate method, so that either a book or a journal is deleted from the catalogue.

Inheritance is a central feature of object-oriented languages and dynamic binding removes the drawbacks found with Ada. Classes are organized in a hierarchy: class *publication* is called a **superclass** of classes *book* and *journal*, which are in turn called **subclasses** of class *publication*.

When a message is sent to an object of a class such as *book*, the object consults the method table for class *book* to find if a suitable method is available. If there is no suitable method, then the method table of the superclass is consulted. This is continued until the **root class** – that is, the class that has no superclass – has been consulted. If no suitable method can be found, an error is returned.

Classes *book* and *journal* inherit the methods associated with *title*, *catalog_no* and *publisher* from the *publication* superclass and replace the method associated with *mk_volume* with more specialized versions. The code for inherited methods is held in the superclass rather than being duplicated for each new subclass. This is shown in Figure 7.5. Hence, if the message *publisher* is sent to the book object *bk*:

> *bk* : *publisher*( )

the appropriate method would not be found in class *book*, but in the *publication* superclass.

Software reuse is central to the object-oriented philosophy. Hence, new classes can be constructed by extending simpler existing classes, rather than starting from scratch. Object-oriented systems typically provide several hundred predefined classes for concepts such as character arrays, sets and trees which can be enhanced to give the particular class required. In addition, facilities are usually available for the user to *browse* through the collection of available classes.

Smalltalk was designed to be used with powerful personal computers complete with windows, pop-up menus, icons and mouse pointing devices, and a large part of the Smalltalk system is devoted to supporting such an environment. This, together with the fact that dynamic binding is less efficient in terms of machine resources than static binding, has meant that Smalltalk is relatively slow. However, with the continued drop in the price of hardware, this is no longer the barrier it was in the 1970s and so the Smalltalk approach is likely to become increasingly attractive.

C++

A recent development is the extension of the C language with object-oriented features to give a new language C++. The assumption here is that the object-oriented approach is useful for some, but not all, parts of the software development process. By having a single language that combines conventional imperative and object-oriented features, programmers can get the best of both worlds.

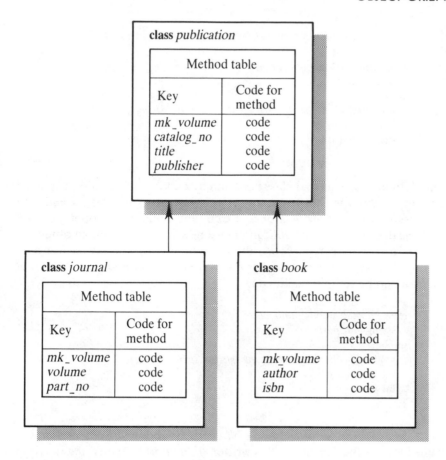

FIGURE 7.5
Class hierarchy.

Modules in C++ are called classes and, as is the case in Euclid, CLU and Alphard, they introduce a new type. The publications problem would be tackled in C++ in the following way. Class *publication* could be defined as:

```
class publication {
   string ti, cat_no, pub;
public:
   void mk_volume(string, string, string);
   string title();
   string catalog_no();
   string publisher();
};
```

The string variables *ti*, *cat_no* and *pub* are called private instance variables and their values may only be accessed or changed through the exported (public) operations *mk_volume*, *title*, *catalog_no* and *publisher*. As in Ada and Modula-2, the implementation part of the class is given separately.

A *book* subclass can be derived from *publication* as follows:

```
class book: public publication {
   string au, isbn_no;
public:
   void mk_volume(string, string, string, string, string);
   string author();
   string isbn();
};
```

This definition means that class *book* inherits all the information exported by class *publication*, has two extra private instance variables *au* and *isbn_no*, has new operations *author* and *isbn*, and replaces the operation *mk_volume* declared in class *publication* by a new version. When an object *bk* is declared to be of type *book*, the operations available on *bk* are *title*, *catalog_no* and *publisher* as well as *mk_volume*, *author* and *isbn*. A *journal* subclass can be similarly defined as:

```
class journal: public publication {
   string vol, part;
public:
   void mk_volume(string, string, string, string, string);
   int volume();
   int part_no();
};
```

In Ada, the author of book *bk* can be found by writing *author(bk)* while in C++ the function call is written *bk.author()*; that is, the message *author* is sent to the object *bk*. The implementation details of the library catalogue are hidden in the Ada solution, but a possible approach would be to have a list of objects of type *publication*. In C++, the catalogue would be implemented as a list of pointers to objects of type *publication*. The type checking rules in C++ are less strict than they are in Ada and when it is manipulated through a pointer, an object of a subclass can be treated as if it were an object of its superclass. Hence, pointers to objects of class *book* and pointers to objects of class *publication* can be dealt with in a similar way. This gives C++ some of the advantages of dynamic binding.

To illustrate this, consider a class *catalog* which exports the operations *add_to_catalog*, *del_from_catalog*, *item_in_catalog* and *item_with_title* and has *cat* as an object. Consider now the expression:

```
cat.del_from_catalog(cat.item_with_title(name));
```

The result of evaluating:

```
cat.item_with_title(name)
```

is a pointer to an object whose class is either *journal*, *book* or *publication*. The full expression then deletes that object from the catalogue.

C++ also has what are known as **virtual functions**. For example, suppose that different *publisher* functions are to be executed depending on whether the class of the object is a *journal*, *book* or *publication*. This can be achieved by declaring different *publisher* functions in classes *book*, *journal* and *publication* and indicating that these are virtual functions by writing in each case:

>   **virtual string** *publisher*( );

The particular version of *publisher* used is decided at run time.

C++ is therefore closer to being an object-oriented language than Ada. Its main drawback is that as the object-oriented features are grafted on top of C, the syntax is messy and the resulting programs are difficult to read.

This section has aimed to show the similarities between object-oriented design in languages like Ada and C++ and object-oriented programming in languages like Smalltalk. It should be pointed out, however, that many adherents of the Smalltalk school would suggest that the differences are more significant than has been indicated here and that dynamic binding is an essential part of the object-oriented approach.

SUMMARY

- To solve a large problem, it must be possible to divide it into separate parts that only interact with one another through small strictly defined interfaces.

- To ensure that a program can be easily modified, it must be designed so that the effect of any change is localized.

- Modules consist of a collection of related subprogram, type and object declarations.

- A module is usually divided into two parts. The interface part describes 'what' the module does while the implementation part gives details of 'how' the operations are to be carried out and is hidden from the user.

- In Ada these two parts are called the package specification and body while in Modula-2 they are called the definition and implementation modules.

- Modules support information hiding. Identifiers declared in the interface part can be used in other modules while identifiers declared in the implementation part are hidden.

- Modules are compiled separately, but in the context of the other modules from which they import information. In this way, type checking can be performed across module boundaries.

- If the interface part stays the same, changing and then recompiling the implementation part of a module does not require any other module to be recompiled.

- A type is characterized by its range of values and the operations that can be performed on objects of that type. Ada packages or Modula-2 modules can be used to extend the range of types available in the language. The allowed operations are given in the interface part while the implementation of the operations and the representation of the objects are hidden. Types defined in this way are called abstract data types.

- Generic packages in Ada allow the implementation of parameterized abstract data types.

- Abstract data types are central to the design method known as object-oriented design. To solve a problem using this method, the real-world objects concerned are identified and then a high-level solution designed, which is expressed in terms of these objects and their associated operations.

- Object-oriented design in Ada uses the data abstraction, information hiding and operation overloading features of the language.

- Object-oriented languages such as Smalltalk also support inheritance and dynamic binding. Objects interact by sending messages. When a message is received by an object, the object decides which method – that is, which piece of code – is to be executed.

- The language C++ attempts to combine the advantages of object-oriented languages and conventional imperative languages.

EXERCISES

7.1 Large programs are usually implemented as separate modules. In early languages, subprograms were used as modules. What were the deficiencies of this approach?

7.2 What is meant by information hiding and why is it important in the construction of large programming systems?

7.3 The two principles of information hiding given by Parnas (1972a) are:

(a)   The intended user must be provided with all the information needed to use the module correctly, and nothing more.

(b)   The implementor must be provided with all the information needed to complete the module, but should be given no information about the structure of the calling program.

Describe how packages in Ada and modules in Modula-2 support these two principles.

7.4 Compare the relative advantages of the private part of an Ada package specification with the use of export lists in Modula-2 definition modules.

7.5 How have the problems that arise with the use of ALGOL 60 own variables been tackled in Ada and Modula-2?

7.6 Distinguish between independent and separate compilation.

7.7 If the definitions of Ada and Modula-2 were changed so that they no longer had local modules or packages, would the power and ease of use of the languages be significantly reduced? If so, in what way?

7.8 What are the essential features of an abstract data type? What language facilities to support the implementation of abstract data types are available in Ada, but are absent from Pascal?

7.9 A queue differs from a stack in that items are added at one end and are deleted from the other. Design a queue abstract data type.

7.10 Construct an Ada package and a Modula-2 module that will implement a rational number abstract data type. Compare the two solutions. Is the ability to overload operators important?

7.11 In Chapters 3 and 5, you were asked to define a type *month* together with a suitable set of operations on objects of type *month*. Construct an Ada package and/or a Modula-2 module to implement a *month* abstract data type.

7.12 Discuss the advantages and disadvantages of the notation used to define an abstract data type in Euclid, where a module definition introduces a new type, compared with the notation used in Ada.

7.13 In Section 7.2, package *retrieve* was defined to deal with a table of items. Write a generic version of this package in which *item* is a generic parameter.

7.14 Consider how you would go about designing a generic *sort* procedure.

7.15 Discuss the importance of dynamic binding in object-oriented programming.

7.16 What is meant by inheritance? As one is concerned with exporting information and the other with hiding information, is there a conflict between the ideas of inheritance and those of information hiding?

Bibliography

The implementation of modules in modern programming languages is a modification of the SIMULA class concept (Birtwistle, 1975). A very influential paper that discusses the way systems should be designed using modules is 'On the Criteria To Be Used in Decomposing Systems into Modules' by Parnas (1972b). Further details on how modules are used in Ada and Modula-2 are available from the standard language texts while the best description of their use in Euclid is given by Chang (1978).

The design of abstract data types in Ada and their use in object-oriented design is described by Booch (1983). Also recommended is a general article on abstraction by Shaw (1984) and, for those who want an introduction to the theoretical background of abstract data types, the article by Berztiss (1983).

The main text on Smalltalk is by Goldberg (1983) and the original text on C++ is by Stroustrup (1986). A more general introduction to object-oriented programming has been given by Cox (1986).

Birtwistle, G. M., Dahl, O.-J., Myhrhaug, B. and Nygaard, K. (1975), *Simula Begin*, Auerbach.

Berztiss, A. and Thatte, S. (1983), 'Specification and Implementation of Abstract Data Types' in *Advances in Computers* 22, Academic Press, pp. 296–353.

Booch, G. (1983), *Software Engineering with Ada*, Benjamin/Cummings.

Chang, E., Kaden, N. and Elliott, W. (1978), 'Abstract Data Types in Euclid', *ACM SIGPLAN Notices*, **13**(3), pp. 34–42.

Cox, B. J. (1986), *Object Oriented Programming*, Addison-Wesley.

Goldberg, A. and Robson, D. (1983), *Smalltalk-80: The Language and its Implementation*, Addison-Wesley.

Parnas, D. L. (1972a), 'A Technique for Software Module Specification with Examples', *Comm. ACM*, **15**, pp. 330–336.

Parnas, D. L. (1972b), 'On the Criteria To Be Used in Decomposing Systems into Modules', *Comm. ACM*, **15**, pp. 1053–1058.

Shaw, M. (1984), 'Abstraction Techniques in Modern Programming Languages', *IEEE Software*, **1**(4), pp. 10–26.

Stroustrup, B. (1986), *The C++ Programming Language*, Addison-Wesley.

CHAPTER 8

Concurrency

This chapter looks at the language features that are used to support concurrent programming. It starts with a description of the concepts involved and how processes can pass information to one another and synchronize their actions.

The two main methods of communication are through shared variables and by message passing. This chapter looks at how the problems associated with shared variables can be overcome using critical regions and monitors and how this is implemented in Modula-2. As an example of message passing, Ada and occam are discussed and it is shown how the rendezvous mechanism achieves both communication and synchronization.

Finally, the chapter considers the problems encountered in real-time systems and the facilities that Ada provides in this area.

8.1   Introduction

During the execution of a sequential program, statements are executed one at a time in some predefined order. In a concurrent system, several sequential programs or program fragments are viewed as being executed in parallel. Each of the sequential programs or program fragments is usually called a **process** or a **task**.

An obvious use of concurrency is to make a program run faster. Often, the precise order in which certain program statements are to be executed is unimportant. For example, if a, b, c and d refer to different variables, and it is assumed that there is no aliasing, the order in which the assignments:

$$a := a + 5; b := d * 6; c := d - 94$$

take place does not matter; so, if three processors are available, the three statements could be performed in parallel. An optimizing compiler can be used to determine which statements do not interfere with one another or, alternatively, this decision can be left to the programmer using a notation like the ALGOL 68 **collateral** statement. When statements in ALGOL 68 are separated by commas instead of semicolons, the order of execution is not specified. Hence, the statement:

> **begin**
> $a := a + 5, b := d * 6, c := d - 94$
> **end**

can be used as an indication to the compiler that code can be generated for parallel execution. However, care must be taken when using such constructs. As the statements in:

> **begin**
> $a := a + 5, b := d * 6, c := b - 94$
> **end**

are not independent of one another, the result depends on the precise order in which the assignments are carried out.

In the language occam, each statement is considered to be a process. The construction:

```
SEQ
  a := a + 5
  b := d * 6
  c := d - 94
```

indicates that three processes are to occur in sequence while:

```
PAR
    a := a + 5
    b := d * 6
    c := d - 94
```

indicates that they may occur in parallel.

A common construct in programming is a loop in which the same calculations are performed in turn on the different elements of an array, as in:

for i := 1 **to** 100 **do**
    $a[i]$:= 3 * $b[i]$

Although languages like Pascal impose an order on the processing of the elements in arrays a and b, the order does not in fact matter: given 100 processors, each of the 100 assignment statements could be performed in parallel.

High-performance computers sometimes include what are known as **array processors**, which allow the same operation to be applied simultaneously to different pieces of data – for example, array elements. In applications where a large amount of time is spent processing arrays, the use of an array processor can therefore significantly speed up the processing.

Several extensions to FORTRAN have been designed to aid the identification of loops in which an array processor can be used, but the simplest language solution is to allow complete arrays as operands. The loop given earlier would then reduce to the single statement:

a := 3 * b

which can be evaluated using a loop on a single processor machine, while it is clear that it is safe to perform the operations on each of the elements in parallel when an array processor is available. APL, which has many operations that act on complete arrays, is well suited for use with an array processor.

So far, the discussion has concentrated on how concurrency can be used to improve efficiency. There are, however, situations in which the solution to a problem is most easily expressed in terms of concurrent processes. A good example of this is simulation which attempts to model a real-life situation in which several activities occur in parallel and interact with one another. When used in simulation, concurrency is not being used to promote efficiency; rather, it is being used because it leads to a more natural representation of the solution to a problem. Writing a solution as a concurrent program may be the best approach even when the execution of the program is carried out on a computer with a single processor and each of the processes is executed in turn. The first language designed to support this approach to simulation was SIMULA.

As the activities in a simulation need not be independent, there must be some means through which the activities can pass information to one another and through which their actions can be **synchronized**. For example, one process may have to wait for results to be produced by another process before it is able to continue. A simple way of achieving synchronization is for a process to execute an instruction (often called a **wait instruction**) so that the process is suspended until another process sends a signal to wake it up. However, care must be taken to avoid a situation where two processes are each waiting for a signal from the other and so neither is able to continue. Such a situation is called a **deadlock**.

A major area in which concurrency is important is in the design and implementation of operating systems. Modern operating systems allow many users to interact with a computer simultaneously. When several processors are available, this is called **multiprocessing**; when there is only one CPU, and so there is only pseudo-concurrency, this is called **multiprogramming**. In a multiprogramming system only one process may be active at any given moment while all others are suspended. However, the speed of the computer allows each user to be given sufficient slices of time for them to appear to have sole control of the system.

As it is often the case that there are more processes ready to run than there are available processors, a scheduling algorithm is needed to decide which processes are to be chosen. In the multiprogramming case only one processor is available and so the scheduling algorithm has to choose one process. Simple approaches to this problem include:

- allowing the process that has been waiting longest to go next, or
- attaching a priority to each process and allowing the process with the highest priority to be the one to proceed.

Whichever method is used, it is important that it allows what is called **fair scheduling** to operate, where all waiting processes are eventually given a chance.

There are two main ways in which processes communicate with one another. The simpler method is to have **shared variables**. The problem with this method is that one process may update a shared variable while another process is examining it. This problem can be overcome by the notion of **critical regions** of programs within which any access to shared variables takes place. At any one time only one process may access a particular critical region. If a second process wishes to access the region, it is suspended until the first process has left the critical region. This is called **mutual exclusion** and is often implemented by means of a **monitor module**, which provides procedures for the safe updating of shared variables. An important feature of a monitor is that the critical regions are collected together in a module rather than being distributed throughout a program. (Monitors are discussed in detail in Section 8.2.)

The other method of communication is for the processes to pass **messages** to one another. In this case, synchronization can be achieved if one process has to wait for a message to be sent to it and if the sender process has to wait for its message to be accepted. This approach was proposed by Hoare in the experimental language CSP (Communicating Sequential Processes) and is the basis for both the Ada **rendezvous** mechanism and for communication in occam. (This mechanism is described in Section 8.3.)

Concurrency and process interaction introduce many new problems into programs, such as the management of shared resources and the possibility of deadlocks. Another major problem is that when several processes are executing concurrently, it is not always possible to predict their relative speeds or, on a single processor system, the order in which they may be scheduled, and this may change with the system load. Running the same program with the same data may not, therefore, always give the same results. Such programs are said to be **non-deterministic** and are clearly very difficult to debug.

Ways in which process synchronization and communication can be implemented in a safe and efficient way are still being actively researched. The usual assumption is that processes normally proceed independently and only interact with one another infrequently. This is the origin of ideas such as that of **communicating sequential processes**.

The marked reduction in the cost of computer hardware has led to multiprocessor systems becoming much more common. Two kinds can be identified: those in which the processors have access to a shared store and those in which they do not. With the growing interest in networks and distributed computing, the latter type of system is increasing in importance. Communication using shared variables is obviously much more suited to systems in which the processes can physically share store.

8.2 Communication and Synchronization

This section uses the standard consumer/producer example to illustrate how the passing of information and process synchronization are implemented in Modula-2. A consumer process must wait for a piece of information to be produced while a producer process cannot pass a new piece of information until the previous piece has been consumed. The standard solution is to have a buffer between the two processes.

In Modula-2, processes communicate with one another through shared variables with monitors being used to guarantee mutual exclusion. Signals may be used to synchronize processes. A process may SEND a signal to wake up another process and it may WAIT until another process sends a signal to it.

Signals are not part of the language, but are defined in a special library module called Processes. This module is used to implement the abstract data type SIGNAL together with the operations SEND, WAIT and Init, which initializes a signal. Another exported procedure StartProcess is used to start a new process running. A possible implementation of Processes is described by Wirth (1982).

Monitors are part of Modula-2 and are implemented as modules. They differ from ordinary modules in that they have a number in the heading which can give a priority to the monitor. Although the number must be present, it has no effect in many implementations of Modula-2! The important point about a monitor is that it guarantees that only one process may be actively executing a procedure in the monitor at any one time.

A possible Modula-2 program is given below:

```
MODULE ProduceConsume;
  FROM Processes IMPORT
        StartProcess, SEND, WAIT, SIGNAL, Init;
  TYPE Item = ...;
  ...


  MODULE Buffer[1];
    IMPORT SEND, WAIT, SIGNAL, Init, Item;
    EXPORT Give, Take;

    VAR TheBuffer : Item;
        Empty, Full : SIGNAL;
        BufferFull : BOOLEAN;


    PROCEDURE Give(x : Item);
    BEGIN
      IF BufferFull THEN
        WAIT(Empty)
      END;
      TheBuffer := x; BufferFull := TRUE;
      SEND(Full)
    END Give;
```

```
    PROCEDURE Take(VAR x : Item);
    BEGIN
      IF NOT BufferFull THEN
        WAIT(Full)
      END;
      x := TheBuffer; BufferFull := FALSE;
      SEND(Empty)
    END Take;


BEGIN
    Init(Empty); Init(Full);
    BufferFull := FALSE
END Buffer;

PROCEDURE Producer;
  VAR Info : Item;
BEGIN
  LOOP
    (*Code to produce an item*)
    Give(Info)
  END
END Producer;

PROCEDURE Consumer;
  VAR NewInfo : Item;
BEGIN
  LOOP
    Take(NewInfo);
    (*Code to consume an item*)
  END
END Consumer;

BEGIN
  StartProcess(Producer, 300);
  StartProcess(Consumer, 300);

  ...

END ProduceConsume.
```

Although, in most implementations, the execution of this Modula-2 program would not be carried out using true concurrency, when designing programs of this nature it is better to consider that processes such as Producer and Consumer actually run in parallel. In this way, the problem can be approached from a more abstract level and implementation details can be ignored.

Consider the execution of this program. The body of module Buffer is first executed and this causes the variables Empty and Full of type SIGNAL to be initialized and the variable BufferFull to be set to FALSE. The Consumer and Producer processes (procedures) are then explicitly started by calls of

StartProcess. The number in the call of StartProcess specifies how much work-space is required by the process. This is a surprisingly low-level feature and ideally the compiler should be able to determine a suitable figure rather than leaving it to the user.

Now consider the execution of the Producer process. After executing the code to produce an item, this procedure calls procedure Give. As BufferFull is FALSE, the WAIT statement is not executed and execution proceeds. Mean-while, process Consumer will have called procedure Take and will be suspended at WAIT(Full) waiting for a Full signal to be sent.

Before the Producer process leaves Give, the statement SEND(Full) is executed, thereby waking up the Consumer process. The two processes are now able to proceed in parallel with Producer producing the next item while Consumer is consuming the last one. The use of WAIT together with the Boolean BufferFull means that Producer cannot give a new item until Consumer has removed the previous one, and that Consumer cannot attempt to take an item that has not yet been produced.

Monitors have been found to be an effective way of implementing mutual exclusion. A major advantage is that, as they are implemented as a module, their internal details are hidden and protected from the processes that use them. However, as they are concerned with protecting access to shared variables, they are not well suited to systems where the processors do not physically share memory.

8.3   Rendezvous Mechanism

Unlike Modula-2, Ada and occam have built-in features to support true concurrency involving multiprocessors with no shared memory. In Ada, each process is described by means of a task and, like packages, tasks have both a specification and a body.

As two Ada tasks can be declared within the same procedure, they can share access to non-local variables and, therefore, communicate through shared variables. However, the preferred method of inter-task communication in Ada is to avoid the use of shared variables and to use the rendezvous mechanism.

A task is entered by means of an **entry call**. An entry is similar to a procedure, the difference being that an entry call cannot proceed until the called task is ready to accept the call – that is, when there is a rendezvous. An entry call is, therefore, used both for inter-task communication and for synchronization.

A similar method operates in occam but instead of a rendezvous consisting of an entry call and an accept statement, processes in occam communicate through named **channels**. One process writes information to a channel and the other process reads information from that channel. For example, one process may execute the occam command:

```
link ! val
```

to put the value of val on channel link, while a second process reads the value into variable info by executing the command:

```
link ? info
```

Communication is synchronized since neither process can proceed until the information transfer has taken place. This is the only way in which two processes can communicate in occam – there are no shared variables.

The rendezvous mechanism can be illustrated by looking at an Ada solution to the producer/consumer problem. The buffer monitor in the Modula-2 solution is replaced by a buffer task in Ada. This task has two entries, *give* and *take*, which, as they are given in the specification, are visible from outside the task and so may be called by other tasks. The bodies of the *give* and *take* entries are written as **accept** statements in the task body. The tasks *producer* and *consumer* closely parallel the two processes of the Modula-2 solution.

```
procedure produce_consume is
  type item is …;

  task buffer is
    entry give(x : in item);
    entry take(x : out item);
  end buffer;

  task body buffer is
    the_buffer : item;
  begin
    loop
      accept give(x : in item) do
        the_buffer := x;
      end give;
      accept take(x : out item) do
        x := the_buffer;
      end take;
    end loop;
  end buffer;
```

```
task producer;

task body producer is
  info : item;
begin
  loop
    --code to produce an item
    buffer.give(info);
  end loop;
end producer;

task consumer;

task body consumer is
  new_info : item;
begin
  loop
    buffer.take(new_info);
    --code to consume an item
  end loop;
end consumer;

begin
  ...
end produce_consume;
```

Tasks are automatically started when the procedure in which they are declared is called. Hence, tasks *buffer*, *producer* and *consumer* are started by calling procedure *produce_consume*. If three processors are not available, then a decision must be made about which task is to be scheduled for execution first. As the three tasks have equal priority, the scheduling order is not defined by the Ada program, although in circumstances where it is important, it is possible to allocate different priorities to different tasks. The order in which the tasks are executed in this case does not matter.

First, consider task *buffer*. The entry *give* and the entry *take* are given in the specification of *buffer* and can be called by other tasks. An entry is called in the same way as a procedure with information being passed by parameters. The statements to be executed when an entry is called are given by an **accept** statement in the task body.

In the execution of the body of task *buffer*, the first statement in the loop is:

```
accept give(x : in item) do
  the_buffer := x;
end give;
```

This indicates that *buffer* is ready to accept a call of the *give* entry. As no such entry call has been made, the execution of task *buffer* is suspended.

Next, consider the execution of the task *consumer*. After entering the loop, the first statement is:

> *buffer.take*(*new_info*);

Task *consumer* therefore wishes to make a call of entry *buffer.take*, but as *buffer* is not ready to accept this call, task *consumer* has to be suspended.

Meanwhile the *producer* task will have been executing the code to produce an item before eventually executing the statement:

> *buffer.give*(*info*);

As *buffer* is waiting to accept this call, a rendezvous exists between the tasks *buffer* and *producer*. Task *producer* is suspended while the body of the **accept** statement is executed. This ensures that the body of the **accept** statement acts as a critical region where access to shared variables can take place. If this critical region did not exist, the value of *info* might be changed by subsequent execution of instructions in *producer*, before the parameter passing had been successfully completed.

To ensure that the execution of *producer* is not delayed for too long, the critical region should be kept as short as possible. Once the body of the **accept** statement has been executed, the rendezvous is over and both tasks are free to continue in parallel.

Task *producer* starts producing the next item while task *buffer* proceeds to accept the call of *take* from *consumer*. As the *consumer* task is suspended while the body of the *take* **accept** statement is executed, this guarantees that the value of the actual parameter *new_info* is updated before execution of *consumer* resumes. Once that rendezvous has been completed, *consumer* executes code to consume the item while *buffer* waits for the next call of *buffer.give*.

Thus, Ada uses the rendezvous mechanism to achieve both communication and synchronization with messages being passed as the parameters of an entry call. Message passing can be implemented on distributed systems as well as on systems involving shared memory.

A much shorter implementation of the producer/consumer problem can be given in occam. This implementation requires three processes each with a channel parameter and a local variable. Each process consists of an infinite loop. The occam process definitions are as follows:

```
PROC buffer(CHAN give, take) =
  WHILE TRUE
    VAR thebuffer:
    SEQ
      give ? thebuffer
      take ! thebuffer :
```

```
PROC producer(CHAN tobuff) =
  WHILE TRUE
    VAR info:
    SEQ
      --code to produce info
      tobuff ! info :

PROC consumer(CHAN frombuff) =
  WHILE TRUE
    VAR newinfo:
    SEQ
      frombuff ? newinfo
      --code to consume newinfo:
```

Occam uses indentation to show program structure and variables do not have a type.

A fourth process is now required to show that the three processes are to be executed in parallel and to declare the channels through which the processes are to interact. Hence:

```
CHAN in, out:
PAR
  producer(in)
  buffer(in, out)
  consumer(out)
```

Information is passed from producer to buffer via channel in and from buffer to consumer via channel out. Interaction between the three processes is very similar to the Ada inter-task communication described earlier although there is no need for the concept of a critical region.

Ada versus occam

This section compares the approaches of Ada and occam to inter-process communication. A process initiates communication by making an entry call in Ada or by putting information on a channel in occam. In the case of Ada, the called task does not know the identity of the caller and an **accept** statement can accept entry calls from several different tasks. This is not possible in occam where a channel only enables communication to take place between two processes. Also, in occam, it is the initiating process that transfers information. There is no equivalent of the Ada **out** parameter where an initiating process receives information. Two-way transfer of information between occam processes requires a second rendezvous, as is shown in Figure 8.1. The occam approach is, therefore, at a lower level, but has the advantage that it can be implemented more efficiently.

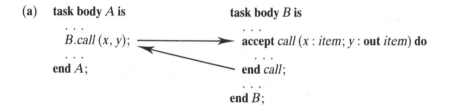

(a)   **task body** *A* **is**
    . . .
      B.call (*x*, *y*);
    . . .
    end *A*;

task body *B* **is**
    . . .
    accept *call* (*x* : *item*; *y* : **out** *item*) **do**
    . . .
    end *call*;
    . . .
    end *B*;

(b)
    PROC A =
    . . .
    call ! *x*
    . . .
    reply ? *y*
    . . .

    PROC B =
    . . .
    call ? *x*
    . . .
    reply ! *y*
    . . .

FIGURE 8.1

Data transfer between processes in Ada and occam.

The main disadvantage of the rendezvous approach is that it often requires a larger number of processes than that required when monitors are used. In the producer/consumer example, a passive buffer monitor in the Modula-2 solution was replaced by an active buffer process in the Ada and occam solutions. Therefore, although the Ada and occam solutions are simpler, they would seem to lead to higher run-time overheads when insufficient processors are available.

The approach in occam is that inter-process communication should be simple and fast and that having a large number of processes is not a problem. Indeed, this idea is central to the occam programming style. In Ada, however, the tasking overhead is high as the language is much more complex and is implemented on general-purpose computers, unlike occam which is implemented on an 'occam machine' (the **transputer**).

Because a source program describes a solution in terms of three processes, this does not mean that it must be implemented in that way. It is possible for an optimizing Ada compiler to remove processes, such as an active buffer, and to move the code to the calling tasks. This gives the advantage of being able to view a solution as if it involved separate processes without this necessarily leading to slower execution.

Larger buffers

When the Ada buffer can contain only one item, the *give* and *take* entries must be accepted alternately, but this is not the case when the buffer is larger. The buffer can then be filled by a sequence of *give* entries or emptied by a series of *take* entries, as long as there are safeguards against adding an item to a full buffer or taking an item from an empty buffer.

To implement this, *buffer* must be modified so that it is capable of accepting either a *give* or a *take* entry. This is achieved by what is known as a **select** statement, which in this case contains two **select alternatives**. Only the body of task *buffer* needs to be changed; the task specification and tasks *producer* and *consumer* remain the same. Hence:

```
task body buffer is
    size : constant integer := 10;
    the_buffer : array (1 .. size) of item;
    no_of_items : integer range 0 .. size := 0;
    in_index, out_index : integer range 1 .. size := 1;
begin
  loop
    select
      when no_of_items < size =>
        accept give(x : in item) do
          the_buffer(in_index) := x;
        end give;
        no_of_items := no_of_items + 1;
        in_index := in_index mod size + 1;
      or when no_of_items > 0 =>
        accept take(x : out item) do
          x := the_buffer(out_index);
        end take;
        no_of_items := no_of_items − 1;
        out_index := out_index mod size + 1;
    end select;
  end loop;
end buffer;
```

The buffer acts like a queue with the first item inserted in the buffer being the first item to be removed. Each of the **select** alternatives is *guarded* by a **when** condition to ensure that items cannot be added to a full buffer or removed from an empty one. Statements guarded in this way are called **guarded commands**.

To execute the **select** statement, the guards are first evaluated. If the value of a guard is 'false', the select alternative is said to be 'closed' and the corresponding **accept** statement is not considered further. If the value of a guard is 'true', the select alternative is said to be 'open'. When only a *give* entry call has been made and *no_of_items* is less than *size*, then the *give* entry is accepted. Similarly, when a *take* entry call has been made and *no_of_items* is greater than zero, the *take* entry is accepted. In the situation when both entry calls have been made and both guard conditions are satisfied, one of the calls is selected arbitrarily (that is, in a non-deterministic manner) and the other has to wait. If no *give* or *take* entry call corresponding to an open **select** alternative has been made, the *buffer* task is suspended until one is.

Occam has an ALT construct that allows guarded alternatives in a similar way to the Ada **select** statement and this makes it possible to write an occam process to implement the larger buffer. Hence:

```
PROC buffer(CHAN give, take, signal) =
  DEF size = 10 :
  VAR inindex, outindex, noofitems, thebuffer[size] :
  SEQ
    noofitems := 0
    inindex := 0
    outindex := 0
    WHILE TRUE
      ALT
        noofitems < size & give ? thebuffer[inindex]
          SEQ
            noofitems := noofitems + 1
            inindex := (inindex + 1)\size
        noofitems > 0 & signal ? ANY
          SEQ
            take ! thebuffer[outindex]
            noofitems := noofitems − 1
            outindex := (outindex + 1)\size :
```

Arrays in occam are like arrays in C: the subscripts start at zero. The operator \ is the remainder operator.

The guards used in the occam example are a combination of Boolean expressions and an input from a channel. In the guard:

```
noofitems < size & give ? thebuffer[inindex]
```

when the value of noofitems is less than size and information has been sent from process producer and is waiting on channel give, the guard is satisfied and the information can be read into thebuffer[inindex].

A problem arises in the second alternative as in this case it is the buffer process that initiates the action and sends information to process consumer, but it must be known when consumer is ready to take this information. The solution to this is for the consumer process to first send a message along another channel to indicate that it is ready. This requires the consumer process to be changed to:

```
PROC consumer(CHAN frombuff, signal) =
  WHILE TRUE
    VAR newinfo:
    SEQ
      signal ! ANY
      frombuff ? newinfo
      --code to consume newinfo
```

The reserved word ANY indicates that the nature of the information being passed is unimportant – it is merely a signal.

This section has only provided a very brief introduction to process interaction in Ada and occam, but it is hoped that it has given the reader a flavour of the rendezvous mechanism and shown how it differs from the approach where explicit *send* and *wait* signals have to be sent.

8.4   Real-Time Programming

The central feature of a real-time system is that it must respond to external inputs or events such as **interrupts** in 'real time'. After all, if a computer system was controlling a chemical process and its sensors showed that pressure was building up to an unacceptable level, then the computer system would have to initiate action such as opening valves or lowering the temperature within a very short time period. It is therefore essential that the input of information and the resulting calculations are completed sufficiently quickly so that a suitable response can be made before the chemical plant blows up.

Real-time programming is one of the last bastions of the assembly language programmer as it usually requires access to low-level machine facilities. This includes the ability to access absolute memory locations, such as those used in handling external devices and in processing interrupts. Few high-level languages, with the notable recent exceptions of Ada and occam, have these facilities although several others, such as C and Coral 66, achieve some of the effects through calls to special system routines. A further problem occurs in multiprocessor systems when trying to define what exactly is meant by time – each processor is likely to have its own internal clock and they may all 'tick' at different rates.

When a computer is embedded in, and used to control, non-computer equipment, the system is known as an **embedded system**. An example of such a system is process control in a chemical plant where the computer system is part of a much larger control system. Most embedded systems are also real-time systems and, indeed, some writers treat the two words synonymously. Ada was specifically designed for use in real-time embedded systems.

In general, real-time programming has all the problems of concurrent programming with the added problem of time. To help solve such problems, Ada and occam allow different processes to be given different priorities, for clearly the process handling an emergency situation such as the one described for the chemical plant must be given top priority and must not be suspended to make way for routine processing.

To give a specific example of real-time programming, suppose that when a sensor in the chemical plant detects abnormal pressure levels, it sends an interrupt to the computer system. This interrupt appears to a running Ada program as an entry call. Each possible hardware interrupt is associated with a memory address and this association is shown in the specification of the task that is to handle the interrupt by a:

for ... **use at** ...

definition. This allows hardware interrupts to be dealt with in exactly the same way as an ordinary entry call. Such a task specification has the form:

```
task pr_interrupt_handler is
    entry pressure_warning;
    for pressure_warning use at allocated_location;
end pr_interrupt_handler;
```

In occam, a channel can be associated with a memory address:

```
PLACE pressurewarning AT allocatedlocation
```

giving a similar effect. For an interrupt to be handled in Ada, there must be a task body waiting to make a rendezvous with the *pressure_warning* entry call. The Ada task body will have the form:

```
task body pr_interrupt_handler is
begin
    accept pressure_warning;
    --appropriate action
end pr_interrupt_handler;
```

There must be a waiting **accept** statement for each interrupt that may be received by the system. By using a **select** statement, one task can be used to handle several interrupts. The occam equivalent is to have a process waiting to receive information on channel pressurewarning.

Time can be introduced into an Ada program through the **delay** statement. Execution of the statement:

```
delay 4.0;
```

will delay a task by at least four seconds. Note that there is no guarantee that the task will be started immediately after four seconds have elapsed for, in a multiprogramming environment, some other task may be chosen by the scheduler. A similar delay in a C program is achieved by the library routine call *sleep*(4).

In occam, the current time can be found by interrogating the special TIME channel. Execution of:

```
TIME ? now
```

sets now to the current value of the processor clock. The command:

```
TIME ? AFTER expression
```

suspends execution until the current time is after the value of expression.

To guarantee that some operation is carried out every four seconds, a simple solution in Ada would seem to be:

```
loop
    --code to carry out some operations
    delay 4.0;
end loop;
```

The problem with this solution is that the time to go round the loop is:

4 seconds + time for operations + delay due to scheduler

which together could be considerably more than four seconds.

The answer to this problem is to use *absolute* rather than *relative* time. Absolute time is provided in Ada by the predefined package *calendar*, which defines the abstract data type *time*. The representation of type *time* is implementation dependent and is hidden, but functions in package *calendar* allow the extraction from values of type *time* the components *year*, *month*, *day* and the time within a day in *seconds*. Absolute time is provided by the function *clock*, which returns the current value of *time*. The package also provides overloaded definitions of $+$, $-$ and the relational operators, so that *time* arithmetic may be carried out.

With *start_time* having been declared as a variable of type *time*, the problem of carrying out an operation every four seconds may now be programmed as:

```
start_time := clock;
loop
    --code to carry out some operations
    start_time := start_time + 4.0;
    delay start_time − clock;
end loop;
```

The value of the expression:

```
start_time − clock
```

will be less than four seconds as it takes into account the time spent in carrying out the operations. It has, of course, been assumed that the operations in the loop are executed in less than four seconds.

delay statements may also be incorporated into select statements. Hence, in the process control example, the action to be taken by the interrupt handler when the pressure is too high might be to reduce the temperature knowing that when the process returns to normal a second interrupt will be received. If this interrupt is not received within 20 seconds, the task will initiate emergency action. This could be programmed as the Ada task body:

```
task body pr_interrupt_handler is
begin
  loop
    accept pressure_warning;
    reduce_temperature;
    select
      accept pressure_ok_signal;
    or
      delay 20.0;
      emergency_shut_down;
    end select;
  end loop;
end pr_interrupt_handler;
```

The loop ensures that once this body has finished handling a *pressure _warning* interrupt, it is ready to handle a similar subsequent interrupt.

Delay guards are also possible in occam. The Ada **select** statement translates into:

```
TIME ? start
ALT
  pressureoksignal ? ANY
    SKIP
  TIME ? AFTER start + (20 * second)
    --emergency shutdown action
```

The value of second is the number of clock ticks in a second and is implementation dependent. SKIP is the null process. If a signal is not received on channel pressureoksignal within 20 seconds, the second guard is satisfied and emergency action can take place.

SUMMARY

- In a concurrent program, several sequential program fragments (processes) are viewed as being executed in parallel. The processes are not independent of one another and so a mechanism is needed through which they can communicate and through which their actions can be synchronized.

- Many concurrent programs run on single processor machines and so only pseudo-concurrency exists. In such circumstances, concurrency is not being used to promote efficiency, but because it leads to a more natural solution.

- Processes can communicate through shared variables or by message passing.

- To get round the problem of one process updating a shared variable while another process is examining it, the notion of critical regions is used. In languages like Modula-2, such regions are implemented by means of a monitor module. Only one process may be executing a procedure in a monitor module at any one time.

- In Ada, processes are implemented by tasks. A task is entered by means of an entry call which must then be accepted by means of an **accept** statement.

- Two Ada processes can only communicate when one process executes an entry call that the other is ready to receive. If one process is not ready to take part in this rendezvous, the other process must wait. Synchronization is thereby achieved. Communication between processes is achieved by passing messages as the parameters of an entry call.

- In occam, processes communicate through named channels. Communication is synchronized as neither process can proceed until the information transfer has been completed.

- The Ada **select** statement enables a task to be in a position to accept alternative entry calls. The **select** alternatives may have Boolean guards. The ALT construct of occam has a similar effect.

- The central feature of a real-time system is that it must respond to external events in 'real time'.

- Hardware interrupts are dealt with in Ada programs as entry calls.

- Delay statements delay a process by at least the stated time. There is, however, no control over how quickly the process will be reactivated after the delay has expired.

EXERCISES

8.1 Should a language include constructs to indicate that certain program segments may be executed in parallel or should such decisions be left up to the compiler?

8.2 Identify the features of languages such as Pascal, FORTRAN and Ada that make it difficult to determine which parts of a program are independent of one another and so may be executed in parallel.

8.3 Outline the problems associated with shared variables and indicate how they may be overcome.

8.4 The hardware of some existing computers may be able to handle the Ada rendezvous efficiently while others may not. Is it therefore sensible to have notions of concurrency as part of a high-level language?

8.5 Is it reasonable to expect computer design to change to fit high-level languages or should high-level languages always be designed to fit existing hardware?

8.6 Design two outline Ada tasks, one for an alarm and one for a person. The sleeping person task should be ready to receive a call from the alarm task and will either return the value *off* and get up or return the value *snooze* and go back to sleep. The alarm task will terminate when the value *off* is returned. If *snooze* is returned, it will delay for two minutes before calling the person task again. This is repeated until alarm is switched off.

8.7 How many channels would be required in an occam solution to the problem in Exercise 8.6?

8.8 Compare inter-process communication in Ada and occam from the point of view of efficiency, flexibility and ease of use.

Bibliography

An important early synchronization primitive was the semaphore which was introduced by Dijkstra (1968). Monitors were introduced and developed by Brinch Hansen (1973) and Hoare (1974) and are based on the SIMULA class concept (Birtwistle, 1975). Guarded commands were introduced by Dijkstra (1975) and a full description of CSP has recently been given by Hoare (1985).

The survey by Andrews (1983) is recommended for those readers who want a more detailed introduction to the concepts of concurrency, while an excellent description of concurrency within operating systems is given by Holt (1978). Processes in Modula-2 are described by Wirth (1982), and the rendezvous concept and buffering between producers and consumers are described in most Ada texts, including the reference manual (Ichbiah, 1983). A good description of Ada's real-time features is given by Booch (1983).

Andrews, G. and Schneider, F. (1983), 'Concepts and Notations for Concurrent Programming', *ACM Computing Surveys*, **15**, pp. 3–43.

Birtwistle, G. M., Dahl, O.-J., Myhrhaug, B. and Nygaard, K. (1975), *Simula Begin*, Auerbach.

Booch, G. (1983), *Software Engineering with Ada*, Benjamin/Cummings.

Brinch Hansen, P. (1973), *Operating System Principles*, Prentice-Hall.

Dijkstra, E. W. (1968), 'Cooperating Sequential Processes' in *Programming Languages* (F. Genuys, Ed.), Academic Press.

Dijkstra, E. W. (1975), 'Guarded Commands, Nondeterminacy and Formal Derivations of Programs', *Comm. ACM*, **18**, pp. 453–457.

Hoare, C. A. R. (1974), 'Monitors: An Operating System Structuring Concept', *Comm. ACM*, **17**, pp. 549–557.

Hoare, C. A. R. (1985), *Communicating Sequential Processes*, Prentice-Hall.

Holt, R. C., Graham, G. S., Lazowska, E. D. and Scott, M. A. (1978), *Structured Concurrent Programming with Operating Systems Applications*, Addison-Wesley.

Ichbiah, J. *et al.* (1983), *Reference Manual for the Ada Programming Language*, ANSI MIL-STD-1815A-1983.

Wirth, N. (1982), *Programming in Modula-2* (Second Edition), Springer-Verlag.

CHAPTER 9

Functional Languages

Up till now, the discussion has concentrated on imperative languages with only passing references to languages such as LISP. This chapter looks at languages that achieve their effect by the application of functions, rather than by changing the value of existing objects through assignment. It starts by introducing the concepts of functional programming using a functional subset of Ada. This approach has been taken in an attempt to pinpoint and discuss features, such as the absence of side effects, the presence of higher order functions and operations on structured objects, that are absent from most imperative languages without the issues being confused by the introduction of the syntax of a new language.

LISP is described in some detail and it is shown that although LISP contains all the necessary features of a functional language, it also contains imperative features such as assignment. LOGO, which can be regarded as a dialect of LISP and is best known in connection with turtle graphics, is also discussed and although it too is not a purely functional language, its mode of use is much closer to the functional paradigm than it is to that of traditional imperative programming.

The chapter then goes on to consider FP whose main impact has been in exploring new ideas in functional programming rather than as a practical system. The chapter concludes with an examination of Hope as a representative of a modern functional language.

9.1 Von Neumann Influence

The languages discussed so far in this book are often referred to as imperative or procedural languages. A program written in an imperative language achieves its effect by changing the values of variables by means of assignment statements. The design of imperative languages has been closely tied to the design of conventional computers, which follow what is known as the von Neumann design, where a store has individually addressable locations. Since machine code programs achieve their effect by changing the contents of store locations, a variable in an imperative programming language can be regarded as an abstraction of the von Neumann computer store location.

Machine code programs are executed by carrying out machine code instructions in sequence with conditional and unconditional jump instructions being used to alter the flow of control. Similarly, the execution of a program in an imperative language is carried out by executing statements in sequence with conditional and loop statements being used to alter the sequence of control. The influence of the von Neumann computer on the design of imperative languages is therefore clear. As imperative languages are closely tied to the design of conventional computers, they can be implemented efficiently.

With the decreasing cost of computer hardware, radically different designs have become possible. One likely outcome of this is that multiprocessor systems will become the norm. It is even possible that conventional machines of the future will have as many processors as store locations or that the whole concept of the store location will disappear.

It is therefore clear that using currently available hardware as a model is not the only way to design a computer language. Other computational models can be used and if they are found to provide a successful way of describing computations, it may be possible to design computer hardware to fit the computational model, rather than the other way round.

Functional languages

An alternative model on which to design a programming language is the mathematical function. A function definition such as:

$$f(x) = 10 * x$$

gives a rule showing how each element in the **domain** of the function f can be mapped to an element in the **range** of the function by multiplying it by 10. If the domain of this function is the set of all integers, then the range will also be the set of all integers. For example, $f(1) = 10$, $f(2) = 20$ and $f(30) = 300$; so the **application** of the function f to the integer 2 results in the integer 20. This corresponds closely to function calls in imperative languages. Languages based on mathematical functions are said to be **functional** or **applicative** as they achieve their effect by the application of functions.

What then are the significant differences between a functional and an imperative programming language? The most important is the concept of assignment: this is fundamental to imperative languages while it does not exist in a purely functional language. Assignment causes a change in the value of an existing object. Application of a function, on the other hand, causes a new value to be returned.

The problem with assignment is that when it is used in conjunction with reference parameters or non-local variables in subprograms, it can lead to side effects and aliasing. As a simple example of this, consider the following Ada function that modifies a non-local variable:

```
function strange return integer is
begin
  a_global := a_global + 1;
  return a_global;
end strange;
```

Different calls of *strange* return different results and so the relational expression:

```
strange = strange
```

gives the value false! Side effects of this nature make it difficult to reason about the correctness of programs and therefore to ensure that they are reliable.

By doing away with assignment, it is possible to ensure that functions do not have side effects and behave like mathematical functions. The precise order in which functions are called then no longer matters; calling a function with a certain parameter will always give the same answer. This is called **referential transparency** and it makes it possible for different expressions to be evaluated concurrently on a multiprocessor system. Determining which parts of an imperative program may be executed concurrently is, on the other hand, very difficult due to the interaction of their various parts via shared store locations.

Language structure

The main components of a functional language are a series of primitive functions together with a mechanism for defining new functions from existing ones. A functional program usually consists of a series of function definitions followed by an expression that involves application of the functions. To illustrate the structure of a functional program, consider the problem of finding the difference between the largest and the smallest of three integer numbers. A solution to this problem can be written in a functional subset of Ada:

```
function max(a, b : integer) return integer is
begin
  if a > b then
    return a;
  else
    return b;
  end if;
end max;

function min(a, b : integer) return integer is
begin
  if a < b then
    return a;
  else
    return b;
  end if;
end min;

function difference(a, b, c : integer) return integer is
begin
  return max(a, max(b, c)) − min(a, min(b, c));
end difference;

put(difference(10, 4, 7));
```

A function definition that only contains function calls does not specify an order in which the calculation must be carried out. The calls of *min* and *max* can therefore occur in any order or they may be carried out concurrently. Synchronization, which is often a problem in concurrent systems, is automatically dealt with. Consider that in the execution of:

```
max(a, max(b, c))
```

both calls of *max* were taking place concurrently. When the value returned by the inner call is required by the outer call, execution of the outer call is suspended until the inner call is completed. Execution of the outer call is then reactivated.

Operations on lists

As programs in functional languages state 'what' is to be done rather than 'how' it is to be done, they are at a higher level than imperative languages, and this makes it possible to produce simpler solutions for many problems, espccially problems involving symbolic manipulation. Another major reason for this is the central position of the list data structure. Languages like LISP are list-processing languages while most imperative languages can be considered to be scalar-processing languages, since their built-in operations act on scalar rather than on structured objects.

Objects in most functional languages can either be atoms, lists or functions. There are usually two kinds of atoms: symbolic atoms that correspond to identifiers and numeric atoms that correspond to numbers. The elements of a list are either atoms or they are other lists. Lists will be written in brackets with the elements separated by a space or a new line. Hence:

```
(ALPHA BETA GAMMA)
(12 14 16)
((A B) (HELLO THERE) 94)
```

are all lists with three elements. A diagrammatic representation of these lists is shown in Figure 9.1. Lists allow the straightforward representation of hierarchical symbolic information and, as they can be defined recursively, they are ideally suited to being taken apart and constructed by recursive functions.

Most modern imperative languages such as Pascal, Modula-2, C and Ada allow linked-list structures to be created, but as list processing in such languages involves the direct manipulation of pointers, it is largely concerned with details of 'how' linked lists can be represented and manipulated rather than the higher level of 'what' they represent.

In imperative programs, structured objects are usually declared and then given initial values. Then, during program execution, the values of individual elements of a structured object are changed. In functional programs, in contrast, where the concept of modifying store locations does not exist, new copies of an object (that is, new values) are created, rather than an existing object modified. This results in run-time overheads and the need for garbage collection, but leads to conceptually simpler solutions.

As lists are of such importance in functional languages, it is important to have functions to extract elements from a list and to construct a list from its components. Two important functions are *head*, which gives the first element in a list, and *tail*, which returns the list containing all elements except the first. Hence, the **head** of the list:

```
(ALPHA BETA GAMMA)
```

is the atom ALPHA while the **tail** of the list is:

```
(BETA GAMMA)
```

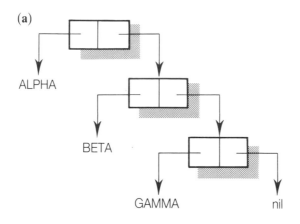

(a)

ALPHA

BETA

GAMMA   nil

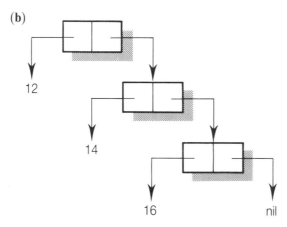

(b)

12

14

16   nil

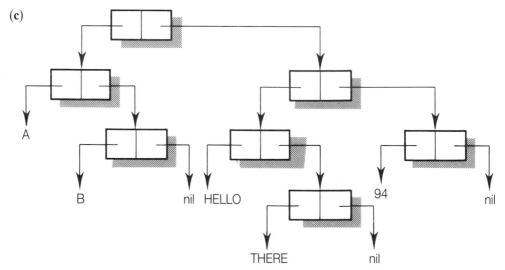

(c)

A

B   nil   HELLO   94   nil

THERE   nil

FIGURE 9.1
List representation.

Note that the head of the list:

((A B) (HELLO THERE) 94)

is the list (A B).

Another important function is *cons* which will put back together a list that has been taken apart by *head* and *tail*. Hence, if *x* is the name of a list, the function call:

$cons(head(x), tail(x))$

produces the original list. The functions *head* and *tail* can be defined in terms of *cons*. Assuming an item *a* and a list *x*, the definitions can be written as:

$head(cons(a, x)) = a$
$tail(cons(a, x)) = x$

If the empty list is represented by *nil*, the following function will test if an integer is a member of a list of integers. (It is assumed here that the type *integer_list* has already been suitably declared.)

```
function is_a_member(x : integer; a : integer_list)
    return Boolean is
begin
    if a = nil then
        return false;
    elsif x = head(a) then
        return true;
    else
        is_a_member(x, tail(a));
    end if;
end is_a_member;
```

Function *is_a_member* is an example of a recursive function. If the list *a* is empty, the value *false* is returned as *x* cannot be a member. If the first element in the list is *x*, then *true* is returned. If neither of these conditions holds, *is_a_member* is applied to the tail of the list. In this way, either *x* is found or the number of elements is exhausted and *is_a_member* is eventually applied to the empty list. Where imperative languages use loops to achieve repetition, functional languages use recursion.

Weakly typed languages

Most modern imperative languages are strongly typed. Although this reduces the flexibility of a language, it allows many logical errors to be picked up at compile time. Many functional languages have opted for flexibility rather than reliability and are weakly typed. This approach is illustrated in the following example.

Using type-free notation, function *is_a_member* could be rewritten as:

```
function is_a_member(x, a) is
begin
  ...
end is_a_member;
```

The body of the function is unchanged. In a call of the function, the actual parameter corresponding to *a* must be a list. If an atom was passed over instead, this would lead to an error when the function was called. The cost of the increased flexibility is, therefore, that some errors, which would be picked up in a strongly typed language at compile time, are not picked up in a weakly typed language until the program is executed.

Weakly typed languages usually include Boolean functions which enable run-time checks to be made on the current type of an expression. This can prevent type errors although at the expense of run-time efficiency.

Higher order functions

An important feature of functional languages that is missing from many imperative languages (with the notable exception of ALGOL 68) is that functions can accept functions as parameters and return functions as results. Functions with this property are called **higher order functions** and the languages **higher order languages**. As an example of a higher order function, consider the problem of applying a function *f* to each element in the list $(x1\ x2 \ldots xn)$ so that the new list $(f(x1)\ f(x2) \ldots f(xn))$ is produced. Using the type-free notation, this could be achieved by the function:

```
function map(f, x) is
begin
  if x = nil then
    return nil;
  else
    return cons(f(head(x)), map(f, tail(x)));
  end if;
end map;
```

map has two parameters, a function *f* and a list *x*. If there is a function:

```
function timesten(x) is
begin
  return 10 * x;
end timesten;
```

and if *a_list* is the list:

   (17 24 59)

the effect of the call:

   map(*timesten*, *a_list*)

would be to produce the list:

   (170 240 590)

Execution of a purely functional program

Due to the absence of side effects, the execution of a functional program can be viewed as replacing a function call by the corresponding body in which formal parameters have been replaced by actual parameters. This process is called **reduction** and can be shown by tracing the execution of the function call given in the previous example:

```
map(timesten, (17 24 59))
=> cons(timesten(17), map(timesten, (24 59)))
=> cons(170, cons(timesten(24), map(timesten, (59))))
=> cons(170, cons(240, cons(timesten(59), map(timesten, nil))))
=> cons(170, cons(240, cons(590, nil)))
=> cons(170, cons(240, (590)))
=> cons(170, (240 590))
=> (170 240 590)
```

Replacing a function call by the corresponding body is referred to as the **application of a rewrite rule**.

9.2   LISP

To most people outside the functional programming community, the language regarded as the archetypal functional programming language is LISP, and so it comes as a surprise to find that LISP is not a purely functional language. It does have a functional core and this is considered before some of its imperative features are examined.

One striking difference between LISP and imperative languages is the simplicity of its syntax. In place of a large number of language constructs, LISP has function application.

Objects to be manipulated by a LISP program are known as **symbolic expressions** or **S-expressions**. An S-expression is an atom or a list where a list is written as a sequence of atoms or lists, separated by spaces and enclosed in brackets. The S-expression:

```
(TIMES 10 2)
```

is interpreted as applying the built-in function TIMES to the two numerical atoms 10 and 2.

Certain atoms in a LISP system represent predefined functions while others represent what are called **special forms**. Special forms do not follow the usual rules of function application and, indeed, their effect often differs from one system to the next.

New functions can be defined using the special form LAMBDA. The function to multiply a value by 10 can, for example, be written as:

```
(LAMBDA (X) (TIMES 10 X))
```

An S-expression whose first element is LAMBDA is called a **LAMBDA expression**. The LAMBDA special form takes two parameters, in this case the lists (X) and (TIMES 10 X). The first parameter gives the parameters of the function being created while the second parameter gives the function body.

To give a function a name, the special form DEF is used, as in:

```
(DEF TIMESTEN (LAMBDA (X) (TIMES 10 X)))
```

DEF has two parameters. The first is an atom representing the new name and the second is a LAMBDA expression indicating the function to which the name is to be bound. The value of TIMESTEN is, therefore, a function. In some LISP implementations, DEF takes as its parameter a list of functions to be defined. However, for the purposes here, it is assumed that DEF can only deal with one function at a time.

LISP systems are normally interactive with functions being defined and then applied. For example, once TIMESTEN has been defined, either of the following two S-expressions could be used to multiply the number 2 by 10:

```
(TIMESTEN 2)
((LAMBDA (X) (TIMES 10 X)) 2)
```

A typical LISP session will continue with the definition and application of other functions. As the definition of a function can use any existing function, complex new functions can be built up in a hierarchical manner.

In most imperative languages, expressions are written using infix notation. In LISP, prefix notation is used. Hence, instead of $A + B$, the built-in function PLUS is used to add two numbers and it is written as (PLUS A B). The S-expression:

(PLUS A (TIMES B C))

corresponds to the infix expression $A + B * C$. There is no need in LISP to define an order of evaluation of operators as all expressions are fully parenthesized. In the purely functional subset of LISP, there is no assignment. Hence, once parameters such as X have been bound to a value in the call of a function, that value may not be changed.

The S-expression is central to LISP. It is the only data structure in the language and a LISP program is itself an S-expression. This allows LISP functions to be manipulated or even created by other LISP functions. Although it is a powerful feature of LISP, this facility is not available in all functional languages, and so is not a central feature of functional programming.

Due to the importance of lists quite a few of the predefined functions manipulate lists; for example CAR and CDR are the head and tail functions, and CONS is the list constructor function. The names CAR and CDR are not meaningful and are a hangover from the machine code instructions used to implement these functions in the first implementation of LISP! The names *head* and *tail* are much more expressive.

When an S-expression such as (A B C) is written, it is interpreted as a request to apply the function A to the arguments B and C. To treat (A B C) as a list that can be passed as an argument to a function, the special form QUOTE must be used, as in:

(CAR (QUOTE (A B C)))

No attempt is now made to apply the function A and the function CAR is applied to the list (A B C). The result of the application is the atom A.

The use of QUOTE in this way allows a parameter to be passed over unevaluated and so is similar to call by name. The default mechanism in LISP is call by value. Strictly speaking, numbers should also be quoted, as in:

(TIMESTEN (QUOTE 2))

but most LISP systems do not insist on this. They also usually allow (QUOTE X) to be abbreviated to 'X.

The empty list is referred to by the special form NIL. Other predefined functions are the predicates or Boolean functions. ATOM tests if its argument is an atom, NULL tests if its argument is NIL, EQ compares two atoms for equality and NUMBERP tests if its argument is a numeric atom. The special form T represents true while NIL can be used to represent false.

Instead of the notation **if** ... **then** ... **else**, LISP has the special form COND. This takes a list of pairs where the first element of each pair is a predicate. COND is evaluated by evaluating the first element of each pair in turn until one is true. The result is the value of the corresponding second element of the pair. The following function to test for membership of a list of atoms makes use of COND:

```
(DEF ISMEMBER (LAMBDA (X A)
   (COND ((NULL A) NIL)
           ((EQ X (CAR A)) T)
           (T (ISMEMBER X (CDR A)))
    )
))
```

If the list A is empty, NIL (false) is returned, while if the head of the list is X, T is returned. If neither of these conditions is true the third condition T, which is always true, is evaluated and this leads to a recursive call of ISMEMBER where X is tested to see if it is a member of the tail of the list. The effect of evaluating:

```
(ISMEMBER 24 '(17 24 59))
```

will therefore be T.

The predefined function MAPCAR corresponds to the function *map* defined earlier. The effect of evaluating:

```
(MAPCAR 'TIMESTEN '(17 24 59))
```

is the list (170 240 590). An advantage of using higher order functions such as MAPCAR is that they reduce the need to program recursion explicitly. Another useful function is LIST which takes a list and returns a new list, each of whose elements is the result of evaluating the corresponding element in the original list. The effect of evaluating:

```
(LIST (TIMESTEN 17) (TIMESTEN 24) (TIMESTEN 59))
```

is the same list as that obtained from the MAPCAR example.

Having looked at the functional core of LISP, consider now the LISP solution to a simple problem. Given an S-expression such as:

```
(TIMES 4 (POWER X 3))
```

the aim is to produce the S-expression that represents its derivative with respect to X; that is, in this case, to produce the list:

```
(TIMES 12 (POWER X 2))
```

The program should also be able to handle expressions in the form (POWER X 3), but to keep the program simple it is assumed that it only has to deal with correctly formed expressions and that special cases are dealt with normally. Hence, the result of differentiating:

```
(TIMES 3 (POWER X 1))
```

will be:

```
(TIMES 3 (POWER X 0))
```

which when differentiated gives:

```
(TIMES 0 (POWER X − 1))
```

The proposed solution in LISP uses two functions, the first of which selects the third element from a list:

```
(DEF THIRD (LAMBDA (Y)
  (CAR (CDR (CDR Y)))
))
```

The main function DERIVE consists primarily of an example of the COND special form and carries out different actions depending on whether the first atom in the list Y is POWER or TIMES. The DERIVE function is given below followed by an explanation of its action through an example call.

```
(DEF DERIVE (LAMBDA (Y)
  (COND
    ((EQ (CAR Y) 'POWER)
     (LIST 'TIMES (THIRD Y)
       (LIST 'POWER 'X (DIFFERENCE (THIRD Y) 1))
    ))
    ((EQ (CAR Y) 'TIMES)
     (LIST 'TIMES (TIMES (CAR (CDR Y))
       (THIRD (THIRD Y))) (THIRD (DERIVE (THIRD Y)))
    ))
    (T 'ERROR)
  )))
```

Consider the call:

```
(DERIVE '(POWER X 4))
```

As the first element in the list is the atom POWER, this results in the evaluation of:

```
(LIST 'TIMES (THIRD Y)
   (LIST 'POWER 'X (DIFFERENCE (THIRD Y) 1)))
```

This gives a list whose first element is the evaluation of 'TIMES (that is, the atom TIMES), whose second element is the result of evaluating (THIRD Y), which is 4, and whose third element is the list obtained by evaluating:

```
(LIST 'POWER 'X (DIFFERENCE (THIRD Y) 1))
```

As (THIRD Y) is 4, the value of:

```
(DIFFERENCE (THIRD Y) 1)
```

is 3 and so the final result is the list:

```
(TIMES 4 (POWER X 3))
```

The reader should now trace the effect of the function application:

```
(DERIVE '(TIMES 4 (POWER X 3)))
```

Scope rules

Most imperative languages have static scope where the association of the use of an identifier with its declaration can be seen from the program text. Many versions of LISP, on the other hand, have dynamic scope where the use of an identifier is bound to its most recent definition during program execution. The advantage of dynamic scope is that it is easier to implement.

In most circumstances in LISP, static and dynamic scope have the same effect, but they can give different results with higher order functions. For example, consider the following two definitions:

```
(DEF BASE (LAMBDA (F A)
   (PLUS (F 10) A)
))
(DEF TWODIGIT (LAMBDA (A B)
   (BASE '(LAMBDA (C) (TIMES A C)) B)
))
```

In the function definition:

```
(LAMBDA (C) (TIMES A C))
```

the atom A is what is called a **free variable**. As it is declared within function TWODIGIT, it might be expected to be bound to the value of the first parameter in a call of TWODIGIT. The effect of the function call:

    (TWODIGIT 2 3)

would then be 23. However, this is not the result obtained. Application of the function TWODIGIT in fact gives:

    (TWODIGIT 2 3)
    => (BASE '(LAMBDA (C) (TIMES A C)) 3)
    => (PLUS ((LAMBDA (C) (TIMES A C)) 10) 3)

It is only now that the LAMBDA expression is evaluated and the free variable A is associated with the most recent occurrence of A; that is, its appearance as a parameter of function BASE. As this A has been bound to the value 3, the effect of the function application is 33 not 23, giving:

    => (PLUS (TIMES 3 10) 3)
    => (PLUS 30 3)
    => 33

This problem would not have arisen if the atom A had not been used in two different contexts; for example, if BASE had been defined as:

    (DEF BASE (LAMBDA (F X)
      (PLUS (F 10) X)
    ))

This shows that care must be exercised in writing higher order functions in a language with dynamic binding if unexpected results are to be avoided.

Imperative features

As has already been indicated, LISP is not a purely functional language. It has, for example, two assignment operators SET and SETQ. The function call:

    (SETQ A 'B)

will assign the symbolic atom B to A while:

    (SET A 'C)

will assign the symbolic atom C to the value of A. When the value of A is the symbolic atom B, the effect of the function call (SET A 'C) is to assign the symbolic atom C to B. Note that the immediate effect of assignment is that the order of function application becomes important.

The connection between SET and SETQ is that the effect of:

(SET 'A 'B)

is the same as the earlier use of SETQ.

SET and SETQ are often used in conjunction with the PROG special form which has an arbitrary number of parameters. The first parameter is a list that defines local variables while the other parameters correspond to the statements of an imperative language. There is even a GO function which causes transfer of control to a label!

The following function uses the PROG feature to calculate the sum of the elements in a list X. It can be seen to have more in common with an imperative Pascal solution (with a rather unhelpful syntax) than with a functional solution. Writing the equivalent (and simpler) recursive function is left as an exercise.

```
(DEF SUMLIST (LAMBDA (X)
  (PROG (TOTAL)
    (SETQ TOTAL 0)
    LOOP
    (COND ((NULL X) (RETURN TOTAL))
          (T (SETQ TOTAL (PLUS TOTAL (CAR X)))
    ))
    (SETQ X (CDR X))
    (GO LOOP)
)))
```

Concluding remarks

For programmers brought up in the imperative style, LISP programs are not easy to read. This has led to the suggestion that LISP really stands for *L*ots of *I*nfuriating *S*uperfluous *P*arentheses. However, this situation has been ameliorated by modern LISP systems providing an editor to help ensure that the proper matching of brackets is achieved and a pretty printer, which lays out programs in a readable form.

LISP systems are interactive and support a development environment where new functions can easily be constructed, tested and modified. This gives many advantages, but one of the central themes in the construction of large reliable programs is that they should be easy to read, even if this means that they are more difficult to write. This is evident in both the design of recent imperative languages such as Ada and in how the languages are used. LISP programs have the advantage of being much shorter than their equivalent imperative programs, but ease of understanding is not helped by many LISP programmers who give mathematical conciseness a higher priority than the software engineering concern of ease of understanding.

Having an acknowledged language standard is another area where LISP falls short. There are almost as many dialects of LISP as there are of BASIC, although there has been an attempt to make COMMON LISP the standard. However, COMMON LISP is very large and seems to combine the features of all other LISP dialects rather than being selective.

Many LISP systems treat function calls at the outermost level differently from inner calls. Hence, instead of writing (TIMES 10 2), it is possible to write TIMES(10 2) or use the predefined function EVAL and write:

```
EVAL (TIMES 10 2)
```

Before using a LISP system, a programmer must discover how that particular system deals with such features. Although the differences may be minor they are off putting to the novice or casual user.

9.3   LOGO

The LOGO language has been implemented on many microcomputers. It is best known in connection with turtle graphics where some of the primitive functions are used to draw lines on a VDU screen with a representation of a turtle being used to indicate the current position of the cursor.

Most of the publicity surrounding LOGO has been about its use as a vehicle to help children think about problem solving. As quite complex patterns can be drawn relatively easily using turtle graphics, this can give children a sense of achievement and they are encouraged to learn while having fun.

LOGO can, in fact, be regarded as a dialect of LISP and a child whose first exposure to computer programming is with LOGO may well assume that the normal programming style is a functional one. In the long term, therefore, it may be LOGO that has the greatest impact on functional programming. Like LISP, LOGO is an interactive language and a LOGO session consists of defining procedures and then applying them. In the language:

- there is a set of built-in procedures,
- new procedures are created from existing ones,
- data objects are words (atoms) and lists,
- words may be either symbolic or numeric,
- parameters are passed by value,
- the scope rules are dynamic, and
- recursion is a major tool.

There is no clear distinction between programs and data and it is possible to create a list and then treat it as a series of commands to be executed.

Some procedures return a value while the purpose of others is to achieve a side effect, such as moving a turtle on the screen. Procedures that return a value are called **operations** and procedures whose purpose is to achieve a side effect are called **commands**. The term function is not usually used in LOGO. A LOGO procedure usually consists of a series of commands and consequently has many similarities with the PROG feature of LISP, although all the commands are procedure calls.

LOGO always comes as a complete system with a built-in editor. Although this makes it easier for novices to learn and to use, it results in the disadvantage that no two LOGO systems are the same.

At the start of a LOGO turtle graphics session, the turtle is at the centre of the screen facing towards the top of the screen. To move the turtle forward, say, 50 units the command is FD 50 and to make it turn 90° to the right it is RT 90. FD and RT are both built-in procedures. Hence, the sequence:

```
FD 50
RT 90
FD 50
RT 90
FD 50
RT 90
FD 50
RT 90
```

returns the turtle to its starting point after it has drawn a square of length 50 units.

The sequence of commands just given can be replaced by a REPEAT command which has two parameters. The first parameter indicates the number of iterations and the second is a list giving the commands to be repeated. Hence:

```
REPEAT 4 [FD 50 RT 90]
```

Lists in LOGO are written in square brackets with empty lists being represented by [].

The LOGO interpreter executes a list of commands by working from left to right and associating parameters with commands. Each non-numeric word is assumed to be the name of a procedure and when it is encountered an attempt is made to call it. If there is no procedure corresponding to a name an error will result. Given the list of commands:

```
FD SUM 20 30 RT 90
```

there is first a call of procedure FD, which expects one parameter. The next word is SUM, which is a procedure that takes two parameters and returns their sum. The call of procedure SUM takes the numeric words 20 and 30 as parameters. This gives the result 50, which becomes the parameter for FD. The actual parameter in the call of FD is, therefore, the result obtained by evaluating SUM 20 30. This mechanism is equivalent to call by value. The interpreter then proceeds to execute RT 90.

A list of LOGO commands can be quite difficult to follow, but additional round brackets can be inserted to indicate to the human reader the grouping of procedures and parameters. Also, as alternatives to the prefix operators SUM and PRODUCT, LOGO provides infix operators such as + and *.

To define a new procedure SQUARE, the TO command can be used as follows:

```
TO SQUARE :SIZE
REPEAT 4 [FD :SIZE RT 90]
END
```

The SQUARE command has :SIZE as its single parameter. To show that they are not the names of functions, parameters are prefixed by a colon. The effect of the call:

```
SQUARE 60
```

is to draw a square with sides of length 60 units.

The assignment operator is MAKE and this is quite widely used because the set of primitive functions is not as powerful as the set in an implementation of LISP. The effect of:

```
MAKE "TEMP 1
```

is to give the variable TEMP the value 1. The symbol " is required for the same reason as QUOTE in LISP although, unlike LISP, lists are automatically quoted.

As LOGO deals with lists it has, as one might expect, a series of built-in operations to decompose and construct lists. FIRST and BUTFIRST correspond to CAR and CDR, and FPUT corresponds to CONS. The LIST operation takes two parameters and returns a list that has the two parameters as its elements. The following examples show the differing effect of LIST and FPUT:

```
LIST "A [B]    produces the list    [A [B]]
FPUT "A [B]    produces the list    [A B]
```

A MAP procedure can be written in LOGO as:

```
TO MAP :F :PARAM
IF EMPTYP :PARAM [OUTPUT []]
OUTPUT FPUT (RUN LIST :F FIRST :PARAM)
            (MAP :F BUTFIRST :PARAM)
END
```

The OUTPUT command used here has a similar effect to RETURN in LISP and the effect of the RUN command is to execute a list of LOGO commands. Normally, a LOGO command must be typed all on one line; however, this rule has not been obeyed here to make the program easier to read.

Assuming a LOGO version of the TIMESTEN procedure:

```
TO TIMESTEN :X
OUTPUT 10 * X
END
```

the effect of executing:

```
PRINT MAP "TIMESTEN [17 24 59]
```

is as follows. If the list is not empty, the value returned by MAP is a list whose first element is constructed by executing the command:

```
RUN LIST :F FIRST :PARAM
```

while the rest of the list is produced by applying the MAP function to the tail of the original list. The effect of the RUN command is to construct the list:

```
[TIMESTEN FIRST [17 24 59]]
```

and to then execute it. Application of MAP returns a list. In LISP, the list would then be printed out, but in LOGO an explicit call of the PRINT procedure is required.

As a final example of the similarity between LISP and LOGO, here is a LOGO version of the program to differentiate a simple expression with respect to X:

```
TO THIRD :Y
  OUTPUT FIRST BUTFIRST BUTFIRST :Y
END
TO DERIVE :Y
  IF (FIRST :Y) = "POWER
    [OUTPUT FPUT "TIMES (LIST (THIRD :Y)
      FPUT "POWER (LIST "X (THIRD :Y) - 1))]
  IF (FIRST :Y) = "TIMES
    [OUTPUT FPUT "TIMES (LIST (FIRST BUTFIRST :Y) *
      (THIRD THIRD :Y) (THIRD DERIVE (THIRD :Y)))]
  OUTPUT "ERROR
END
```

Execution of the following two commands takes place in a similar way to the corresponding LISP function applications:

```
PRINT DERIVE [POWER X 4]
PRINT DERIVE [TIMES 4 [POWER X 3]]
```

9.4   FP Systems

The FP language or, more correctly, group of languages have been proposed by Backus as an alternative to the LISP style of functional programming. The intention behind FP is that it is a vehicle for new ideas rather than a language that is to be implemented and used.

Data objects in FP are either atoms or sequences and the elements of a sequence can themselves be a sequence. Sequences are written in <angular brackets> with the elements separated by commas. A sequence in FP is therefore the counterpart of a list in LISP.

FP systems are purely functional languages and so the only operations are the definition and application of functions. Application of a function F to an object X is written as F : X. Higher order functions are replaced by what are known as **functional forms** which provide the main mechanism for creating new functions from existing ones. Functions themselves may not be higher order.

As an example of the use of a functional form, consider the following FP alternative to the LISP MAPCAR higher order function. (It is assumed here that function TIMESTEN has already been defined.) Instead of:

```
(MAPCAR 'TIMESTEN '(17 24 59))
```

the functional form APPLYTOALL is used in FP to create a new function from the existing TIMESTEN. This new function can be given a name such as TIMESTENALL in a function definition:

DEF TIMESTENALL = APPLYTOALL TIMESTEN

The effect of the function application:

TIMESTENALL : <17, 24, 59>

is to apply the function TIMESTEN to each element in the sequence. Hence:

APPLYTOALL TIMESTEN : <17, 24, 59>
=> <TIMESTEN : 17, TIMESTEN : 24, TIMESTEN : 59>
=> <170, 240, 590>

An interesting point to note in the definition of a function in FP is that there is no mention of parameters or variables. There is only the combination of functions. In fact, FP programs do not contain any variables.

Once all the elements have been multiplied by 10, the sequence containing all but the first element could be produced by using the above function combined with the tail function TAIL. The combination is performed by the **composition functional form** ∘:

DEF TAILTENS = TAIL ∘ (APPLYTOALL TIMESTEN)

The effect of applying the function F ∘ G to X is the same as first applying G to X and then applying F to the result. Hence, the effect of:

TAILTENS : <17, 24, 59>

is the same as:

TAIL : (APPLYTOALL TIMESTEN : <17, 24, 59>)

Thus, an FP system contains a set of primitive functions together with a set of functional forms. Existing functions can be combined using functional forms to create new functions, but it is not possible to define new functional forms. The idea behind this is that an FP system will have a large number of primitive functions rather than a small number out of which useful ones can be created.

A function may only have one parameter, but as that parameter may be a sequence, this is not a restriction. The function +, for example, takes as its parameter a sequence of two numbers and returns their sum as a numeric atom.

To create interesting functions, the ability to make choices must exist. This is achieved in FP systems by the **condition functional form** which is written as →. Assuming that the function P is a predicate, the effect of:

(P → F; G) : X

is that if P : X is true, F is applied to X, otherwise G is applied to X.

Another important functional form is **construction**. The result of the function application:

[F1, F2, ... , FN] : X

is the sequence:

<F1 : X, F2 : X, ... , FN : X>

These functional forms can be used to define, for example, a function ISMEMBER, which accepts a sequence consisting of a number and a sequence and determines if the number is a member of the sequence. Hence:

ISMEMBER : <3, <7, 3, 9>>

will give the value true as 3 is a member of the sequence <7, 3, 9>. The definition of ISMEMBER is:

DEF ISMEMBER = (NULL ∘ SEC → F;
             (EQ ∘ [HEAD, HEAD ∘ SEC] → T;
               ISMEMBER ∘ [HEAD, TAIL ∘ SEC]))

The function SEC selects the second element of a sequence while HEAD selects the first element. The atom T represents true and the atom F represents false. The primitive function NULL tests if its argument is the empty sequence while EQ takes a sequence of two elements as its argument and tests if they are equal. Note again that the function definition consists solely of functions and functional forms.

The effect of the function application:

ISMEMBER : <3, <7, 3, 9>>

is to first evaluate:

NULL ∘ SEC : <3, <7, 3, 9>>

to determine if the sequence being examined is empty. This evaluates to:

```
NULL : (SEC : <3, <7, 3, 9>>)
=> NULL : <7, 3, 9> => F
```

As the first predicate has given the value F, the following predicate must now be evaluated:

```
EQ ∘ [HEAD, HEAD ∘ SEC] : <3, <7, 3, 9>>
=> EQ : ([HEAD, HEAD ∘ SEC] : <3, <7, 3, 9>>)
=> EQ : <HEAD : <3, <7, 3, 9>>,
        HEAD ∘ SEC : <3, <7, 3, 9>>>
=> EQ : <3, HEAD : (SEC : <3, <7, 3, 9>>)>
=> EQ : <3, HEAD : <7, 3, 9>>
=> EQ : <3, 7> => F
```

As this predicate has also returned F, the value of the function is obtained by evaluating:

```
ISMEMBER ∘ [HEAD, TAIL ∘ SEC] : <3, <7, 3, 9>>
=> ISMEMBER : ([HEAD, TAIL ∘ SEC] : <3, <7, 3, 9>>)
=> ISMEMBER : <HEAD : <3, <7, 3, 9>>,
              TAIL ∘ SEC : <3, <7, 3, 9>>>
=> ISMEMBER : <3, TAIL : (SEC : <3, <7, 3, 9>>)>
=> ISMEMBER : <3, TAIL : <7, 3, 9>>
=> ISMEMBER : <3, <3, 9>>
```

ISMEMBER is now applied to this new sequence and as the second predicate gives the value T this time, the value returned by ISMEMBER is T.

The advantage of FP systems is that they are amenable to formal mathematical reasoning due to their regular and simple structure. On the other hand, they are perhaps too simple to be effective programming languages and their primary interest may be as a vehicle for the radical re-examination of what languages need to contain. Their major impact is therefore likely to be on the design of more conventional functional languages.

9.5 Hope

One possible method of defining the effect of a function is to give a set of what are known as **recursion equations**. This approach is used in Hope which is presented here as an example of a modern purely functional language.

Hope can be used in the same way as LISP; that is, by interactively defining new functions from existing ones and then applying them. It is, however, more usual in Hope to create modules that can export public types and functions while keeping their definition hidden. A module can also use the information exported from other modules. The overall structure of a Hope program, therefore, has many similarities with the structure of a program in Ada or Modula-2.

A continuing debate in computer science is over the importance of strong typing. As has been shown, LISP and FP are weakly typed, but there has been a move in recent functional languages, such as Hope, towards strong typing.

In Hope, the definition of a function such as *Timesten* is written as:

dec *Timesten* : *num* → *num*;
---*Timesten*(*x*) <== 10 * *x*;

The first part of this definition gives the functionality; that is, the number and type of the parameters and the type of the function result. *Timesten* takes one numerical parameter and returns a numerical result. The second part gives the definition of the function. The symbol −−− means 'the value of' and <== means 'is defined as'. Hence, the value of *Timesten*(*x*) is defined as 10 * *x*. The application of *Timesten* to the number 2 is written as *Timesten*(2) and this results in:

20 : *num*

being typed out – that is, both the type and the result are given.

As one might expect, Hope has lists as a built-in data structure together with operations such as *hd*, *tail* and *cons* (written as the infix operator ::). Lists are written in square brackets and the elements are separated by commas. All the elements must have the same type. The operation :: is an example of what is known as a **constructor operation**. Constructor operations are used on the left-hand side of recursion equations as can be seen from the following definition of *IsMember*:

dec *IsMember* : *num* × *list*(*num*) → *truval*;
---*IsMember*(*x*, *nil*) <== *false*;
---*IsMember*(*x*, *first* :: *rest*) <== **if** *x* = *first* **then** *true*
                                          else *IsMember*(*x*, *rest*);

This definition states that *IsMember* takes two parameters, a number and a list of numbers, and returns a *Boolean* value (called a *truval* in Hope). Two equations are used to define the function. The expression *first* :: *rest* is called a **pattern**. From the type information, it can be seen that this pattern must represent a list of numbers and, due to the properties of the ::

operator, the parameter *first* must represent the head and *rest* must represent the tail of the list.

The appropriate recursion equation is selected by pattern matching of the parameters. If the list being examined is empty (*nil*), the result of the function is *false*. If the list being examined is constructed using :: (is not empty), the second equation is selected with the head of the list being matched with *first* and the tail with *rest*. The result is then *true* when the first element in the list is x, otherwise it is the result of applying *IsMember* to the tail of the list.

A set of recursion equations can be considered as the specification of a problem. The power of Hope is that once the full specification has been given, then that is the solution.

In the earlier definitions of *IsMember* in weakly typed languages, the function was defined for lists of any type. This can be achieved in Hope by the use of type variables. For example:

> **typevar** *alpha*;
> **dec** *IsMember* : *alpha* $\times$ *list(alpha)* $\rightarrow$ *truval*;
> ---*IsMember(x, nil)* $<==$ *false*;
> ---*IsMember(x, first :: rest)* $<==$ **if** x = *first* **then** *true*
>   **else** *IsMember(x, rest)*;

IsMember can now be applied to a list of any type although strong typing is retained as the type of the item being searched for and the type of the list elements must be the same. Functions like this are said to be polymorphic. Although generic functions in Ada are similar, they have to be instantiated with an actual type before they can be applied, as was shown in Chapter 7. This is not necessary in Hope as *IsMember* can be applied directly. Therefore, the test whether a character is present in a list of characters would be written:

> *IsMember('a', ['a', 'e', 'i', 'o', 'u'])*;

As a list of characters is the same as a string of characters, a shorter alternative would be:

> *IsMember('a', "aeiou")*;

Higher order functions are an important feature of Hope. As an example, consider:

> **dec** *map* : (*num* $\rightarrow$ *num*) $\times$ *list(num)* $\rightarrow$ *list(num)*;
> ---*map(f, nil)* $<==$ *nil*;
> ---*map(f, first :: rest)* $<==$ *f(first)* :: *map(f, rest)*;

The first parameter of *map* is a function that has a *num* parameter and returns a *num* result. The effect of the application:

   map(*Timesten*, [17, 24, 59]);

will be to print out:

   [170, 240, 590] : *list num*

Writing a polymorphic version of *map* is left as an exercise for the reader.

Abstract data types

The ability to construct abstract data types is a powerful feature of Hope. Objects are not defined by how they can be represented, but by the constructor operations used to construct them, together with the definitions of selector operations used to manipulate and examine them.

This is best illustrated by looking at the standard example of a stack. A new type is defined by having a data declaration where a type is defined in terms of its constructors. For a stack with items of an unspecified type, this might be written:

   typevar *item*;
   data *stack*(*item*) == *new_stack* ++ *push*(*item*, *stack*(*item*));

Here, a stack has been defined in terms of the constructors *new_stack*, which has no parameters and represents a new empty stack, and *push*, which has two parameters and is the means of constructing a new stack from an item and an existing stack. The definition of the stack is completed by defining *top*, which returns the top element of a stack, *pop*, which returns the stack obtained by removing the top element, and *is_empty*, which tests to see if the stack is empty. The definitions are:

   dec *pop* : *stack*(*item*) → *stack*(*item*);
   ---*pop*(*new_stack*) <== *new_stack*;
   ---*pop*(*push*(*a*, *b*)) <== *b*;

   dec *top* : *stack*(*item*) → *item*;
   ---*top*(*push*(*a*, *b*)) <== *a*;

   dec *is_empty* : *stack*(*item*) → *truval*;
   ---*is_*empty(*new_stack*) <== *true*;
   ---*is_empty*(*push*(*a*, *b*)) <== *false*;

Note that if an attempt is made to try to find the top element of an empty stack, the result is undefined. The two patterns to be matched are: *new_stack*, which represents an empty stack, and *push(a, b)*, which represents a stack with at least one item. Consider the definition:

$$---top(push(a, b)) <== a;$$

This states that for a stack constructed by pushing *a* on to an existing stack, the top element of the resulting stack is *a*.

The definitions of *pop*, *top* and *is_empty*, together with the constructors *push* and *new_stack*, fully define a stack without giving any representation information. Such an approach can be difficult for imperative programmers to get used to as the definition of a stack and its associated operations in a language like Ada or Modula-2 can only be given in terms of some concrete representation.

As with Ada and Modula-2, the definitions can be hidden in a module. The module will have *stack* as a **public type** and the operations *push*, *pop*, *top*, *is_empty* and *new_stack* as **public operations**. This is written as:

```
module anystack;
    pubtype stack;
    pubconst push, pop, top, is_empty, new_stack;
    ...
        the definition of the stack
    ...
end;
```

For another module to use the stack operations, it must contain the line:

```
uses anystack;
```

It is then possible to declare a stack object:

```
dec s1 : stack(num);
---s1 <== push(4, new_stack);
```

The effect of the operation:

$$push(29, s1);$$

is to create a stack of numbers which can be represented as:

$$push(29, push(4, new\_stack))$$

In summary, the main differences between Hope and the other functional languages considered in this chapter are:

- Strong typing: This gives the advantage that many errors are found at compile time instead of run time. As such errors are often logical errors, debugging is made much easier. Furthermore, the existence of polymorphic functions removes many of the problems that arise with strong typing in conventional imperative languages.

- Recursion equations: Using recursion equations with pattern matching as an alternative to conditional expressions allows the different parts of a function definition to be given separately. This makes it easier to construct the definitions and leads to a layout that is much easier to read and understand than LISP's nested parentheses.

- Modules: The module construct allows Hope to be used in the construction of large programs. There are many similarities in the definition of abstract data types in Hope, Ada and Modula-2 but, as has been seen, their definition in Hope is at a much higher and abstract level.

9.6   Concluding Remarks

Functional languages have two features that could lead to them becoming increasingly important.

(1)   As they are at a higher level they can be used to produce a program more quickly than is possible with imperative languages, although the program may run much slower on conventional computers.

(2)   Their lack of side effects, due to the omission of the assignment operator, means that they are more amenable to mathematical reasoning.

These two features allow functional languages to be used in rapid prototyping, where the aim is to provide an initial solution that has the correct effect and can be used to test a design. The experience gained in producing the prototype can then be used to help in the design of an efficient full implementation.

Another consequence of the lack of side effects is that functional languages are much more amenable to having their different parts executed in parallel. If the computers of the future are highly parallel, functional programs could become more efficient than their imperative counterparts due to their ability to exploit parallelism.

SUMMARY

- A program written in an imperative language achieves its effect by changing the values of variables by means of assignment statements. A functional program, on the other hand, achieves its effect by creating new values through the application of functions.

- As side effects cannot occur in a purely functional language, calling a function with a certain parameter will always give the same answer. This is called referential transparency.

- A functional program consists of function definitions followed by an expression that involves application of the functions.

- Functional languages are much better at dealing with structured objects, such as lists, than are imperative languages.

- Most functional languages allow functions to accept functions as parameters and to return functions as results. Such functions are said to be higher order functions.

- Objects manipulated by a LISP program are known as S-expressions. An S-expression is an atom or a list.

- Many of the predefined functions in LISP are used to manipulate lists.

- Expressions in LISP are fully parenthesized and prefix notation is used rather than conventional infix notation.

- LISP is not a purely functional language as assignment is possible.

- LOGO was derived from LISP and is normally used with turtle graphics on a microcomputer.

- FP is a purely functional language and was designed as a vehicle for trying out new ideas in functional programming. Functional forms are used to create new functions.

- FP functions contain neither parameters nor variables. It is only possible to have a combination of functions.

- An advantage of FP systems is that they are amenable to formal mathematical reasoning. This is due to their regular and simple structure.

- Hope is a purely functional language and differs from LISP and FP in that it is strongly typed.

- Functions are defined in Hope by a set of recursive equations. The appropriate recursive equation is chosen by means of pattern matching.

- Hope allows the creation of modules which can export types and functions while keeping their definition hidden. This allows abstract data types to be constructed. Instead of the generics of Ada, Hope supports polymorphic functions.

EXERCISES

9.1 It is possible to write programs in a functional subset of Ada. What features would have to be added to Ada to make it a useful functional language?

9.2 What properties of functional languages make them better able to exploit the parallelism that results from multiprocessor systems than is possible with imperative languages?

9.3 What is the difference between predefined functions and special forms in LISP?

9.4 Evaluate by reduction, the function applications:

      (ISMEMBER 24 '(17 24 59))   (LISP)

      IsMember(24, [17, 24, 59])   (Hope)

9.5 Describe the difference between static and dynamic scope rules. Under what circumstances will they lead to different results?

9.6 A function that used the PROG feature to calculate the sum of the elements in a list was given in Section 9.2. Write the equivalent recursive function.

9.7 Using the definition of DERIVE given in Section 9.3, evaluate the LOGO operation:

    DERIVE [POWER X 4]

by reduction.

9.8 Compare functional forms in FP with higher order functions in LISP.

9.9 What are the differences between polymorphic functions in Hope and generic functions in Ada?

9.10 Write a polymorphic version of the Hope *map* function given in Section 9.5.

Bibliography

Detailed descriptions of functional programming are given by Henderson (1980) and by Glaser (1984). In *Functional Programming: Application and Implementation*, Henderson uses a purely functional subset of LISP called LISPKIT, while in *Principles of Functional Programming* a simple new language is developed and descriptions of newer languages such as Hope and FP are included.

There are many textbooks on LISP. The book by Winston (1984) uses the COMMON LISP dialect, which is the nearest there is to a standard version of the language.

Most books on LOGO concentrate on its use with turtle graphics. An interesting alternative is the book by Harvey (1985).

The paper by Backus (1978) has been very influential. As well as introducing FP, it gives a critique of the advantages of the functional style over imperative von Neumann based languages.

Most of the material on Hope is not readily available with the exception of the tutorial introduction given in the August 1985 edition of *Byte* (Bailey, 1985).

The use of functional languages in prototyping has been described by Henderson (1986).

Backus, J. (1978), 'Can Programming be Liberated from the Von Neumann Style?', *Comm. ACM*, **21**, pp. 613–641.

Bailey, R. (1985), 'A Hope Tutorial', *Byte*, **10**(8), pp. 235–258.

Glaser, H., Hankin, C. and Till, D. (1984), *Principles of Functional Programming*, Prentice-Hall.

Harvey, B. (1985), *Computer Science Logo Style*, MIT Press.

Henderson, P. (1980), *Functional Programming: Application and Implementation*, Prentice-Hall.

Henderson, P. (1986), 'Functional Programming, Formal Specification and Rapid Prototyping', *IEEE Trans. in Software Engineering*, **12**, pp. 241–250.

Winston, P. H. and Horn, B. K. P. (1984), *LISP* (Second Edition), Addison-Wesley.

CHAPTER 10

Logic Programming

Logic programming is almost synonymous with PROLOG. Indeed, the name PROLOG stands for PROgramming in LOGic. This chapter is, therefore, mainly concerned with the PROLOG language.

The chapter opens with a discussion of the goal-oriented approach of PROLOG to problem solving and shows how this can lead to efficiency problems. Methods for solving such problems are briefly considered.

The basics of PROLOG are then illustrated by means of an example program that defines family relations. This example is then extended to show how unification, backtracking, recursion, negation, data abstraction and information hiding are handled in PROLOG.

Backtracking is an important feature of PROLOG and the use of the cut operation to control this process is examined.

Finally, a PROLOG program that performs simple symbolic differentiation is presented.

10.1   The PROLOG Approach

The majority of programming languages concentrate on how operations are carried out. PROLOG, on the other hand, is **goal oriented**; that is, the programmer defines the problem to be solved – the goal. The programmer is not expected to give a detailed solution of how such a goal can be achieved; this is left to the PROLOG system itself. Such a design feature has evolved in part because PROLOG was developed in an artificial intelligence environment where practitioners are encouraged to think in terms of the goals rather than the means of satisfying such goals.

A PROLOG program describes how a goal can be satisfied by giving a list of subgoals whose achievement will result in the fulfillment of the goal. As alternative subgoals can be provided, there may be more than one way in which a goal may be achieved. A subgoal may be an assertion, which evaluates to either true or false, or, alternatively, achieving a subgoal may require the PROLOG system to generate and then try to achieve further subgoals.

Execution of a PROLOG program, therefore, amounts to trying to satisfy a goal. It starts by trying to satisfy the list of subgoals and if failure occurs, it **backtracks** and tries an alternative set of subgoals. If the system runs out of alternatives, then it has failed to achieve the goal. The power of PROLOG lies in the fact that the selection of goals and backtracking are built in, while in most other languages such operations would have to be explicitly programmed.

PROLOG programs have both a *declarative* and a *procedural* meaning. The declarative (or descriptive) meaning is concerned with the objects and their relationships, as defined by the program. The procedural meaning is concerned with how and in what order such relationships are evaluated to obtain a solution. Ideally, programmers would prefer to restrict their attention to the declarative meaning and leave the matter of the efficiency of the search processes to the implementation. Such an approach tends towards pure logic programming, but has as yet not proved very effective.

Early implementations of PROLOG were exceedingly slow, as was Microplanner the first PROLOG-type language developed in the United States. Efficiency is a serious problem for functional and logic languages unless they are used only as specification languages for defining problems and not used in the implemented solution.

There are two methods of tackling the efficiency problems of PROLOG. One is to take a close look at the implementation techniques. Warren (1977) did a lot of work in this area and his ideas led to PROLOG systems of considerably improved efficiency, thereby making the language more accessible to the general programmer. (These ideas are discussed in more detail in Section 10.4.)

The second method of providing efficient PROLOG implementations is the more fundamental one of re-examining basic computer architecture. This approach is strongly advocated in the Japanese Fifth Generation initiative and suggests a move away from the classical von Neumann computer architecture, which has been the basis for most computer designs since the 1950s. Just how successfully a new computer architecture can be designed to support logic languages like PROLOG is, however, still a matter of speculation.

10.2   The Basics of PROLOG

This section gives an overview of PROLOG, looking at its basic mechanisms and illustrating them by an example. As with most programming languages, problems can be solved in PROLOG in many different ways. Perhaps because of its novelty for most programmers, no definitive PROLOG style has yet emerged that has had general approval, like structured programming for imperative languages.

Problem solving in PROLOG is achieved by identifying the basic objects to be manipulated and describing the relationships between these objects. This is accomplished by **facts** and **rules**.

- The facts about objects are declared to be always true.
- The rules about objects and their relationships state that a statement is true if certain stipulated goals and subgoals are satisfied.

Finally, a PROLOG program can be asked **questions**. These questions may be about objects and their relationships and are concerned with the satisfying of goals. A question may be concerned with a single goal or a series of goals. In some circumstances, more than one answer will satisfy the goals and PROLOG can be programmed to find as many solutions as the programmer desires, and are available.

To illustrate how PROLOG programs are written, here is an example that defines family relations. The details of the family can be described by the following facts:

```
male(philip).
female(elizabeth).
male(charles).
female(anne).
male(andrew).
male(edward).
female(diana).
female(sarah).
```

```
male(mark).
male(william).
male(harry).
parents(charles, elizabeth, philip).
parents(anne, elizabeth, philip).
parents(andrew, elizabeth, philip).
parents(edward, elizabeth, philip).
parents(william, diana, charles).
parents(harry, diana, charles).
```

where **parents(A, B, C)** means the parents of A are mother B and father C. Such facts can be represented in many different ways. For example, instead of:

```
parents(charles, elizabeth, philip).
```

the following two binary relationships could be used:

```
mother(charles, elizabeth).
father(charles, philip).
```

Similarly, **male(philip)** could be expressed as the binary relationship:

```
sex(philip, masculine).
```

The information on this family can be extended by adding new facts and also by adding rules. For example, the concept of a person being someone's brother can be introduced. This could be defined by the following rule:

```
brother(X, Y) :- male(X),
                 parents(X, M, F),
                 parents(Y, M, F).
```

In contrast to a fact, which is always true, the result of evaluating a rule is only true when the conditions are satisfied. In this case, all three conditions (subgoals) must be satisfied before the rule (the goal itself) evaluates to true. Note that the commas between the conditions are the same as the logical *and*. Note also that PROLOG has the convention of starting variables with capital letters and values with lower case letters.

Questions, unification and backtracking

A PROLOG program can be asked questions at any stage. Writing:

> ?– parents(william, diana, charles).

asks the question 'Is it the case that the parents of William are Diana and Charles?'. In this case, the answer to the question is 'yes' as the question can be matched to one of the set of facts.

Facts, rules and questions are examples of **clauses** in PROLOG. A PROLOG program consists of a set of clauses with each clause being terminated by a full stop. A clause is considered to have a **head** and a **body**. Facts are clauses with a head but no body; questions have no head only a body; and rules have both a head and a body. The body part of a clause gives a list of the subgoals. If it is a question, then it asks if such goals are true; if it is a rule, then it is defining the goals that can be satisfied to make the clause head true.

Here is a slightly more complicated question:

> ?– brother(edward, anne).

The PROLOG proof process involves generating subgoals and instantiating (that is, replacing) PROLOG variables by values. Using the rule:

> brother(X, Y) :– male(X),
> parents(X, M, F),
> parents(Y, M, F).

the substitutions X ← edward and Y ← anne are made and the following subgoals attempted:

> male(edward),
> parents(edward, M, F),
> parents(anne, M, F).

The first subgoal is true, as it matches one of the facts. The program must now find values for M and F so that it can match:

> parents(edward, M, F)

The substitutions M ← elizabeth and F ← philip allow this subgoal to be matched to the fact:

> parents(edward, elizabeth, philip)

The same substitutions for **M** and **F** must be made in the third subgoal giving:

> parents(anne, elizabeth, philip)

which can be seen to match one of the facts. As the three subgoals have been satisfied, so has the original goal. The process of finding a suitable set of values that can be substituted for variables, so that a goal can be matched to a fact or to the head of a rule, is called **unification**. The matching used by PROLOG systems does not exactly correspond to unification in logic. However, the differences are minor and subtle and interested readers are referred to *Prolog for Programmers* (Kluzniak, 1985).

Straightforward questions such as the one just examined would be of little interest in a general problem-solving situation and the questions asked would almost certainly contain variables. Thus, a question like:

> ?− brother(X, anne).

would require a slightly more complex matching process, since it requires the value for X that satisfies the goal. After making the substitution Y ← anne, the subgoals are:

> male(X),
> parents(X, elizabeth, philip),
> parents(anne, elizabeth, philip).

The first fact with which **male(X)** can be matched is **male(philip)**. Therefore, the substitution X ← philip is made and the following goal attempted:

> parents(philip, elizabeth, philip)

As there is no fact that matches this goal, it fails. The program must now backtrack and attempt an alternative way of achieving the goal **male(X)**. This time, the substitution X ← charles is tried, which satisfies both the subgoals **male(charles)** and **parents(charles, elizabeth, philip)**. As the third subgoal also matches one of the facts, the PROLOG system will respond with something like:

> X = charles

If a semicolon is typed in response to this answer, the system will attempt to find further matches for the original question by backtracking to find other ways of matching the subgoals. In this case, the other solutions are **andrew** and **edward**. The semicolon is the logical *or* and can be used elsewhere in PROLOG with this meaning.

An alternative to asking 'Who is the brother of Anne?' is 'Who is Edward the brother of?':

?— brother(edward, X).

The matching process will again give the answer:

X = charles

If the system is asked for further matches, it will eventually give the match **edward**. Such a result means that the original rule for **brother(X, Y)** was insufficiently specified, so it must be redefined to exclude people being considered brothers of themselves.

As backtracking is such an intrinsic part of PROLOG, here is a more complicated example to show how the backtracking process operates. Suppose that the facts are:

mother(jane, george).
father(john, george).
brother(bill, john).

and the rules are:

parent(X, Y) :— mother(X, Y).
parent(X, Y) :— father(X, Y).
uncle(Z, Y) :— parent(P, Y), brother(Z, P).

If the goal is:

?— uncle(X, george).

the steps in the solution process are as follows.

(1)   The substitutions Y ← george and Z ← X result in the subgoals:

parent(P, george), brother(X, P).

(2)   Using the rule:

parent(X, Y) :— mother(X, Y).

the goal **mother(P, george)** is attempted and as this is matched by the fact **mother(jane, george)**, the substitution P ← jane takes place.

(3)   The subgoal **brother(X, jane)** is now attempted, but it fails as there is no supporting fact with which X can be matched.

(4)   The system must now backtrack to **parent(X, Y)** and try the alternative rule:

> **parent(X, Y) :− father(X, Y).**

The goal is now **father(P, george)** and this is matched by the fact **father(john, george)** and so P ← **john**.

(5)   The goal **brother(X, john)** is now attempted, which is matched with the fact **brother(bill, john)** giving X ← **bill**.

(6)   The goal in the original question is now satisfied since both its subgoals are satisfied. The PROLOG system will respond with something like:

> X = **bill**

An important factor in all backtracking techniques is the ordering; in PROLOG's case, the ordering of the subgoals and the facts. Order is necessary so that the search can be carried out systematically and to prevent the occurrence of infinite loops. Ordering also influences the speed of the searching process and good choices can have a considerable effect on the efficiency. For example, a good heuristic is to place those subgoals that are liable to be the most difficult to satisfy as early as possible since this will normally reduce the amount of backtracking.

Recursion in PROLOG

Recursion plays a central role in PROLOG, as it does in functional languages. As with all recursive situations, there must be a rule to halt the recursion in addition to a recursive rule. For example, the rule:

> **child(X, Y) :− mother(Y, X).**
> **child(X, Y) :− father(Y, X).**

says that X is a child of a parent Y. Such a relation can be generalized to X is a descendant of Y, and this can operate over as many generations as necessary. In PROLOG, **descendant** could be defined as follows:

> **descendant(X, Y) :− child(X, Y).**
> **descendant(X, Y) :− child(X, Z),**
> $\qquad\qquad\qquad\qquad$ **descendant(Z, Y).**

This defines both the recursive definition and the definition that halts the recursion. Both of these definitions are needed, since without the first one, the recursion will be infinite, while the first one alone is an incomplete and restricted definition of descendant. The two definitions are often considered together to form a *procedure*.

Negation

Some PROLOG implementations provide **not** as a built-in procedure. If such a facility is available, it is used as a prefix operator, as in:

?− **not typhoid(bill).**

However, care must be taken in interpreting the answer to this question, since negation is not the same as in mathematics.

PROLOG uses the **closed-world assumption** and thus assumes that all the facts about the world are included in the model. Anything not derivable is therefore false. When PROLOG has to process **not typhoid(bill)**, it tries to prove that Bill has typhoid and it then negates the result. The **not** goal therefore succeeds in two situations:

(1)   When Bill has definitely not got typhoid.
(2)   When it cannot prove Bill has typhoid.

The problem of using the closed-world assumption with negation is that the negation of anything not derivable is considered true.

10.3   Data Objects

As in most languages, both simple and structured data objects are allowed in PROLOG. Simple data objects are numbers and character strings (also known as atoms).

Chapter 6 showed how records in Pascal (or structures in PL/I) can be represented by a tree. Structured data objects in PROLOG are also of this nature. The Pascal record:

```
type name = packed array [1 .. 12] of char;
     fullname =
        record
          forename : name;
          surname : name
        end;
     student =
        record
          person : fullname;
          age : integer
        end;
```

could be represented in PROLOG as an object with the structure:

    student(fullname(Forename, Surname), Age)

Such a structure can be used in facts and rules, as in:

    attends(student(fullname(mary, smith), 20), stirling).
    attends(student(fullname(joe, brown), 25), stirling).
    maturestudent(Surname) :− attends(student(fullname(Forename,
                                     Surname), Age), University), Age > 23.

PROLOG can then be asked questions like:

    ?− maturestudent(X).

to which the answer is:

    X = brown

The name part of a structure in PROLOG is called a **functor**. Hence, **student** and **fullname** are functors. The components of a structure are given in brackets.

A database can be built up from a collection of PROLOG facts and the questioning facility used to query the database and the matching mechanisms used to retrieve structured information.

An important structure in PROLOG is the list. It is defined using the special functor **.** as is shown in the following list representation, which is built from the four atoms **p**, **q**, **r** and **s**:

    .(p, .(q, .(r, .(s, [ ]))))

where [] represents the empty list. As lists are used so frequently in PROLOG, a special notation is available. The above list can be written as:

    [p, q, r, s]

As is the case in functional languages, a PROLOG list consists of a head, which may be any PROLOG object, in this case **p**, and a tail which must also be a list, in this case [q, r, s]. A list with the head X and the tail Y can be written as [X|Y], which allows pattern matching operations on lists in the same way as is done with the :: operator of Hope. PROLOG considers all structures to be binary trees and the list [p, q, r, s] is represented as the tree shown in Figure 10.1.

It should be noted that structures and facts have the same form. Each clause is an example of a structure. As in LISP, this allows programs to be manipulated as data.

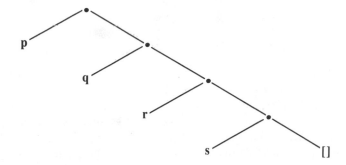

FIGURE 10.1
The structure of a list.

PROLOG can be used to support the ideas of data abstraction and information hiding by means of what are called **selector relations**. Such relations are used to access components of a structure as illustrated in the following example which selects the **forename** of a **student**. The selector **forename** can be defined by means of the clause:

> forename(student(fullname(Forename, Surname), Age), Forename).

although, as the definition of **forename** does not depend on the values of **Surname** and **Age**, this would normally be written as:

> forename(student(fullname(Forename, _), _), Forename).

where each occurrence of the underscore character represents a different (anonymous) variable. In PROLOG, the scope of a variable is restricted to the clause in which it is used. Hence, both occurrences of **Forename** refer to the same variable, but the identifier **Forename** has no significance outside this clause, and of course it has no connection with the functor **forename**. Conventional software engineering wisdom would suggest that it is inadvisable to use two identifiers that only differ in the case of their first letter. Such usage does, however, seem to be common practice in PROLOG.

The result of asking the question:

> ?– S1 = student(fullname(john, smith), 18), forename(S1, X).

will be:

> X = john

while the answer to:

> ?– attends(Person, stirling), forename(Person, mary).

is:

Person = student(fullname(mary, smith), 20)

This illustrates that once selectors such as **forename** have been defined, the user no longer needs to know about the structure of student. If, during the development of a program, the structure is changed, then all that is needed is a change to the definitions of selectors such as **forename**. Their use could continue unchanged. Hiding the representation of a structure in this way does, however, remove some of the advantages of pattern matching.

10.4   Efficiency in PROLOG

From a theoretical standpoint, all the user needs to know when using a PROLOG question clause is that it terminates. It is not too difficult for logic languages to attain this goal in theory, but if they wish to be considered seriously as practical programming languages, they must do more than guarantee termination – they must search reasonably efficiently.

When PROLOG is asked a question, a simple backtracking strategy is instituted which is normally **depth-first tree search** with subgoal evaluation from left to right. It is, therefore, of some importance to think about the order in which the goals are listed, as the ordering of the subgoals in a rule is likely to have a considerable bearing on its speed of execution. Such considerations are far from trivial and in complex search problems of the type likely to be encountered in an Expert System, the ordering and methods of searching are often the crux of the solution process.

Allowing automatic backtracking relieves the programmer of the problems of designing a detailed search algorithm. This is satisfactory in small problems or when the searching is not too deep. However, it soon becomes clear to a programmer that complete reliance on the PROLOG search mechanisms produces some very inefficient programs. Efforts have been made to try to improve this situation by allowing the programmer some control over the backtracking process by the **cut** facility. The cut operation, indicated in a PROLOG program by !, is used to stop backtracking. For example, consider the rules:

R :– G1, G2, !, G3.
R :– G4.

where **G1**, **G2**, **G3** and **G4** are goals and ! is a cut (or pseudo-goal). When the cut is encountered, **G1** and **G2** will have already been satisfied. The cut ensures that they are frozen in that state, since no further backtracking is allowed. If goal **G3** fails, PROLOG will not therefore try to achieve either **G1** or **G2** in some other way. Furthermore, it will not consider the other rule for **R**; that is, it will not try to achieve goal **G4**.

One example where cuts are useful is in rules that have mutually exclusive clauses. A function which is -1, 0, $+1$ when its argument is negative, zero or positive, respectively, can be expressed in Pascal as:

if $x < 0$ **then** $F := -1$
else if $x = 0$ **then** $F := 0$
else $F := +1$;

The PROLOG rules without cuts could be:

f(X, −1) :− X < 0.

f(X, 0) :− X = 0.

f(X, 1) :− X > 0.

but this could lead to unnecessary inefficiencies and backtracking due to the exclusive nature of the three clauses. A more efficient PROLOG implementation would be:

f(X, −1) :− X < 0, !.

f(X, 0) :− X = 0, !.

f(X, 1).

Here, the use of cuts prevents the program from trying alternatives that cannot succeed. Hence, if the condition **X < 0** is satisfied, neither of the alternatives will ever be tried.

The objection to cuts is that they can change the nature of a PROLOG program. Provided that it terminates, a PROLOG program without cuts has the same declarative and procedural meaning. As has been seen, the procedures may be slow, but they will arrive at the correct answer. When cuts are included, there is no longer a guarantee that the declarative and procedural meaning are the same. When the use of cuts does not affect the declarative meaning, they are called **green cuts**. In other words, if the cuts are removed the answers will be unchanged, and so the cuts are achieving improved efficiency without any disadvantages. Cuts that affect the declarative meaning are called **red cuts**. The use of these types of cuts is more dangerous and they can easily lead to errors since the program's meaning cannot be deduced from the program without cuts.

10.5   A PROLOG Example

Chapter 9 looked at LISP and LOGO programs that performed simple symbolic differentiation. This section looks at a PROLOG solution to this problem.

Suppose that an expression such as:

4 * power(x, 3)

is to be converted into 12 * power(x, 2) and:

power(x, 3)

is to be converted into 3 * power(x, 2). To differentiate an expression Y with respect to X giving the result E, the head of the rules will have the form derive(Y, X, E). A first attempt at the rules might be:

derive(A * F, X, A * C) :− integer(A), derive(F, X, C).
derive(power(X, N), X, N * power(X, N − 1)) :− integer(N).

where the goal integer(N) succeeds when N is instantiated to an integer number. The first rule defines the derivative of A * F with respect to X (where A is an integer) to be A times the derivative of F with respect to X. The second rule defines the derivative of power(X, N) with respect to X to be N * power(X, N − 1). These rules deal with the differentiation, but do not carry out the necessary arithmetic. Using these rules, the result of:

?− derive(4 * power(x, 3), x, E).

is:

E = 4 * (3 * power(x, 3 − 1))

Although arithmetic is not one of PROLOG's strong points, the necessary evaluation can be performed by means of the is operator. The effect of:

P is N − 1

is to evaluate the expression N − 1 and associate its value with P. The is operator is used in the following two modifications to the rules for derive:

derive(A * F, X, G * B) :− integer(A), derive(F, X, D * B), G is A * D.
derive(power(X, N), X, N * power(X, P)) :− integer(N), P is N − 1.

The required PROLOG program is therefore short, although its effect is not immediately obvious. Consider the matching process for the question:

?– derive(4 * power(x, 3), x, E).

The aim here is to match this with:

derive(A * F, X, G * B)

which means that after the substitutions:

A ← 4   F ← power(x, 3)   X ← x

the three subgoals to be achieved are:

integer(4),   derive(power(x, 3), x, D * B),   G is 4 * D

The first subgoal is achieved, but the second subgoal:

derive(power(x, 3), x, D * B)

does not match with the first rule for derive and so PROLOG tries to match it with the second:

derive(power(X, N), X, N * power(X, P))

On making the substitutions:

X ← x   N ← 3   D ← 3   B ← power(x, P)

the new subgoals are:

integer(3),   P is 3 − 1

The goals integer(3) and P is 2 are achieved. PROLOG has, therefore, succeeded in matching D * B to:

3 * power(x, 2)

The third of the original three subgoals is:

G is A * D

and so G is 12. E has, therefore, been matched with:

12 * power(x, 2)

The PROLOG program to solve this problem is much shorter than either the LISP or LOGO solution, which are in turn much shorter than a solution in an imperative language like Pascal. This is because much more of the processing is carried out behind the scenes by the PROLOG system.

10.6   The Future of PROLOG

Although PROLOG has been available for many years, it was only in the mid 1980s that large numbers of users started to use it for programming. Fortunately PROLOG is an attractive language and is not off putting to the beginner. However, the newcomer does face problems in trying to acquire a PROLOG programming style and technique.

The recent book by Bratko (1986) includes a chapter on the subject and suggests that clauses should be short with only a few goals in their body. The more general guidance in Bratko's book is not dissimilar from the advice on structuring a program that would be given to a new programmer using any language. PROLOG does support the implementation of top-down design principles with the subgoals acting as subdivisions of the tasks. Each subgoal can then be subdivided again if further refinements are required.

Case analysis can be implemented conveniently by alternative rules or clauses for the same predicate. Since there is no such thing as a global variable in PROLOG, the ideas of information hiding are easier to implement than in many imperative languages.

For many programmers, PROLOG often poses readability problems which is partly due to the fact that it can be highly recursive. Although recursion is a powerful and useful programming tool, it does not always aid the transparency of the code. Large PROLOG programs can also lack structure and indeed there is nothing in the language to match the module facilities of Modula-2 and Ada, which impose form and structure on the programmer. This seems an area where improvements are required.

Objections to PROLOG have mainly come from three types of programmer. Firstly, the users of imperative languages have attacked its inefficiences and claimed that it is unrealistic to consider PROLOG as a serious language for the practical programmer. They may be currently correct, but PROLOG needs time to develop. If its potential can be assessed, then some of the inefficiency caused by the von Neumann architecture of traditional computers could be removed by new hardware configurations.

The second group of objectors are the orthodox mathematicians and logicians who find that the use of cuts and negation take PROLOG away from the realm of a pure logic language. Their objection is valid, but misplaced, since programming languages are not pure mathematical objects, but practical tools for solving problems, and a pure logic language can never be that.

Finally, there have been a lot of objections to PROLOG from the artificial intelligence community. This is ironic because it is in AI that many of the most suitable applications for the language exist. The reason for such objections is probably due to the strong hold that languages like LISP have for AI practitioners. It does seem that in the last few years there have been serious attempts to look at both functional and logic languages objectively and examine their strengths and weaknesses. Such moves are welcome and will help to remove the attitude of mind that sees PROLOG and LISP as competitors. These two languages take different approaches to problem solving and should be viewed as alternatives rather than rivals.

SUMMARY

- Logic programming is almost exclusively carried out in PROLOG.

- PROLOG is a declarative language and is goal oriented.

- A program in PROLOG consists of clauses, which can be of three types: facts, rules and questions.

- Facts about objects are declared to be always true.

- A rule about objects and their relationships gives the goals and subgoals that must be satisfied to make the rule true.

- Questions require a goal or a series of goals to be satisfied and invoke a process of matching. If a goal fails, an alternative is tried by backtracking.

- The operations of selecting goals and backtracking are carried out by the PROLOG system itself. However, the efficiency of these operations can be influenced by the ordering of the subgoals in a rule.

- Recursion is an important feature of many PROLOG rules.

- Structured data objects in PROLOG have the same form as facts.

- PROLOG is well suited to applications involving database queries.

- Efficiency in PROLOG can be improved by cuts, which are used to limit backtracking.

- PROLOG uses the closed-world assumption and assumes that anything not derivable is false.

EXERCISES

10.1   Using the facts and rules given at the beginning of Section 10.2 for family relations:

   (a)   Explain in detail how the goals in the following PROLOG questions are achieved:

   ?– brother(william, harry).

   ?– brother(X, william).

   (b)   Define a rule for **sister** and show the steps in answering the questions:

   ?– sister(X, edward).

   ?– sister(X, william).

   (c)   How can the **brother** and **sister** rules be altered so that a person is not considered to be their own brother or sister?

10.2   Given the facts:

   loves(john, jane).
   loves(bill, jane).
   loves(james, jane).
   loves(mary, bill).
   loves(jane, james).

and the rule:

   goodmatch(X, Y) :– loves(X, Y), loves(Y, X).

show the backtracking involved in answering the question:

   ?– goodmatch(A, B).

10.3   Given the facts:

   district(stirling, dunblane).
   region(central, stirling).
   country(scotland, central).
   continent(europe, scotland).

define a rule whose head is **within**(X, Y) and which expresses the fact that Y is within the geographical region X. Show how this can be done using **district, region, country** and **continent**. How can the facts be redefined and recursion used to simplify the definition of **within**?

10.4 An object X is a member of a list L if X is the head of L or if X is a member of the tail of L. Use this definition of membership to define **member(X, L)** and then trace the actions required by the PROLOG question:

?— **member(X, [john, bill, fred, peter]), X = fred.**

10.5 Compare and contrast functional languages, logic languages and object-oriented languages as exemplified by LISP, PROLOG and Smalltalk, respectively. Discuss areas in which they each have particular strengths and weaknesses.

10.6 Give an example to show how the ordering of a PROLOG rule can make a significant difference in the efficiency of processing of a question.

10.7 Define the minimum function as a rule whose head is **minimum(X, Y, Minval)**. Give an initial definition without a cut and then show how its efficiency can be improved by using a cut.

10.8 Discuss the differences between green and red cuts and give an example of each.

10.9 Compare the use of pattern matching in Hope and PROLOG.

Bibliography

An introduction to the use of logic in problem solving has been given by Kowalski (1979), whose ideas were a major influence in the development of PROLOG. For many years, the only book on PROLOG was Clocksin (1984), although several user manuals were also available. Recently, several new books have appeared, one of the most interesting being that by Bratko (1986).

Implementation techniques for compiling PROLOG programs were studied by Warren (1977) and his ideas led to much more efficient PROLOG systems.

Bratko, I. (1986), *PROLOG: Programming for Artificial Intelligence*, Addison-Wesley.

Clocksin, W. F. and Mellish, C. S. (1984), *Programming in Prolog* (Second Edition), Springer-Verlag.

Kluzniak, F. and Szpakowicz, S. (1985), *Prolog for Programmers*, Academic Press.

Kowalski, R. (1979), *Logic for Problem Solving*, North Holland.

Warren, D. H. D. (1977), 'Implementing PROLOG: Compiling Predicate Logic Programs', *Dept. of Artificial Intelligence Reports* 39, 40 and 44, University of Edinburgh.

CHAPTER 11

Input and Output

This chapter looks at the Cinderella of language design – input and output (I/O) – and shows how the input and output of textual information is handled in several languages, including those such as C, Modula-2 and Ada where I/O is not really part of the language at all, but is handled by a set of predefined routines.

I/O routines must be able to deal with a wide range of different peripheral devices, but for reasons of simplicity, languages abstract away from the physical details of particular peripheral devices and deal with both input and ouput in terms of sequences of records. When the information is in human readable form, each record usually corresponds to a line of text. The problems that arise when interactive I/O is dealt with in the same way as accessing sequential files on disk are discussed.

Binary files and direct access files, where records may be written or read in any order, are then considered.

A robust program must be able to respond to input errors made by human operators. In languages like Pascal, this requires special numerical input routines to be written to replace the predefined ones. It is shown how, in Ada and PL/I, the exception mechanism can be used to handle this problem.

An alternative model of I/O, where the program and the user are considered as two concurrent interacting processes, is examined in the final section.

11.1 Introduction

The most effective way in which human users can interact with computers has only recently received a significant amount of attention with the advent of menu-driven systems, mouse input, multiple windows and icons. Such systems are often aimed at non-experts using a personal or business computer where the facilities are regarded as being part of the operating system or an application package, rather than being features of a high-level language. However, they are also a feature of the powerful workstations used by more specialized users and are of course central to the Smalltalk environment, from which many of the ideas originated. Fourth-generation languages also exploit the sophisticated facilities available on workstations and PCs.

In traditional languages, the commands for reading and writing human readable information deal in terms of lines of text and although human interaction now usually takes place at a terminal, PC or workstation, the language facilities have not changed much from the days when the standard devices were a card reader and a line printer.

Although information is usually presented to and received from a computer as lines of text, this is not how the information is held within the computer. Part of the reading process is, therefore, to convert information from an external human readable form (usually text) to a suitable internal representation. With integer data, for example, the external representation is a series of digit characters with a possible leading + or − sign. A command to read an integer will read such a character string and convert it into the computer's internal representation for integer numbers (for example, two's complement). Similarly, when results are output the internal representation has to be converted back into the appropriate character string.

Input and output devices (I/O devices) are much slower than the central processor. To prevent I/O instructions slowing down the operation of the whole computer, they are executed concurrently with processing by the CPU, and buffers are used to hold intermediate information. This process is normally handled by the operating system and is transparent to the programmer, the exception being when the language is to be used for systems programming. Even then, programmers do not need to get involved with low-level detail, unless they wish to, because systems programming languages usually have different levels of I/O instructions.

I/O instructions have to indicate the device to be used as well as the layout and type of the data or results. To avoid the necessity of having a different instruction for each new device, language designers have made an abstraction of the I/O process. In the original definition of FORTRAN, for example, it was assumed that input came from punched cards and output went to a line printer. These devices can be considered as delivering or receiving a series of fixed-length records with each record being regarded as a line of characters divided into fields. Similarly, information held in a file on backing store can be considered as a series of such records and so can be dealt with in the same way.

The abstraction used in Pascal is that all I/O, even when it involves a terminal, is considered to be 'to' or 'from' a sequential file; that is, a file in which the records may only be accessed in the order in which they were originally written. A Pascal program has two standard files, called *input* and *output*, which are attached to what are called the standard input and output devices; usually the keyboard and terminal screen. These logical file names are given in the program heading:

    program *example*(*input, output*);

and are of the predefined type *text*. A file of type *text* is a file of lines where each line consists of a series of characters terminated by an end-of-line indicator. A text file is not the same as a file of characters since the implementation of the end-of-line indicator depends on the particular operating system used, and some systems have no way of representing the end of a line within their character set. This abstraction of text I/O is more or less the same as that used in Ada, Modula-2 and C. Unlike FORTRAN, the lines are not of a fixed length in these languages.

Files are not only used for communication between different programs on the same computer, but for the transfer of information between computers with different operating systems. For the reasons just stated, this type of transfer can cause problems. However, it is usually possible to achieve the transfer of a file of records, where each record consists of a line of printable (non-control) characters. If the end-of-line indicator used in the transmitting system is known to the network, a series of records can be sent. On receipt of each record, the receiving system can insert its own end-of-line indicator.

File transfer is not within the realms of language design, but what is important is that a language's abstract model for files of text should fit the scenario described here. The next section looks at how sequential input and output of textual information is handled in FORTRAN, ALGOL, Pascal, Ada, Modula-2, C, PROLOG and LISP.

11.2   Input and Output of Text

FORTRAN

FORTRAN uses FORMAT statements to specify the layout of data and results, and channel numbers to specify their source or destination. The channel number corresponding to the standard input device depends on the operating system. Assuming that it is channel 5, the statement:

```
READ (5, 50) ITEM, NUMBER
```

causes two values to be read into the integer variables ITEM and NUMBER with a layout as specified by the FORMAT statement labelled 50. This could have the form:

```
50    FORMAT (I8, I7)
```

where the I8 indicates that an integer value is to be found in the first eight columns of the input record and the I7 that a second integer value is to be found in the next seven. Leading blanks are ignored, but trailing blanks are treated as zeros.

The command for writing information is similar. Hence:

```
      WRITE (6, 51) ITEM, NUMBER
51    FORMAT (' ANSWERS =', I9, I7)
```

causes a character string and two integer values to be written out on a new line on channel 6 with the layout specified by the FORMAT statement labelled 51. This format specifies that after ANSWERS =, the next nine columns should be used to contain an integer value (with leading blanks if required) and the next seven used for a second integer value. It has been assumed that channel 6 corresponds to the standard output device.

Format specifications are available to read and write integer, real, character, complex and logical values. The FORTRAN FORMAT statements make it relatively straightforward to print out tables of information although, as many different kinds of format specification are possible, novice programmers tend to make mistakes.

Reading in data in a fixed format was sensible when cards were the main input mechanism, but it is inconvenient when input occurs at a terminal. List-directed I/O was therefore introduced in FORTRAN 77. The statement:

```
READ (5, *) ITEM, NUMBER
```

will read from channel 5 two integer values into ITEM and NUMBER, respectively. These values must be separated by a comma or by spaces. No FORMAT statement is required.

Instructions to transfer information to and from sequential files of text have the same form as ordinary input and output instructions. However, it is also necessary to have a way of associating the physical file on backing store, usually disk, with the channel number used in the program. The statement:

```
OPEN (2, FILE = 'INFO', STATUS = 'OLD')
```

associates an existing (OLD) disk file called INFO with channel 2. Ordinary READ statements can then be used to read information on this channel. The statement:

```
OPEN (4, FILE = 'MOREINFO', STATUS = 'NEW')
```

creates a new file called MOREINFO which can then have information written to it on channel 4. The file associated with a channel may be closed by a command such as:

```
CLOSE(2)
```

after which another file may be connected to that channel or the original file may be connected to another channel.

ALGOL 60

FORTRAN I/O is simple and powerful and machine dependence is limited to the channel numbers. One of the aims of the designers of ALGOL 60 was to produce a language that was machine independent, and as I/O requires interaction with the operating system, it was completely ignored in the design of the language. This had exactly the opposite effect to that intended. Since read and write instructions are essential each implementor of ALGOL 60 devised a different mechanism with the result that ALGOL 60 programs are less portable than FORTRAN ones.

Pascal

To write a character string, followed by the values of the integer variables *item* and *number*, to the standard output device in Pascal, the following statement is used:

write(' ANSWERS =', *item*, *number*)

which is shorthand for:

write(*output*, ' ANSWERS =', *item*, *number*)

There are no FORMAT statements in Pascal and the default layout is implementation dependent, although the number of columns to be used in writing a value can be specified, as in:

   write(' ANSWERS =', *item* : 9, *number* : 7)

which will give the same layout as the FORTRAN WRITE statement given earlier.

Unlike FORTRAN, where each new WRITE statement causes information to be written on a new line, values are written on the current line in Pascal. To output an end-of-line indicator, *writeln* is used. The statements:

   write(*item*); *write*(*number*)

will cause two values to be written on the current line while:

   writeln(*item*); *write*(*number*)

will cause the first value to be written on the current line and the other on the next line. The end-of-line indicator can only be written using *writeln*.

To read two values, the statement is:

   read(*item*, *number*)

which is shorthand for:

   read(*input*, *item*, *number*)

The statement:

   readln(*item*, *number*)

will read two values and then skip all the remaining characters in the line up to and including the end-of-line indicator. When reading data, it is possible to find out if the current position is at the end of a line by using the predefined Boolean function *eoln*. The end-of-line indicator itself is read as the space character.

Associated with a file *x* is the file buffer variable *x*↑. The standard file buffer variables *input*↑ and *output*↑ are of type *char*. The *read* and *write* statements can be defined in terms of the more fundamental I/O statements *get* and *put*. If *ch* is a character variable, the effect of *read*(*ch*) is defined as:

   ch := *input*↑ ; *get*(*input*)

which sets *ch* equal to the current value of the file buffer variable *input* ↑ and then uses *get* to read the next character into *input* ↑ . The effect of *write*(*ch*) is defined as:

output ↑ := *ch*; *put*(*output*)

The value of *ch* is assigned to *output* ↑ and *put* is then used to add the value of *output* ↑ to the end-of-file *output*. After a call of *put*(*output*), the value of *output* ↑ is undefined.

As, after a call of *read* or *readln*, the file buffer variable contains the next character to be read, problems can arise with interactive I/O. A statement such as *readln*(*item*) reads the value of *item*, skips the rest of the characters on the line, including the end-of-line indicator, and then inputs the first character on the next line into *input* ↑ . In interactive input, this character may not yet have been typed in and so cannot be read. In early implementations of Pascal, this caused programs to hang up at unexpected times, waiting for input. Most recent implementations of Pascal solve this problem by using what is called **lazy I/O**, where the reading of the next character into the file buffer variable is delayed until it is required.

Interactive I/O is the only place in the semantics of a sequential language like Pascal that two parallel processors must be considered; namely, the computer and the human user. If problems are to be avoided, their synchronization must be explicitly considered in the language design. Unfortunately, this does not happen. I/O is usually the last feature to be considered and it often seems that interactive I/O is not given any special consideration at all.

Items of type *char*, *integer*, *real*, *Boolean* and packed arrays of *char* may be written in Pascal, but *Boolean* values may not be read and strings have to be read in as a series of individual characters.

To read or write information to disk, logical file names must be listed in the program heading along with *input* and *output* and their type given in a declaration:

program *example*(*input*, *output*, *oldfile*, *newfile*);
...
var *oldfile*, *newfile* : *text*;
...

As has been seen, *input* and *output* are automatically associated with the standard input and output devices. The way in which other logical file names are associated with physical files on backing store is up to the operating system. This association is fixed and cannot be changed during program execution, for there is no equivalent in standard Pascal of the *open* and *close* procedures found in many other languages.

To open the file associated with *oldfile* for reading, the command is:

reset(*oldfile*)

and to open the file associated with *newfile* for writing, the command is:

rewrite(*newfile*)

read and *write* statements are then used in the same way as with the standard input and output files; for example:

read(*oldfile*, *item*); *write*(*newfile*, *item*)

When reading a file, it is possible to determine if the end has been reached through the value of the Boolean function *eof*.

Although there is no instruction to close a file in standard Pascal, if *reset* or *rewrite* is applied to an open file, the file is first closed and then opened for reading or writing, respectively.

Ada and Modula-2

I/O in Ada is provided by a hierarchy of predefined packages called *low_level_io*, *direct_io*, *sequential_io* and *text_io*. All validated Ada systems must provide an implementation of these packages, as specified in the Ada Reference Manual.

Modula-2 also provides I/O through a hierarchy of modules, although it differs from Ada in that the module contents are only recommended and are not mandatory. The problem of non-standard implementations and the resulting difficulties in program portability therefore arise, and could be a major obstacle to the acceptance of Modula-2. As the current recommendations correspond to a simplified and incomplete version of Ada I/O, they will not be considered further.

High-level text I/O in Ada is provided by the package *text_io*, which provides facilities at a similar level to Pascal I/O. This package defines procedures called *get* and *put* to read and write characters or strings. The *get* and *put* routines to read and write integers, fixed-point numbers, reals and enumerated types are declared in the local generic packages *integer_io*, *fixed_io*, *float_io* and *enumeration_io*, which are declared within package *text_io*. However, these packages must be instantiated before such I/O can take place. (The instantiation of generic packages was looked at in Section

7.6.) For example, to be able to read and write integers, the following must be written:

```
with text_io; use text_io;
procedure example is
    ...
    package int_io is new integer_io(integer);
    use int_io;
    ...
```

Calls of *get* and *put* to read and write character, string and integer values may now be made in procedure *example*. As Ada allows procedures and functions to be overloaded, the type of the parameter determines which version of *get* or *put* is required. The drawback of this approach is that generic instantiation has to be introduced at the beginning of an Ada course.

A difference between Pascal and Ada is that the Ada I/O routines all follow the ordinary Ada rules for procedures and functions, while Pascal I/O routines only look like ordinary subprograms and can have a variable number of parameters of differing types.

As with Pascal, Ada lines are terminated by an end-of-line indicator, which can only be written by calls of procedures such as *new_line*. The Ada function corresponding to the Pascal *eoln* function is *end_of_line*. In addition, in Ada, lines are grouped into pages. End-of-page indicators are written by calls of *new_page* and are recognized by calls of the Boolean function *end_of_page*.

In Ada, logical file names are declared to be of type *file_type*; for example:

```
old_file, new_file : file_type;
```

Ada files may have the mode *in_file* or *out_file* where type *file_mode* has been declared in *text_io* as:

```
type file_mode is (in_file, out_file);
```

The procedure call:

```
open(old_file, in_file, info);
```

will cause the logical file called *old_file* to be associated with the backing store file whose name is held in the string variable *info* and for that file to be opened for reading. The call:

```
create(new_file, out_file, new_info);
```

will create a new file with the name that is held in the string variable *new_info*. It will then associate that file with the logical file *new_file* so that it can be written to.

As a value can be read into a string variable, the association between logical and physical files can be set up and changed during program execution. In Pascal, on the other hand, all such associations must be set up before execution begins.

Overloaded versions of *get* and *put* are used for file I/O in Ada; for example:

get(*old_file*, *item*); *put*(*new_file*, *item*);

To close the file associated with *new_file*, the command is *close*(*new_file*) and to delete it, the command is *delete*(*new_file*). Files should be explicitly closed before a program is terminated. Many other procedures and functions are available in Ada to manipulate files and to control the layout of data or results. Another difference between Pascal and Ada is that in Ada it is possible to read and write the values of an enumerated type (by instantiating the generic package *enumeration_io* for a particular enumeration type) and to read strings as a single unit as well as write them.

The C language

The definition of the C language does not deal with input and output, but in most implementations high-level I/O is provided by a standard library called *stdio*. To ensure that certain necessary definitions are available, programs using this library should start with:

#include <stdio.h>

To control layout a FORTRAN-like format specification is incorporated within the print statement. Hence:

printf(" ANSWERS =%9d%7d", *item*, *number*);

causes ANSWERS = to be output followed by the value of *item* in the next nine columns and the value of *number* in the following seven. The format %d indicates that an integer number is to be printed. Other formats are also possible, such as %s for string, %c for character and %f for floating-point number.

Input is provided by the *scanf* routine, as in:

scanf("%d%d", &*item*, &*number*);

Instead of having a special end-of-line indicator, lines are terminated by an ordinary character, which is represented in programs as \n. Being at the end of a line is determined by testing for this character.

Logical file names are declared to be pointers to type FILE, as in:

FILE *oldfile, *newfile*;

To associate the logical file called *oldfile* with the backing store file whose name is held in the string variable *info* and to open the file for reading, the call is:

oldfile = *fopen*(*info*, "r");

while to create a new file with the name held in the string variable *newinfo* so it can be written to, the call is:

newfile = *fopen*(*newinfo*, "w");

If a file cannot be opened, the null pointer is returned. Pointers to three standard files (*stdin*, *stdout* and *stderr*) are declared in <*stdio.h*>. These are associated with the standard input, standard output and standard error output files. To close a file such as *newfile*, the command is *fclose*(*newfile*). To read and write files, *fscanf* and *fprintf* are used, as in:

fscanf(*oldfile*, "%d", &*item*); *fprintf*(*newfile*, "%d", *item*);

At a slightly lower level, characters can be read and written by calls of *fgetc* and *fputc*, as in:

ch = *fgetc*(*oldfile*); *fputc*(*ch*, *newfile*);

The function *fgetc* actually returns an integer value, but this can usually be treated as a character. The exception to this is when the end of file is encountered; then, the integer constant EOF is returned. The value of EOF is defined in <*stdio.h*> and is implementation dependent.

As with the other languages discussed, I/O is buffered in C. It is often necessary to be able to 'peek' ahead at the character following the item currently being read. Pascal uses the file buffer variable for this while in C it is possible to read a character as normal and then, after examining it, to put it back by means of the *ungetc* function! The next call of *fgetc* will then read the character that was put back.

PROLOG and LISP

PROLOG and LISP are normally used interactively. A PROLOG session often consists of a series of questions to which the system is required to respond. Similarly, a LISP session consists of a series of function definitions and expressions which are to be evaluated. The LISP system responds to a request to evaluate an expression by printing the result. More conventional I/O is, however, possible in both of these languages.

In PROLOG, as in Pascal, the user's keyboard and screen are treated as sequential files. Only one input and one output file are active at any one moment and at the beginning of a PROLOG session these are the user's keyboard and screen. To change the current input file to file **oldfile**, the following clause is used:

> **see(oldfile)**

while to change the output file to file **newfile**, the following clause is used:

> **tell(newfile)**

These goals succeed when it is possible to open the relevant file, otherwise they fail. To return to the standard input file, the goal **see(user)** is attempted; to return to the standard output file, the goal **tell(user)** is tried.

The effect of **read(X)** in PROLOG is to read a value (terminated by a full stop) from the current input file and attempt to match it with the variable **X**. Similarly, **write(X)** will write out the value of **X**. There is no restriction on the complexity of the data object associated with **X**. Input and output in PROLOG is, therefore, relatively simple, the main aim being to read and write values for the data objects that are manipulated by the PROLOG program. There is automatic translation between the internal representation and some suitable external form.

LISP systems have functions READ and PRINT which achieve their effect by side effects. Like PROLOG, the values input or output are the basic data objects of the system, which in the case of LISP are S-expressions. Input from or output to a file is achieved by calls to predefined functions and these differ from one implementation to the next.

Thus, the I/O facilities of LISP and PROLOG are aimed at supporting the interactive environment in which they are usually used, rather than supporting sophisticated file handling facilities.

Scanning strings

From a programmer's point of view, reading a line of text and converting it into some internal representation is not too different from scanning a string of characters. Hence, C and Ada have routines, analogous to their I/O routines, for converting strings of, for example, digits into the internal representation of a number. If *str* is the string "34 42 -181 853", the effect of:

>   *get*(*str*, *item*, *pos*);

in Ada is analogous to:

>   *get*(*old_file*, *item*);

when 34 is the next string of characters in the file associated with *old_file*. The variable *pos* is set equal to the position in the string *str* of the last character read so that, by using array slices, the next item from the string can be read. The effect of executing the code segment:

```
pos := 0;
for count in 1 .. 4 loop
   get(str(pos + 1 .. str'length), item, pos);
   put(item);
end loop;
```

is to write out the four numerical values which were in the string *str*. The value of *pos* will be in turn 2, 5, 10 and 14. *str'length* is an array attribute that has as its value the length of the string *str*.

It can at times be useful to read a complete line of numerical data into a string before extracting its contents. By doing this, it is possible to build in an error recovery routine if an input error is detected.

11.3   Binary and Direct Access Files

Binary files

Up till now, the discussion on I/O has concentrated on text files. However, when a file is created by one program, so that it can be read by another, there is no need for conversion between some internal representation and a human readable external form.

In Pascal, instead of declaring a file to be of type *text*, it can be declared to be a file of, for example, *integer*:

>   **var** *old* : **file of** *integer*;

The exact way in which the integers are represented in the file is implementation dependent, although the probability is that they will be in binary; that is, in the same form as their internal representation. All that can be guaranteed here is that a file written by a Pascal program on a particular system as a file of *integer* can be read as a file of *integer* by another Pascal program on the same system.

A file can be considered to consist of a series of records where each record consists of a series of fields. This structure can be represented in Pascal by declaring a record type with the appropriate field structure. Assuming a record type *recorditem*, file variables can then be declared as:

> **var** *datafile*, *resultfile* : **file of** *recorditem*;

If the variable *thisrecord* has been declared to be of type *recorditem*, the following loop will cause the contents of file *datafile* to be copied to file *resultfile*:

```
reset(datafile); rewrite(resultfile);
while not eof(datafile) do
begin
  read(datafile, thisrecord);
  write(resultfile, thisrecord);
end;
```

Each call of *read* reads the contents of the next complete record in file *datafile* into the record variable *thisrecord*, while each call of *write* outputs the contents of a complete record.

In FORTRAN, binary files are said to be UNFORMATTED. A binary file called BIN can be associated to channel 2 and opened for reading by:

```
OPEN(2, FILE = 'BIN', STATUS = 'OLD', FORM ='UNFORMATTED')
```

READ and WRITE statements are declared as before except that no format number need be given, as in:

```
READ (2) ITEM, NUMBER
```

In Ada, the generic package *sequential_io* contains the definition of I/O for sequential files. To deal with a sequential file of items of the record type *recorditem*, this package has to be instantiated as:

> **package** *seq_int_io* **is new** *sequential_io(recorditem)*;

The package contains definitions of file management procedures such as *open*, *create* and *delete* similar to those declared in *text_io*. One difference is that reading and writing is done by calls to *read* and *write* instead of *get* and *put*.

Direct access files

As well as having sequential files, many languages support direct access files where items may be read or written in any order. Thus, there must be some means of indicating which position in the file is being referred to.

Such facilities are available in FORTRAN 77, C and Ada, but not in Pascal.

To illustrate how direct access is handled, consider the facilities available in the Ada generic package *direct_io*. This is very similar to *sequential_io* except that as well as having procedures *read* and *write* with the specification:

> **procedure** *read*(*file* : **in** *file_type*; *item* : **out** *element_type*);
>
> **procedure** *write*(*file* : **in** *file_type*; *item* : **in** *element_type*);

which transfer an item to or from the current position in a file, it also has:

> **procedure** *read*(*file* : **in** *file_type*; *item* **out** *element_type*;
>   *from* : *positive_count*);
>
> **procedure** *write*(*file* : **in** *file_type*; *item* **in** *element_type*;
>   *to* : *positive_count*);

in which the position of the item can be specified. The subtype *positive_count* is an implementation-defined integer subrange.

This package also has a file of mode *inout_file* as well as *in_file* and *out_file*, which allows the contents of a file to be updated while it is still open for reading.

11.4   Errors on Input

As users of computer systems often make mistakes when typing in data, robust programs must be able to respond to such errors in a sensible way and not immediately crash. If, in Pascal, for example, a letter is typed in response to a request for a numerical value, then the program will be terminated with control being passed to the operating system. If a programmer wishes control to remain within the program, then he or she must define special procedures to read the group of characters from which the numerical value is to be constructed character by character. The programmer can then program in the appropriate action which is to be taken when an unacceptable character is encountered. This approach is far from satisfactory in a high-level language.

In Ada, the exception mechanism can handle such errors. If a letter is typed in response to *get(x)* when a number is expected, a *data_error* exception is raised. Control is then passed to the appropriate exception handler where remedial action can take place, as in:

```
loop
  begin
    get(x);
    exit;
  exception
    when data_error =>
      skip_line;
      put_line("Error in number, try again");
  end;
end loop;
```

If an error is detected on reading x, the exception handler causes all the remaining characters on the current line to be skipped and then gives a new prompt. The loop then allows a second attempt to be made to read x.

Other I/O errors that can cause exceptions to be raised include trying to open files that are already open or trying to close, read from or write to files that are not open. These errors all raise *status_error* exceptions. If an attempt is made to read past the end of a file, an *end_error* exception is raised.

The ON-condition facility in PL/I allows similar control of I/O errors.

11.5 Concluding Remarks

This chapter has shown how several languages handle I/O and how, in general, I/O is not a central part of the language, but is implemented by means of a series of predefined subprograms. In languages like Pascal, these subprograms allow a variable number of parameters of varying types and so do not follow the usual language rules for subprograms. In more recent languages such as Ada and Modula-2, modules are used to encapsulate the subprograms that implement I/O, but the general approach remains the same. This leads to the question of whether there is a simple conceptual model that would allow I/O to be brought into the mainstream of language design.

One novel approach has been receiving attention. In a concurrent system, sequential processes can communicate with one another by passing messages. The output of information to, or input of information from, a peripheral device has a marked similarity with a process passing information to, or receiving information from, another process. This similarity underlies the approach taken in inter-process communication in the language CSP and implemented in occam. The command:

keyboard ? ch

means read a value from a keyboard and assign it to the variable ch. The command:

vduscreen ! ch

means send the value of the variable ch to a VDU screen. It is assumed here that keyboard and vduscreen are peripheral devices. However, they could equally well have been the names of processes, and in that case the form of the CSP command would have been the same.

The identification of I/O with inter-process communication is useful at the implementation level, since a process controlled by the CPU really is operating concurrently with a peripheral device. It is also useful when thinking about the effect of a user program. In interactive I/O, for example, the two communicating sequential processes can be considered to be the program and the activities of a human being sitting at a terminal. Furthermore, if a user is to take part in a dialogue at a terminal, then this requires that input and output are not independent of one another, but are synchronized.

Although Ada adopted the CSP model as the basis for task communication and synchronization it, unlike occam, uses the conventional approach to I/O. There is, however, no reason why an alternative set of I/O packages could not be defined to make explicit use of tasking. It would in fact be interesting to see if such an approach resulted in an improved way of defining interactive I/O.

When dealing with I/O, it is often unclear where language issues end and the operating system begins. This is especially true with C due to its intimate connection with the UNIX operating system. To illustrate the situation in C, suppose that the program *first* outputs results to a terminal while the program *second* inputs data from a terminal. Program *first* can be made to output its results to a file called *intermediate* by 'redirecting' the output by means of the UNIX command line:

first > *intermediate*

Similarly, *second* can be made to read its input from the file *intermediate*, instead of from a terminal, by means of the command line:

second < *intermediate*

Neither of these commands would change the C program in any way.

To make the two programs communicate with one another without having to specify an intermediate file, a UNIX **pipe** is used. The command line is:

first | second

The output from *first* is taken as the input to *second*. The same mechanism is, therefore, used in UNIX for I/O and for the communication between two independent processes.

SUMMARY

- After information in human readable form has been input into a computer, it must be converted into a suitable internal representation. Conversion in the opposite direction is required on output.

- FORTRAN uses FORMAT statements to specify the layout of data and channel numbers to specify the peripheral device. Pascal has no FORMAT statements and uses symbolic names to specify the peripheral device. C uses FORTRAN-like format specifications but, unlike FORTRAN, they are incorporated into the appropriate I/O routine.

- In Pascal, all I/O, including interactive I/O, is considered to be 'to' or 'from' a sequential file. A Pascal text file is a file of lines. This approach has been followed in Ada and in Modula-2.

- In standard Pascal, the association between logical file names and particular physical files cannot be changed during program execution. This is in contrast to many other languages which have explicit open and close instructions.

- I/O in Ada is provided by a hierarchy of predefined packages called *low_level_io*, *direct_io*, *sequential_io* and *text_io*. *text_io* is for human readable text, *sequential_io* for binary files, *direct_io* for direct access files while *low_level_io* allows direct control of peripheral devices.

- The exception-handling mechanism of Ada allows the programmer to catch input errors that might otherwise lead to program termination.

EXERCISES

11.1 Compare the relative ease of presenting the results of executing a program as a table in Pascal and FORTRAN.

11.2 What I/O instructions would have to be added to Pascal so that it could be used as a systems programming language?

11.3 Languages like FORTRAN have special I/O instructions while later languages use predefined procedures and functions to handle I/O. Which approach is to be preferred and why?

11.4 Many languages treat all I/O as if it were 'to' or 'from' a sequential file. What difficulties does this cause with interactive I/O?

11.5 Should languages like Pascal and Ada have features that directly support menus, icons and the movement of turtles about a VDU screen? Pascal systems on microcomputers often have enhanced screen handling facilities. Collect as much information as you can on existing systems, compare their facilities and design a suitable set of machine-independent routines.

Bibliography

Input and output in the various languages is described in the language texts listed at the end of this book. The text on C by Kernighan (1978) also describes the interface between C and UNIX. CSP was introduced by Hoare (1978).

Hoare, C. A. R. (1978), 'Communicating Sequential Processes', *Comm. ACM*, **21**, pp. 666–677.

Kernighan, B. W. and Ritchie, D. M. (1978), *The C Programming Language*, Prentice-Hall.

CHAPTER 12

The Future

The first part of this chapter looks at the development of programming languages through the 1980s and into the 1990s. Speculation beyond this point is probably too unreliable to be useful to current computer users.

The second part of the chapter then looks at language design in general and examines how it is likely to develop. Particular attention is paid to those features that support the production of reliable programs such as the need for language structures that make it easier to reason about a program's effect and the move towards declarative languages where more of the details are handled by the system rather than by the programmer.

12.1   Imperative Languages

Current imperative languages can be divided into three categories. The old languages (FORTRAN and COBOL) which were developed in the 1950s and early 1960s but which are still in use in a revised form; the middle-aged languages (Pascal, BASIC and C) which were developed in the 1960s and early 1970s and which are still going strong; and, finally, the new languages (Modula-2 and Ada) whose share of the market is likely to grow.

Old imperative languages

Given the far-reaching changes that have occurred in both hardware and software design, it is surprising to find that 30 years on the old war horses, FORTRAN and COBOL, still hold a sizeable share of the scientific and business programming markets, respectively. As was stated at the beginning of this book, there is a great deal of inertia in the computing world and so once a language has been accepted and a large body of algorithms, systems and programs developed, it is difficult (if not impossible) to replace it. Certainly, FORTRAN and COBOL will continue to be used in the foreseeable future, although the attitude of most programmers is one of acceptance of them with all their warts, rather than true love. Newer versions (for example, FORTRAN 8X replacing FORTRAN 77) will no doubt continue to emerge but few people believe that such updates will produce more than a temporary life extension for these languages since it is the basic structure that needs to be replaced.

Middle-aged imperative languages

The languages Pascal, BASIC and C are likely to extend their useful lives well into the 1990s, but for quite different reasons.

Pascal was developed as a language for teaching good programming practice and after a somewhat slow start, it convinced a fair body of opinion of its ability to do just that. Hence, at most universities it is the first language taught to students and this is almost invariably so for those taking specialist computing degrees. As Pascal is backed up by efficient compilers for the majority of computers, its role in this area is hardly being challenged. Indeed, the major new imperative languages, Modula-2 and Ada, are Pascal based. Hence, Pascal is an excellent first language if it is intended to move on to Modula-2 or Ada.

BASIC's surprising success in the 1970s was due to its simplicity and the fact that it contained sufficient operating system features for it to be self-contained. Such features enabled BASIC to take full advantage of the opportunities in the small computer market. However, its hold on the microcomputer market is not likely to be as long lasting as that of FORTRAN and COBOL in their areas. One reason for this is that the small computer market does not have the same strong inertia factor for systems written in BASIC. When users move from small computers, they do not normally insist on a large body of algorithms, systems and programs moving with them. Another factor is that with the reduction in hardware costs, the power and size of microcomputers has increased substantially. In the early 1980s, micros typically had main memory sizes of 16, 32 or 64 kbytes while in the latter half of the 1980s main memory sizes of one or more megabytes have become commonplace. This change has meant that micros are now capable of handling more sophisticated languages than BASIC and so has given other languages a chance to challenge BASIC in the small computer market.

Thus, at one end, there is an erosion as more users prefer the precision and structure of Pascal, a trend that has been helped by the development of Pascal extensions, such as Turbo Pascal, which are designed specifically for use on microcomputers. At the other end, there have been several attempts to produce languages simpler than BASIC, usually at a higher level and for specific applications.

C is a difficult language to assess as it has serious deficiencies, particularly in the area of typing and abstract data structures. However, systems programmers, particularly those using the UNIX operating system, find it a most attractive language, and some of its deficiencies are dealt with in extensions such as C++. In the United States, its impact in the systems area has been considerable and, although not quite as widely used in the UK, it still is an important systems language. The looser typing of C tends to go against modern trends but no doubt this has a lot of appeal to the professional systems programmer who feels that he or she can use the flexibility and is sufficiently experienced to cope with the disadvantages. A major factor in the rise of C is that it is the host language for UNIX; how pervasive this operating system will become is a matter for speculation but its rise has enhanced that of C.

Newer imperative languages

Ada and Modula-2 seem the most likely heirs to the imperative language empire. Of these two languages, Ada is an obvious candidate since it underwent a rigorous selection procedure at birth and has the backing of the US Department of Defense (DOD). Doubts about Ada mainly stem from its large size and, while appreciating that complex problems may well need more than a simple language, it still worries many computer scientists that Ada could well encounter the size and complexity problems that beset PL/I.

It is perhaps unfair to associate Ada with the problems of PL/I, particularly as the design of Ada was dealt with in a much more effective and professional manner. Ada compilers are, however, large and expensive and require substantial computing power due to the size and complexity of the language. In addition, the widespread adoption of the language is not helped by the inflexibility of the DOD in not allowing any subsets. A sensible approach to this problem would be to have a small teaching subset of Ada – in essence, the part of Ada that is similar to Pascal with the addition of packages. Other useful subsets could also be evolved, but at present official policy is to ban all subsets of Ada.

The other new imperative language that is gaining in popularity is Modula-2. As Modula-2 does not have the complexity of Ada, the compiler difficulties are much less serious. Of course, Modula-2 has no large backing organization like the DOD, and this has its drawbacks, but it also allows experimentation and an ability to take opportunities when they arise. There are, however, reservations amongst programmers as to whether Modula-2 has the right features to make a significant impact in the embedded systems and concurrency areas.

12.2   Fourth-Generation Languages

The so-called fourth-generation languages (4GLs) have not been discussed in any depth in this book, a detail that will no doubt confirm James Martin's view that academics have not realized the true importance of these languages. It is indeed the case that universities have done little to advance the cause of 4GLs, but their reasons are not just ignorance and prejudice. Although 4GLs cover a wide range of programming activity, their most obvious area of application is in the business programming area; they are, in effect, attempts to produce a higher level COBOL. Perhaps what is required is for the business programming fraternity to sit down together and design one 4GL for their field of computing. So far, however, this has not happened and the net result is a whole mass of 4GLs, each purporting to do everything that one could possibly wish for. Alas, the reality is that while these languages have some strong high-level features, they are incomplete and never comprehensive. It seems that manufacturers, in an attempt to catch the market, produce them too quickly and before they are wholly and consistently specified. Nevertheless, the fact that the current incomplete and often ill-designed 4GLs are making a considerable impact in the market place suggests that there is indeed a need for a high-level business-oriented language – this is hardly surprising since COBOL was a product of the late 1950s and computers have advanced considerably since then. Perhaps what is needed is a development on the business side similar to the development of Ada. However, there is no sign of such a move and so the probable outcome will be the emergence of the best of the current business-oriented 4GLs.

12.3   Declarative Languages

The main declarative languages are the functional subset of LISP, the newer functional languages such as Hope and ML and the logic language PROLOG. It is clear that the supremacy of imperative languages is being seriously challenged by declarative languages, although both functional and logic languages are at a considerable disadvantage when they are used on current computer architectures. Furthermore, although they have shown their ability to specify problems, particularly in artificial intelligence, they have revealed a major weakness when attempts have been made to use them on large problems.

There are two approaches to these difficulties. The first is to use the declarative language to specify the problem and then convert the specification, perhaps automatically, to an imperative language for running on the computer. A more fundamental approach is to seek alternative architectures that support concurrent activities and thus build computers more attuned to declarative languages. This latter approach is the basis of the Japanese Fifth Generation initiative and it will be some time before the success or otherwise of this idea can be evaluated.

For a long time, functional languages and PROLOG were seen as competitors, and this may have been partly due to the fact that they both arose in artificial intelligence research activities. A fair amount of wasted effort and energy went into attempts to prove that the functional approach was superior to the logic method and vice versa. However, these efforts did help to identify the strengths and weaknesses of each language and have led to more constructive research aimed at finding a compromise based on the strong points of each. This is a welcome development and could perhaps be taken further by adding some of the better features of more modern imperative languages to declarative languages. As was seen in Chapter 9, progress in providing structure in functional languages has already been achieved in languages like Hope. Similar extensions to PROLOG would be of great interest.

12.4   Language Design

The aim of this section is to look at language design in general to see if any conclusions can be made about the features that are central to the design of a modern language. To some extent, this will of course depend on what the language is to be used for, but it should be possible to identify common goals.

A principal aim of a programming language should be to support the development of reliable programs. This means that it should be a help to the designer or programmer during the development process and should lead to programs that are straightforward to read and understand. It is, of course, possible to write obscure programs in any language, but there can be no doubt that the development of techniques such as programming by stepwise refinement, coupled with the introduction of languages such as Pascal that support the systematic development of programs, has led to an improvement in programming standards.

What then are the features that support the production of reliable programs? One approach is to use high-level constructs where the programmer states 'what' is to be done rather than 'how' it is to be achieved. By removing such details, the opportunity for error is reduced. Short high-level programs are generally easier to read, write and understand than long low-level programs. This factor has led to the great interest in functional and logic languages, but unless radically new computer hardware is developed, it seems likely that imperative languages will remain dominant for the foreseeable future.

Reliable programs should be straightforward to read and understand. Ideally, a language should contain a minimum number of independent concepts that can be combined according to simple rules. As there will then be few, if any, special cases to be considered, such a language should be simple. Unfortunately, the combination of independent concepts in all possible ways usually leads to certain features that are of dubious value and which are difficult and expensive to implement, as was found with ALGOL 68. An example of such a feature is arrays of procedures.

In certain cases, the introduction of restrictions on how features may be combined can actually increase the simplicity of a language. After all, a feature of high-level languages is that they do restrict usage, examples being strong typing, restrictions on the arbitrary transfers of control and on performing arithmetic on addresses.

A programming language's design must, therefore, exhibit a proper sense of balance. On the one hand, it is important to have a small set of concepts that can be combined, since this leads to a set of regular rules that can be learned and used much more easily than a set of *ad hoc* rules. On the other hand, it is important to have a small set of restrictions that outlaw those constructs that few, if any, people would ever want to use.

Another important feature of language design is that there should be no surprises. Features that are similar should look similar; for example, procedure and function declarations should have the same structure. Conversely, features that are different should look different so that similarities are not sought where none exist; for example, the notation used in Pascal to indicate a file buffer variable (*filename* ↑) is the same as that used with pointers and students are often misled into pushing the analogy further than is useful.

Reliability is greatly enhanced if most errors can be detected by a static scan of the program text rather than having to wait till program execution. This suggests the need for strong typing so that certain logical errors, which would otherwise lie dormant until run time, show up during program translation.

It is also important that a simple typing mistake should cause a syntax error rather than leading to a program which, although logically wrong, is syntactically correct. The classic example of this is the FORTRAN statement:

```
DO 20 I = 1.6
```

where a decimal point has mistakenly been typed instead of a comma. Thus, the statement, instead of describing the beginning of a loop, represents an assignment statement where 1.6 is assigned to the variable DO20I. Errors of this nature cannot occur when spaces are significant in the program text and when all identifiers are declared before being used, rather than being implicitly declared by their first use.

Security is also enhanced by the introduction of redundant reserved words so that errors can be detected as soon as they occur. For example, in the Pascal statement:

if $a > 2$ **then** $b := 47$

the reserved word **then** is not strictly necessary. In a statement such as:

if $a > 2$ $b := 47$

it is always possible to tell when the end of the Boolean expression has been reached. The appearance of **then** is not therefore necessary, but it does help readability.

If a language is to be used in the development of reliable large programs, it is essential that it contains some mechanism to support modular decomposition. In general, this is achieved by programs being organized into a collection of modules. Each module is then divided into two parts: a visible part that defines its interface with other modules and an implementation part that is hidden. Such modules are included in languages as diverse as Ada and Hope, and their main purpose is information hiding. If a user of a module cannot see, and therefore cannot use, the information in the implementation part then, provided that it has no effect on the module interface, a change in the implementation part cannot have an effect outside the module. The consequences of change are therefore localized and this is essential if reliability is to be maintained when a large system is modified.

12.5   Implementation Considerations

This book has not been concerned with language grammars, but as stated in Chapter 1 the syntax of modern programming languages are formally and unambiguously defined by meta-languages, such as Backus-Naur Form (BNF), or graphically by means of syntax diagrams. Having a language syntax defined in this way leads to a regular language structure. Modern compilers directly use a language's syntax rules to translate a source program into machine code. It is therefore important that the syntax can be defined in such a way that it can be easily handled using conventional compiler techniques. This really means that the language should be defined by either an LL(1) or an LR(1) grammar. Such languages are always unambiguous and can be parsed by efficient standard techniques.

The needs of the compiler and the human user as regards the definition of a language's syntax appear to exactly coincide since language constructs that can be easily translated also seem to be simple for humans to understand whereas constructs that are difficult to translate are also difficult for humans to comprehend. Indeed, Wirth suggests that the process of language design and language implementation should go together for this very reason, and he has followed this approach in the design of Pascal, Modula and Modula-2. Given the success of these languages, Wirth's views must be taken seriously, although concern with implementation issues can be taken too far.

Often, when a language is being designed, a lot of pressure is placed on the designer to include additional features because they might be useful. Such pressures can be balanced by requests to keep things simple if the language implementation team are in day-to-day contact with the design team.

The importance of size should not be underestimated. The size and complexity of a language affects the speed at which it can be translated and the size of machine required to host the translation. The relative ease with which Pascal could be implemented, coupled with the existence of a portable compiler, greatly enhanced its acceptance while the size and complexity of ALGOL 68 and PL/I led to their relative lack of success. Similarly, the widespread adoption of Ada is being hampered by the size, cost and lack of speed of its compilers and is helping C and Modula-2 gain a niche in the market place.

12.6   Reasoning about Programs

Once a program has been produced, it is important to ensure that it satisfies its specification. The usual way of doing this is to run the program with suitably chosen data. Although testing is an important stage of the software development process, it does suffer from one major drawback: it can show the presence of errors, but it cannot prove that no errors remain. The ideal approach is therefore to verify a program; that is, to *prove* that the program conforms to its specification. A specification is often written in an informal notation although the trend is increasingly towards the use of a formal (mathematical) notation, which has led to the development of special specification languages. Such languages are beyond the scope of this book but the interested reader is referred to the collection of papers edited by Gehani (1986).

A lot of research has gone into proving that programs meet their specifications and into how specifications can be automatically transformed into executable programs. Although progress has been made, this research is still a long way from either being able to prove the correctness of large programming systems or automatically generating them from their specification. However, it is at present possible to reason about the effect of programs and thereby to increase one's confidence that the specifications are met. To reason about the effect of a large program, it is important that it has been constructed in such a way that it can be decomposed into separate components. It is then possible to reason about these components independently and so use the separate results when reasoning about the program as a whole.

Among the language features that help support this approach are the structured control statements introduced in ALGOL 60 and refined in later languages. Each structured statement has only one entry and one exit point. A program constructed from such statements consists of a linear sequence of program components and the flow of control closely follows the program text. The reason for the unpopularity of the **goto** statement is that the arbitrary transfer of control that is then possible makes reasoning about programs much more difficult.

The ability to modify global variables means that one program component can have an unforeseen effect on another and is an obstacle to the decomposition of large programs into self-contained units that can be reasoned about independently. This is especially so when aliasing is involved.

Two approaches can be taken in language design. One is to offer sufficiently powerful language constructs so that programmers can produce well-structured programs; the other is to restrict languages so that the offending constructs are outlawed. These two approaches can, of course, be considered to be complementary.

One of the recently identified villains in the programmer's repertoire is the assignment statement, as without this it would not be possible to have global variables or aliases. Although pure functional languages manage without assignment, it is central to imperative languages and so curbing its abuses seems more appropriate than total abolition.

12.7   Efficiency Versus Ease of Use

An important practical concern of a language is its efficiency at run time, both in terms of speed and the amount of store required. Associated with this, are the data types allowed and their built-in operations.

An important reason for the success of functional languages is that they treat structured data types, such as lists, as primitive types. Conventional imperative languages, on the other hand, tend to have a much richer set of operators available on scalar types than they do on structured types. In Pascal, for example, a function cannot return a structured value and, with the exception of strings, structured constants are not possible.

Having either built-in operators on structured types or the ability to easily create such operators leads to shorter programs, which should therefore be easier to understand. Detailed programming no longer has to be done by the programmer, but is handled automatically by the language system. The drawback of this approach is that in many cases heap storage allocation must be used with the attendant need for garbage collection and the reduction in execution speed.

Strong typing has been criticized for its lack of flexibility. For example, to sort an array of reals and an array of integers in Pascal, two separate sort procedures are required. In Ada, on the other hand, this can be achieved by generic subprograms and packages and it is no longer necessary to write two separate sort procedures. Instead, there are two instantiations of a generic sort procedure: one for integers and one for reals. This means, however, that two separate sort procedures still exist. In a language like Hope, a single polymorphic sort procedure can be used and there is no need to create special-purpose forms.

There has been a long debate about the need for types in programming languages. The balance seems to have swung decisively towards the strong typing school on the grounds that the need for reliability is more important than flexibility. The functional language ML makes an interesting contribution to this debate. It has types, but the types of objects do not have to be declared. The ML system deduces what the type of objects must be from their use and can report on inconsistent use. Thus, ML attempts to give the advantages of being weakly typed together with the security of type checking. It is not, however, clear that the extra complexity in the ML system is worthwhile.

Finally, the development of multiprocessor systems makes it likely that languages of the future will have to have a high-level way of handling concurrency. Perhaps the most interesting development (Yonezawa, 1987) is the generalization of the Smalltalk object so that systems are composed of objects that can execute independently and in parallel with all the others. The objects then interact with one another by passing and receiving messages. This concurrent object-oriented approach has a lot in common with the process model used in occam and Ada, and so yet again there is a convergence of the developments in different areas. It is therefore important that all computer scientists have a working knowledge of the imperative, functional, logic and object-oriented programming paradigms so that they can make such connections instead of acting as a series of non-communicating sequential processes.

SUMMARY

- Languages such as FORTRAN, COBOL and LISP, although developed in the 1950s and early 1960s, are still in widespread use.

- C is currently the most widely used systems programming language although both Modula-2 and Ada have much better features for the support of reliable programming.

- Declarative languages may require the development of new architectures if they are to become dominant.

- The principal aim of a programming language should be to support the development of reliable programs.

- There is a correlation between language constructs that are simple for a human to understand and those that are easy for a compiler to translate.

- There is still much research to be done before it will be possible to prove the correctness of large programs or to automatically generate them from their specifications. Reasoning about the effect of a program can, however, increase one's confidence that it meets its specification.

- Run-time efficiency and ease of use are often incompatible language design goals. The current trend is towards ease of use.

Bibliography

The book by Gehani (1986) contains a large collection of papers on specification languages and methods. Three more recent references are the book on VDM by Jones (1986), the collection of papers on Z edited by Hayes (1987) and the paper by Henderson (1986).

Gehani, N. and McGettrick, A. D. (Eds.) (1986), *Software Specification Techniques*, Addison-Wesley.

Hayes, I. (Ed.) (1987), *Specification Case Studies*, Prentice-Hall.

Henderson, P. (1986), 'Functional Programming, Formal Specification and Rapid Prototyping', *IEEE Trans. in Software Engineering*, **12**, pp. 241–250.

Jones, C. B. (1986), *Systematic Software Development Using VDM*, Prentice-Hall.

Yonezawa, A. and Tokoro, M. (1987), *Object-Oriented Concurrent Programming*, MIT Press.

APPENDIX 1

Language Summaries

This appendix summarizes the features of the principal languages dealt with in the text. The languages are given in alphabetical order and are Ada, ALGOL 60, ALGOL 68, C, C++, COBOL, FORTRAN 77, LISP, Modula-2, Pascal, PL/I, PROLOG and Smalltalk. References to these and all the other languages referred to in the text are given in Appendix 2.

Ada

Ada is a large and powerful language based on Pascal. It includes features to support data abstraction, concurrency and the production and maintenance of large systems.

Program structure and visibility

An Ada program is a collection of modules (subprograms or packages) whose interdependency is given by context clauses. One of the modules is the main program and it must be a procedure. A module is compiled in the context of those modules from which it imports information. A package is in two parts: a specification, which gives its interface with the rest of the program, and a hidden implementation part. This allows separate compilation.

Data types

The predefined types are *integer*, *float*, *character*, *Boolean* and *string*. Scalar user-defined types are the derived subrange types and the enumeration types. Structured types can be defined using arrays, records and pointers. Abstract data types can be implemented using packages and parameterized abstract data types using generic packages.

Type checking

Ada is strongly typed.

Manipulation of structured objects

Arrays and records can be passed as parameters and returned as function values. Fixing the size of an array can be delayed until block entry. Dynamic data structures are created using records that have one or more fields of a pointer type. Strings are arrays of *character*.

Control structures

Structured control statements have explicit terminators. The conditional statements are **if** and **case**. The iterative statements are **while**, **for** and a **loop** ... **end loop** construct that may be left using an **exit** statement. Exception handling is also supported.

Concurrency

Parallel processing is achieved using tasks. Message passing is used both to pass information and to achieve synchronization.

Input/output

I/O is supported by a hierarchy of packages whose specifications are given in the Ada Reference Manual. At the highest level, text I/O is supported while the lowest level supports direct access to peripheral devices.

ALGOL 60

ALGOL 60 was the original block-structured language and is the direct ancestor of Pascal and most modern imperative languages. It was the first language to have its syntax defined formally using BNF.

Program structure and visibility

It is block structured with blocks inheriting declarations made in enclosing blocks. Procedures may be recursive in ALGOL 60 and all its descendants.

There are no facilities for dealing with very large programs or for separate or independent compilation.

Data types

The predefined types are *real*, *integer* and *Boolean*. The only structured type is the array. User-defined types are not available.

Type checking

Implicit conversions are allowed between numeric types.

Manipulation of structured objects

Arrays may be passed as parameters, but may not be returned as the value of a function. The bounds of an array do not have to be fixed until block entry.

Control structures

The **if** statement has been copied in most ALGOL-like languages. Iteration is performed by the **for** statement which has several forms, one of which includes a **while** variant.

Concurrency

Not supported.

Input/output

Not defined in the language. Each implementation introduced its own statements.

ALGOL 68

ALGOL 68 was designed as the sophisticated and elegant successor to ALGOL 60, but although it proved popular with theoreticians it was far less popular with programmers. Its definition was difficult to follow and no concessions were made to ease the implementation – a compiler writer's nightmare.

Program structure and visibility

It is a block-structured language. There are no facilities for dealing with very large programs or for separate or independent compilation.

Data types

Predefined types are *int*, *real*, *char*, *bool* and *string*. Array, pointer and structure (record) types can be user defined.

Type checking

It is strongly typed.

Manipulation of structured objects

There are better facilities for the manipulation of structured objects in ALGOL 68 than in most other languages. The size of a (flexible) array can be changed during program execution. Strings are implemented as flexible character arrays. Subprograms can have subprograms as parameters and functions can return subprograms as values.

Control structures

Unlike ALGOL 60, control statements in ALGOL 68 have explicit terminators. The conditional statements are **if** and **case**, but as all statements have values, they are also conditional expressions. As in ALGOL 60, loops are constructed from the many variants of the **for** statement, which include a **while** statement.

Concurrency

Parallel processing is supported with semaphores being used for synchronization.

Input/output

I/O (called transput) is by a set of predefined routines. Files may be opened and closed at run time and formatted, unformatted and binary transput is supported.

C

C is a systems programming language and is at a lower level than the other languages dealt with in this book. It has the control and data structures found in modern high-level languages and as its wide range of operators mirror the machine code instructions found in many computers, C programs are comparable in efficiency to assembly language programs. C is closely identified with the UNIX operating system.

Program structure and visibility

The source text of a C program can be distributed among several files, each of which can be compiled independently. Full type checking is not possible, however, across these boundaries. Although it has some features of a block-structured language, subprograms may not be nested.

Data types

The predefined data types are *int*, *char* and *float* together with *short* and *long* (for integers) and *double* (for floating point). User-defined types are enumeration types, arrays and structures (records). Dynamic data structures can be created using pointers.

Type checking

As it is a relatively low-level systems programming language, strict type checking is not imposed.

Manipulation of structured objects

This is largely achieved by manipulating pointers to structured objects. Strings are implemented as arrays of character, but there are no built-in operators on strings.

Control structures

It has structured control statements. The conditional statements are **if** and **switch** (similar to **case** in Pascal) and the iterative statements are **while** and **for** together with a **do** ... **while** construct which tests at the end of a loop.

Concurrency

Not supported directly, but new processes can be created through calls to UNIX system routines.

Input/output

I/O is not directly defined in the language, but is implemented by means of a standard library.

C++

C++ was designed to add object-oriented features to C.

Program structure and visibility

Classes support the decomposition of large programs into self-contained units.

Data types

The types are as in C with the addition of classes. This gives information hiding and allows the definition of abstract data types.

Type checking

The type checking of C has been tightened up significantly.

Manipulation of structured objects

As in C, this is largely done using pointers. Objects are allocated space dynamically.

Control structures

As in C.

Concurrency

As in C.

Input/output

A library of predefined routines is available.

COBOL

COBOL is the most extensively used programming language in data processing and is oriented to dealing with large files of data. It has been revised several times, but these revisions, like the FORTRAN revisions, have been unable to take into account in any sensible way the new programming concepts of structure and modularity.

Program structure and visibility

A COBOL program is divided into four divisions. The IDENTIFICATION DIVISION provides commentary and is essentially program documentation; the ENVIRONMENT DIVISION contains machine-dependent program specifications relating logical and physical entities; the DATA DIVISION describes the data and its structure; and, finally, the PROCEDURE DIVISION gives the algorithms. Subprograms do not exist as such although it is possible to use labelled sequences of statements. There is no recursion.

Data types

The basic types are character strings and numbers whose precision is defined by the programmer in the DATA DIVISION. Arrays exist, but the main structured variables are records, which can be combined together to make files. Dynamic data structures are not supported.

Type checking

Since implicit type conversions are an integral part of COBOL, little type checking is possible.

Manipulation of structured objects

The REDEFINES clause allows more than one data structure to be mapped to the same piece of storage. Array bounds are fixed.

Control structures

There is a restricted IF ... THEN ... ELSE statement, but most control is exercised by the PERFORM statement, which can be used as an iterative statement or as a primitive form of subprogram call. There are labels and GOTO statements.

Concurrency

Not supported.

Input/output

Extensive read and write facilities are provided for both sequential and random access to the records of a file.

FORTRAN 77

FORTRAN is still widely used for numerical applications by scientists and engineers, but although it has been revised to take account of some of the ideas of structured programming, it lacks the regular structure of languages such as Pascal.

Program structure and visibility

A FORTRAN program consists of a set of independently compiled sub-programs. There is no block structure and subprograms communicate through parameter lists and COMMON lists. Recursion is not supported.

Data types

The predefined data types are INTEGER, REAL, DOUBLE PRECISION, LOGICAL, CHARACTER and COMPLEX. The only structured types are fixed-size arrays. User-defined types are not available.

Type checking

Type checking of actual and formal parameters cannot take place due to the requirements of independent compilation. There is implicit conversion between integer and real in assignment statements.

Manipulation of structured objects

Arrays can be passed as parameters, but may not be returned as the value of a function. Strings are character arrays.

Control structures

Early versions of FORTRAN did not have structured control statements. This was remedied in FORTRAN 77 with the block IF statement. Iteration is provided by the DO loop, which corresponds to the **for** loop of Pascal.

Concurrency

Not supported.

Input/output

Special read and write statements with channel numbers to indicate the device and optional FORMAT statements are provided.

LISP

LISP is primarily used in artificial intelligence applications and although it is not a purely functional language, it has all the features needed for functional programming. It syntax is simple although it is rather off putting to the beginner.

Program structure and visibility

A program consists of a set of function definitions. There is no support for dealing with very large programs.

Data types

The objects manipulated in the language are S-expressions, which can be lists, atoms or functions. Atoms may be symbolic or numerical.

Type checking

Lisp is weakly typed.

Manipulation of structured objects

Lists are first-class objects and so they can be manipulated as easily as scalar objects in imperative languages. Functions may be higher order. Automatic garbage collection is supported by LISP systems.

Control structures

Recursion is used instead of iteration.

Concurrency

Not dealt with explicitly although, as pure functions have no side effects, they may be executed in parallel.

Input/output

A set of predefined functions are used to read and write S-expressions.

Modula-2

Modula-2 can be regarded as Pascal extended with modules and with low-level features to support systems programming.

Program structure and visibility

A Modula-2 program consists of a series of modules that can be divided into a definition and an implementation part. Modules interact by importing information exported by other modules. Modules support the creation of large programs as they are the basis of information hiding, data abstraction and separate compilation. Procedure declarations may be nested within modules.

Data types

The predefined types are INTEGER, CARDINAL, REAL, CHAR and BOOLEAN together with LONGINT, LONGCARD and LONGREAL. Scalar user-defined types are subrange and enumeration types. Structured types are arrays, records and sets. Dynamic data structures can be constructed using pointers. Abstract data types can be implemented using modules.

Type checking

The language is strongly typed with the exception of variant records, although Modula-2 systems usually include a SYSTEM module, which includes definition of system-dependent types such as BYTE, WORD and ADDRESS and which allow all kinds of unsafe type conversions.

Manipulation of structured objects

As in Pascal, except that string comparisons are not allowed.

Control structures

Structured control statements have explicit terminators and so compound statements are not required. There are **if** and **case** conditional statements. As well as the Pascal-like iterative statements, **while**, **repeat** and **for**, there is a LOOP ... END statement, which may be left by execution of an EXIT statement.

Concurrency

Processes communicate through shared variables with monitors being used to guarantee mutual exclusion. Signals are used to synchronize processes.

Input/output

I/O is not defined in the language, but is provided by a set of library modules.

Pascal

Pascal was designed as a vehicle for the teaching of good programming style. Its emphasis on the importance of types and data structures has been very influential and virtually all recent imperative languages can be classified as Pascal derivatives. It is relatively small and, partly as a consequence of it being designed so that it would be easy to implement, it is available on most computers.

Program structure and visibility

It is a block-structured language, but as there is a single outermost block, neither independent nor separate compilation is supported. The only inner blocks are procedures and functions. Inner blocks inherit all declarations made in enclosing blocks.

Data types

The predefined data types are *integer*, *real*, *Boolean* and *char*. Array, record, set, pointer, subrange and enumeration types can be user defined.

Type checking

It is strongly typed, apart from variant records.

Manipulation of structured objects

Arrays and records may be parameters, but may not be returned as function values. Dynamic data structures are created using records, which have one or more fields of a pointer type. The size of arrays is fixed at compile time, although arrays of different sizes may be passed as parameters. Strings are packed arrays of *char*.

Control structures

It has structured control statements. The conditional statements are **if** and **case**; the iterative statements are **while**, **repeat** ... **until** and **for**. The compound statement is used to group statements together.

Concurrency

Not dealt with.

Input/output

Handled by a set of predefined procedures and functions that do not follow the usual language rules. The association of internal file names with physical external files is not handled in the language. Interactive I/O is dealt with in the same way as I/O to a sequential file.

PL/I

PL/I is a large general-purpose language that was designed to be suitable for both scientific and data processing work. It brought together ideas from FORTRAN, ALGOL and COBOL, but turned out to be large and unwieldy.

Program structure and visibility

A program consists of a set of external procedures, which may be compiled independently. External procedures may communicate with one another by passing parameters or through EXTERNAL variables. Within an external procedure, the declarations of internal procedures may be nested. Internal procedures inherit declarations from their enclosing blocks.

Data types

Types may be defined in great detail. For example, numeric types can have a mode (REAL or COMPLEX), a scale (FIXED or FLOAT), a base (DECIMAL or BINARY) and a precision. However, the default options are heavily used in defining types. Structured types are arrays and structures (records). Dynamic data structures can be created using pointers. Character strings can be defined to have either a fixed size or to be variable up to a fixed maximum size.

Type checking

When types do not match, implicit conversion rules are applied.

Manipulation of structured objects

Structured objects can be parameters of procedures, but they may not be returned as values of user-defined functions. There is an extensive set of operators and built-in functions for string handling.

Control structures

A structured **if** statement is available and the DO (**for** loop) can include a WHILE variant. Exception handling is also available.

Concurrency

Primitive tasking facilities are defined, but seldom used.

Input/output

Extensive facilities are available to support data processing work as well as the simpler requirements of scientific programmers.

PROLOG

PROLOG is a logic programming language in which the programmer states what is to be done rather than how it is to be carried out. The PROLOG approach is goal oriented and along with LISP dominates the artificial intelligence scene.

Program structure and visibility

A PROLOG program consists of a database of facts and a series of rules. Although programs can be easily extended by adding new facts and rules, there is no support for the creation of very large programs.

Data types

PROLOG has (symbolic) atoms, numbers and structures.

Type checking

It is weakly typed.

Manipulation of structured objects

Structures (which are similar to records in Pascal) can be manipulated as easily in PROLOG as can lists in LISP. Structures are mainly used to represent lists, trees and graphs.

Control structures

To achieve a goal, subgoals are generated and achieved. Tree searching and associated backtracking are built into the interpreter and are not explicitly programmed.

Concurrency

Not dealt with.

Input/output

All data objects in PROLOG programs can be directly read or written. The standard input and output streams can be redirected to give access to disk files.

Smalltalk 80

Smalltalk is the archetypal object-oriented language. It is not just a language, but is a complete programming environment. Everything in a Smalltalk system is an object, which means that the number of separate concepts are kept to a minimum.

Program structure and visibility

Objects support information hiding. Data local to an object may only be accessed by sending a message to the object. An object responds to a message by selecting a procedure (called a method) to carry out the requested task. Objects give a hierarchical structure to large programs.

Data types

The only type is the object. Objects belong to a class, which is itself an object. New classes (subclasses) can be defined that inherit the properties of an existing class (their superclass) which they extend through the definition of new methods. There is automatic garbage collection of inaccessible objects.

Type checking

When messages are sent to an object, the required method is selected dynamically at run time. The nearest thing to a type error is when an object is unable to respond to a message.

Manipulation of structured objects

As the Smalltalk approach is centred on the manipulation of objects, its facilities are excellent in this area.

Control structures

Control structures are implemented as messages involving objects of class *block*. A *block* object represents a sequence of instructions which are to be executed when a suitable message is received.

Concurrency

A concurrent system can be built as a collection of concurrent objects that communicate with one another by sending messages.

Input/output

The Smalltalk environment introduced windows, icons and the mouse.

APPENDIX 2

Language Texts

Ada

After several earlier editions, the Ada Reference Manual was published in 1983. There are a large number of Ada texts, three of which are given below.

Barnes, J. G. P. (1984), *Programming in Ada* (Second Edition), Addison-Wesley.

Booch, G. (1983), *Software Engineering with Ada*, Benjamin/Cummings.

Clark, R. G. (1985), *Programming in Ada: A First Course*, Cambridge University Press.

Ichbiah, J. D. *et al.* (1983), *Reference Manual for the Ada Programming Language*, ANSI MIL-STD-1815A-1983.

ALGOL 60

There are many books on ALGOL 60. Three of the early ones are given below as well as the classic paper edited by Peter Naur which gives the language definition.

Dijkstra, E. W. (1962), *A Primer of Algol 60 Programming*, Academic Press.

Ekman, T. and Froberg, C.-E. (1967), *Introduction to Algol Programming*, Oxford University Press.

Naur, P. (1963), 'Revised Report on the Algorithmic Language Algol 60', *Comm. ACM*, **6**, pp. 1–17.

Reeves, C. M. and Wells, M. (1964), *A Course on Programming in Algol 60*, Chapman & Hall.

ALGOL 68

The original defining document is not easy to read. The description by Lindsey and van der Meulen is more accessible.

Lindsey, C. H. and van der Meulen, S. G. (1971), *Informal Introduction to Algol 68*, North-Holland.

van Wijngaarded, A., Mailloux, B. J., Peck, J. E. L. and Koster, C. H. A. (1969), 'Report on the Algorithmic Language Algol 68', *Mathematisch Centrum*, Amsterdam.

ALGOL W

This language is described in the following paper.

Wirth, N. and Hoare, C. A. R. (1966), 'A Contribution to the Development of Algol', *Comm. ACM*, **9**, pp. 413–431.

Alphard

There is only one text.

Shaw, M. (1981), *Alphard: Form and Content*, Springer-Verlag.

APL

The designer Kenneth Iverson wrote the original book on the language before a computer implementation was considered. The implemented version is somewhat different.

Falkoff, A. and Iverson, K. E. (1973), 'The Design of APL', *IBM Journal of Research and Development*, **17**, pp. 324–334.

Iverson, K. E. (1962), *A Programming Language*, John Wiley.

Polivka, R. P. and Pakin, S. (1975), *APL: The language and its Usage*, Prentice-Hall.

BASIC

The designers John Kemeny and Thomas Kurtz wrote the first book about the language. Since then the market has been flooded.

Kemeny, J. G. and Kurtz, T. E. (1967), *BASIC Programming*, John Wiley.

C

Recently, a large number of C books have been published, but for a long time the only text was by Kernighan and Ritchie. A simpler introduction is given in the book by Kelley and Pohl.

Kelley, A. and Pohl, I. (1984), *A Book on C*, Addison-Wesley.

Kernighan, B. W. and Ritchie, D. M. (1978), *The C Programming Language*, Prentice-Hall.

C++

This is a recent object-oriented extension to C and apart from minor details it is a superset. The only text is as follows.

Stroustrup, B. (1986), *The C++ Programming Language*, Addison-Wesley.

CLU

The most accessible reference is given below.

Liskov, B., Snyder, A., Atkinson, R. and Schaffert, C. (1977), 'Abstraction Mechanism in CLU', *Comm. ACM*, **20**, pp. 564–576.

COBOL

There are many textbooks to choose from, two of which are listed here.

Philippakis, A. S. and Kazmier, L. J. (1981), *Structured COBOL* (Second Edition), McGraw-Hill.

Shelly, G. B. and Cashman, T. J. (1977), *Introduction to Computer Programming Structured COBOL*, Anaheim Publishing Co.

Euclid

A complete issue of *SIGPLAN Notices* was devoted to the language.

Lampson, B. W., Horning, J. J., London, R. L., Mitchell, J. G. and Popek, G. J. (1977), 'Report on the Programming Language Euclid', *ACM SIGPLAN Notices*, **12** (2).

FORTRAN

There are textbooks on FORTRAN to suit all tastes. The following text adopts a structured approach.

Ellis, T. M. (1982), *A Structured Approach to Fortran 77 Programming*, Addison-Wesley.

GPSS

O'Donovan, T. M. (1979), *GPSS Simulation Made Simple*, John Wiley.

LISP

The classic text is written by John McCarthy *et al*. Since then, many texts have been written. The book by Winston and Horn is oriented towards COMMON LISP.

McCarthy, J., Abrahams, P. W., Edwards, D. J., Hart, T. P. and Levin, M. I. (1965), *LISP 1.5 Programmer's Manual*, MIT Press.

Winston, P. H. and Horn, B. K. P. (1984), *LISP* (Second Edition), Addison-Wesley.

LOGO

Early publicity on LOGO was centred on the book by Papert. Since then, many texts have been published, most of which concentrate on turtle graphics.

Papert, S. (1980), *Mindstorms*: *Children*, *Computers and Powerful Ideas*, Harvester Press.

ML

The first book devoted to ML is by Wikstrom.

Wikstrom, A. (1987), *Functional Programming Using Standard ML*, Prentice-Hall.

Modula-2

Books on Modula-2 are now appearing in quantity. The original text is by Wirth and like most books on Modula-2 it assumes prior knowledge of a language like Pascal. The book by Terry is suitable for a first course on programming.

Terry, P. D. (1986), *An Introduction to Programming with Modula-2*, Addison-Wesley.

Wirth, N. (1985), *Programming in Modula-2* (Third Edition), Springer-Verlag.

occam

The first version of the occam programming manual is now rather out of date as the language has continued to be developed. The text by Jones gives a much better intoduction to the language.

INMOS Ltd. (1984), *occam Programming Manual*, Prentice-Hall.

Jones, G. (1987), *Programming in occam*, Prentice-Hall.

Pascal

The original book is by Jensen and Wirth, but many better books are available, such as the ones by Findlay and Watt and by Dale and Weems.

Dale, N. and Weems, C. (1987), *Pascal* (Second Edition), D.C. Heath.

Findlay, W. and Watt, D. A. (1984), *Pascal* (Third Edition), Pitman.

Jensen, K. and Wirth, N. (1974), *Pascal User Manual and Report*, Springer-Verlag.

PL/I

There are many textbooks available. Conway and Gries is worth noting as it contains a well-known and useful subset called PL/C.

Conway, R. and Gries, D. (1979), *An Introduction to Programming – A Structured Approach Using PL/I and PL/C* (Third Edition), Winthrop.

PROLOG

The first book available was by Clocksin and Mellish although other texts are now being published, such as the text by Bratko.

Bratko, I. (1986), *Prolog Programming for Artificial Intelligence*, Addison-Wesley.

Clocksin, W. F. and Mellish, C. S. (1984), *Programming in Prolog* (Second Edition), Springer-Verlag.

RPG

Essick, E. L. (1981), *RPG II Programming*, SRA.

SIMULA 67

The main text is as follows.

Birtwistle, G. M., Dahl, O.-J., Myhrhaug, B. and Nygaard, K. (1975), *Simula Begin*, Auerbach.

Smalltalk

Smalltalk is not just a language, but is a complete programming environment. The main text is given below.

Goldberg, A. and Robson, D. (1983), *Smalltalk-80: The Language and its Implementation*, Addison-Wesley.

SNOBOL

The original designers have written the standard textbook.

Griswold, R. E., Poage, J. F. and Polonsky, I. P. (1971), *The SNOBOL 4 Programming Language*, Prentice-Hall.

Solutions to Selected Exercises

Chapter 3

3.8 **type** *month* **is** (*January*, *February*, *March*, *April*, *May*, *June*, *July*,
August, *September*, *October*, *November*, *December*);
Operations: *next_month*, *last_month*, *month_number*, *month_name*

Chapter 4

4.2 In either of the expressions:

A **or** *B*   where *A* is true

A **and** B   where *A* is false

and *B* contains an expression that cannot be correctly evaluated or whose evaluation has a side effect.

4.5 Ada leads to the more reliable programs as the programmer has to make a positive decision when writing a program about all possible cases. This allows some errors to be picked up at compile time, which in Pascal would lead to run-time errors.

Chapter 5

5.7 The result $j = 2$, $a[1] = 1$, $a[2] = 3$ is obtained except with call by name which gives $j = 2$, $a[1] = 2$, $a[2] = 1$ when the call is *swap*(j, $a[j]$) and the same result as the others when the call is *swap* ($a[j]$, j). As long as the addresses of all the actual parameters are computed on subprogram exit before any of the actual parameters are updated, call by value-result (ALGOL W) gives the same answer as call by value-result. If this is not the case, it gives the same result as call by name.

5.10 **function** *next_month*(*mo* : *month*) **return** *month* **is**
begin
  if *mo* = *December* **then**
    return *January*;
  else
    return *month'succ*(*mo*);
  end if;
end *next_month*;

function *last_month*(*mo* : *month*) **return** *month* **is**
begin
  if *mo* = *January* **then**
    return *December*;
  else
    return *month'pred*(*mo*);
  end if;
end *last_month*;

function *month_number*(*mo* : *month*) **return** *integer* **is**
begin
  return *month'pos*(*mo*) + 1;
end *month_number*;

function *month_name*(*num* : *integer*) **return** *month* **is**
begin
  return *month'val*(*num* − 1);
end *month_name*;

The Pascal implementations are essentially the same with the exception of *month_name* where a **case** statement has to be used as there is no equivalent of the *val* operation.

Chapter 6

6.2 Assume *BA*, the base address, is where the first element of the array is stored and each element occupies *s* locations.

Mapping function for $x[i] = BA + s * (i - 2)$

Mapping function for $a[i, j] = BA + s * (6 * (i - 1) + j)$

Hence:

$x[7]$ is in $BA + 5 * s$

$a[3, 2]$ is in $BA + 14 * s$

6.8   **subtype** *size* **is** *integer* **range** 1 .. *max*;
type *values* **is array**(*size*) **of** *real*;
type *queue* **is**
  record
    data : *values*;
    front, *rear* : *size* := 1;
    --front points to the front of the queue
    --rear points to where the next element will be inserted
  end record;

procedure *add* (*x* : *real*; *q* : **in out** *queue*) **is**
begin
  if (*q.rear* = *max* **and** *q.front* = 1) **or else**
    (*q.rear* + 1 = *q.front*) **then**
    full_error_message;
  else
    q.data(*q.rear*) := *x*;
    if *q.rear* = *max* **then**
      q.rear := 1;
    else
      q.rear := *q.rear* + 1;
    end if;
  end if;
end *add*;

procedure *delete* (*q* : **in out** *queue*) **is**
begin
  if *q.front* = *q.rear* **then**
    empty_error_message;
  elsif *q.front* = *max* **then**
    q.front := 1;
  else
    q.front := *q.front* + 1;
  end if;
end *delete*;

It is assumed that the queue is represented by a circular list and that the element following *q.data*(*max*) is in *q.data*(1). To be able to differentiate between a full and an empty queue, the maximum number of elements that can be held is *max* − 1.

6.10   **procedure** *Polish* (*p* : *ptr*);
  begin
    if p <> **nil then**
    begin
      write(*p* ↑ .*data*);
      Polish(*p* ↑ .*left*);
      Polish(*p* ↑ .*right*)
    end
  end {*Polish*};

6.12 CORRECT

Chapter 7

7.9   **generic**
       type *item* **is private**;
       max : *integer*;
     package *queues* **is**
       type *queue* **is limited private**;
       procedure *add*(*x* : *item*; *q* : **in out** *queue*);
       procedure *delete*(*q* : **in out** *queue*);
       function *first*(*q* : *queue*) **return** *item*;
       function *is_empty*(*q* : *queue*) **return** *Boolean*;
     private
       --implementation of type *queue* as in 6.8
     end *queues*;

7.11 **package** *months* **is**
       type *month* **is** (*January*, *February*, *March*, *April*, *May*, *June*, *July*,
                 August, *September*, *October*, *November*, *December*);
       function *next_month*(*mo* : *month*) **return** *month*;
       function *last_month*(*mo* : *month*) **return** *month*;
       function *month_number*(*mo* : *month*) **return** *integer*;
       function *month_name*(*num* : *integer*) **return** *month*;
     end *months*;

     package body *months* **is**
     --function definitions as in 5.10
     end *months*;

7.13 **generic**
       type *item* **is private**;
     package *retrieve* **is**
       type *table* **is private**;
       procedure *insert*(*x* : *item*; *info* : **in out** *table*);
       function *lookup*(*x* : *item*; *info* : *table*) **return** *integer*;
     private
       type *table* **is array**(1 .. 100) **of** *item*;
     end *retrieve*;

Chapter 8

8.6   Assuming the type declaration:

       type *ready_state* **is** (*off*, *snooze*);

the two task bodies are:

```
task body person is
  state : ready_state;
begin
  loop
    accept alarm_call(response : out ready_state) do
      --determine value for state
      response := state;
    end alarm_call;
    exit when state = off;
    --go back to sleep
  end loop;
  --get up
end person;

task body alarm is
  continue : ready_state;
begin
  loop
    person.alarm_call(continue);
    exit when continue = off;
    delay 2.0;
  end loop;
end alarm;
```

8.7 Two, as a channel will be required for the person's response.

Chapter 9

9.4 (ISMEMBER 24 '(17 24 59))
=> (COND ((NULL '(17 24 59)) NIL)
            ((EQ 24 (CAR '(17 24 59))) T)
            (T (ISMEMBER 24 (CDR '(17 24 59)))))
=> (COND (NIL NIL)
            ((EQ 24 (CAR '(17 24 59))) T)
            (T (ISMEMBER 24 (CDR '(17 24 59)))))
=> (COND ((EQ 24 (CAR '(17 24 59))) T)
            (T (ISMEMBER 24 (CDR '(17 24 59)))))
=> (COND ((EQ 24 17) T)
            (T (ISMEMBER 24 (CDR '(17 24 59)))))
=> (COND (NIL T)
            (T (ISMEMBER 24 (CDR '(17 24 59)))))
=> (COND (T (ISMEMBER 24 (CDR '(17 24 59)))))
=> (ISMEMBER 24 (CDR '(17 24 59)))
=> (ISMEMBER 24 '(24 59))

```
=> (COND ((NULL '(24 59)) NIL)
         ((EQ 24 (CAR '(24 59))) T)
         (T (ISMEMBER 24 (CDR '(24 59)))))
=> (COND ((EQ 24 (CAR '(24 59))) T)
         (T (ISMEMBER 24 (CDR '(24 59)))))
=> (COND (T T)
         (T (ISMEMBER 24 (CDR '(24 59)))))
=> T
```

$IsMember$(24, [17, 24, 59])
=> **if** 24 = 17 **then** *true*
   else $IsMember$(24, [24, 59])
=> **if** *false* **then** *true*
   else $IsMember$(24, [24, 59])
=> $IsMember$(24, [24, 59])
=> **if** 24 = 24 **then** *true*
   else $IsMember$(24, [59])
=> **if** *true* **then** *true*
   else $IsMember$ (24, [59])
=> *true*

9.6 (DEF SUMLIST (LAMBDA (X)
         (COND ((NULL X) 0)
               (T (PLUS (CAR X) (SUMLIST (CDR X))))
         )))

Chapter 10

10.2 The question:

?- **goodmatch (A, B).**

requires the subgoals:

loves (A, B), loves (B, A)

to be satisfied. The substitutions A ←john and B ←jane allow the first subgoal to be matched with the first fact, but the second subgoal then fails. The system backtracks to the first subgoal and tries A ← **bill** and B ← jane so that the second fact is matched. The second subgoal again fails. The system again backtracks and tries A ←**james** and B ←jane which satisfies both subgoals.

10.3   within (X, Y) :− district (X, Y).
   within (X, Y) :− region (X, Y).

   .
   .
   .

   within (X, Y) :− district (Z, Y), region (X, Z).
   within (X, Y) :− region (Z, Y), country (X, Z).

   .
   .
   .

   within (X, Y) :− district (Λ, Y), region (B, Λ), country (C, B),
                   continent (X, C).

Better to define:

   inside (X, Y) :− district (X, Y).
   inside (X, Y) :− region (X, Y).
   inside (X, Y) :− country (X, Y).
   inside (X, Y) :− continent (X, Y).

and then to define:

   within (X, Y) :− inside (X, Y).
   within (X, Y) :− inside (X, Z), within (Z, Y).

Chapter 11

11.2   Instructions are needed to associate named physical files with logical files at run time and to create, open, close and delete such files. Operations on direct access files should also be included.

Index